# RED OVER BLUE

# RED OVER BLUE

## The 2004 Elections and American Politics

JAMES W. CEASER
AND
ANDREW E. BUSCH

ROWMAN & LITTLEFIELD PUBLISHERS, INC.
*Lanham • Boulder • New York • Toronto • Oxford*

ROWMAN & LITTLEFIELD PUBLISHERS, INC.

Published in the United States of America
by Rowman & Littlefield Publishers, Inc.
A wholly owned subsidary of The Rowman & Littlefield Publishing Group, Inc.
4501 Forbes Boulevard, Suite 200, Lanham, Maryland 20706
www.rowmanlittlefield.com

PO Box 317
Oxford
OX2 9RU, UK

British Library Cataloguing in Publication Information Available

**Library of Congress Cataloging-in-Publication Data**

Ceaser, James W.
  Red over blue : the 2004 elections and American politics / James W. Ceaser and
Andrew E. Busch.
     p. cm.
  Includes bibliographical references and index.
  ISBN 0-7425-3496-0 (cloth : alk. paper) — ISBN 0-7425-3497-9 (pbk. : alk. paper)
1. Presidents—United States—Election—2004. 2. United States.
Congress—Elections, 2004. 3. Elections—United States. 4. United
States—Politics and government—2001–  I. Busch, Andrew. II. Title.  JK5262004
.C43 2005
  324.973'0931—dc22

2005001994
Printed in the United States of America

♾ᵀᴹ The paper used in this publication meets the minimum requirements of American
National Standard for Information Sciences—Permanence of Paper for Printed Library
Materials, ANSI/NISO Z.39.48-1992.

To

Carolyn Rebar

and

to the Ceaser brothers blue: Harvey, Richard, and Martin

# Contents

# Acknowledgments

We would like to thank the following individuals for their help in the preparation of this manuscript: Annie Johnson, Daniel DiSalvo, Blaire French, Sam Seeley, Dennis Logue, Mark McNaught, Gregg Lindskog, Sara Henary, Zach Courser, and Jane Carson. Our appreciation also goes to the editorial staff at Rowman & Littlefield, in particular Laura Gottlieb and Terry Fischer, and the the Salvatori Center at Claremont McKenna College and the Program on Constitutionalism and Democracy at the University of Virginia.

*Chapter One*

# The New Face of American Politics

Using colors to describe political divisions is a practice that was employed at least as early as the sixth century, when Byzantine politics was riven by a division between the "blues" and the "greens," rival political factions that based their names on the colors worn by their favorite chariot teams. The political theorist and historian Niccolò Machiavelli records that in his native city of Florence, after a brief period of domestic peace that ended in 1300, "the whole city became divided, the people as well as the nobility, and the parties took the names of the Bianchi (Whites) and the Neri (Blacks)."[1] The labels appear to have originated in an earlier blood feud between two families in the neighboring city of Pistoia, where one of the families descended from a woman named Bianca (White), prompting the other to call itself Blacks. But these origins were quickly forgotten as the factional names of Whites and Blacks spread across Northern Italy.

America's experience with the palette did not begin until just after the 2000 election, when an electoral map appeared in the *New York Times* showing the states that gave a plurality to George W. Bush in red and those going for Al Gore in blue. Other renditions followed illustrating the national vote by counties. The visual impression created by these maps was striking. Given the geographical distribution of the vote, in which most areas favored George Bush, what the viewer saw was a vast sea of red surrounding a few beleaguered islands of blue. In the bitter dispute that followed Election Day in 2000, Republicans seized on this image and circulated these maps on the Internet with great enthusiasm. Democrats dismissed these pictures as wholly misleading, reminding everyone that what counts is the number of inhabitants in a district, not the expanse of its territory; it is people who vote, not rocks or stones or trees.

The battle of the colors in America had begun.

Would the impression have been different if the scheme had been re-versed? Surprisingly, a good deal of speculation has gone into this ques-tion. After all, red is the strongest color on the spectrum, and it was tradi-tionally claimed by the Left. In past elections, cartographers often made Republicans blue. A few writers have therefore alleged a conspiracy, charging that red was stolen by Republicans to bolster their position.[2] But whatever future historical research may eventually uncover, it is unlikely to make much difference. Commentators today, no matter what their per-sonal political hue, are accustomed to using the red-blue labels and could hardly function without them.

Americans in the 2004 election chose red over blue. They made this choice not crushingly or overwhelmingly, but clearly and decisively. No one could call the 2004 election a landslide, but Republicans emerged from the election ascendant as the nation's majority party. Republicans de-feated Democrats across the board and improved their position inside each national institution. President Bush defeated Senator John Kerry in the popular vote 51 percent to 48 percent, increasing the Republican share from the 2000 election by nearly three points. The Republicans won a ma-jority in the House of Representatives, 232 to 201, upping their total by eleven seats from 2000 (and three seats from 2002). Finally, Republicans were victors in 19 of the 34 Senate races, giving them a solid 55-44 ma-jority in that body and increasing their number by five seats from 2000 (and four from 2002). America was not just more red than blue in 2004, but it was considerably redder than it had been in 2000. George W. Bush's personal victory may have been narrow, but the victory he brought his party was substantial indeed.

## The 2004 Presidential Contest

There is a great danger, however, in trying to make political analysis too colorful. Elections in America do not just revolve around partisan choices. Each national election, indeed each separate race within each national election, is a distinct event with its own issues and cast of characters. This is especially so in the presidential contest, where voters are generally known to have their strongest personal reactions. This fact was confirmed in the aftermath of the 2004 election, when large numbers of Democrats reported receiving treatment for a depressive condition that was called Post-Election Stress Trauma (PEST). Diagnostic tests revealed that the cause had little to do with Republican gains in the House or Senate; it derived almost entirely from allergic reactions to the reelection of George W. Bush.

The 2004 presidential race falls in the category of incumbent reelection campaigns, when a sitting president is running for a second term. These races are distinct from what are known as "open-seat" contests, such as 2000, where neither candidate is the incumbent. In an incumbent reelection campaign, the race invariably revolves around the public's judgment of the president. The slogan "Four More Years," which has been chanted now for decades by supporters of presidents from both parties, poses the core question voters must decide: whether the president's performance warrants another term. In the language of electoral analysts, every campaign involving a president is a kind of "referendum" on the health of the nation and on the president's job performance. But a word of caution is appropriate. The term referendum should not be taken to mean that voters are simply rewarding past achievements, like the Oscars. Rather, voters appear to use the past to try to peer into the future. In Alexander Hamilton's classic words from *The Federalist*, people are making "an experimental estimate" of the president's record, so that where "they see reason to approve of his conduct, [they can] continue him in his station, in order to prolong the utility of his talents and virtues."[3] The term referendum can be slightly deceiving in another sense as well. An election is not just about the incumbent. There is that other fellow, too, and the challenger's attributes can also play a role in the voters' calculations, although admittedly sometimes a smaller one.

Over the past half century, from 1956 until the 2004 presidential election, the question of "four more years" was asked in eight of the twelve contests.[4] Three presidents were denied another term: Gerald Ford (1976), Jimmy Carter (1980), and George H. W. Bush (1992). Five prevailed: Dwight Eisenhower (1956), Lyndon Johnson (1964), Richard Nixon (1972), Ronald Reagan (1984), and Bill Clinton (1996). George W. Bush became the sixth on the list of survivors (table 1.1).

Incumbent election campaigns can be analyzed in terms of the two factors just suggested: the strength of the president's record as judged by the American people and the kind of challenger the opposition party presents. Let us consider these in reverse order.

The opposition party in these campaigns can adopt one of two basic strategies. The first is to present a nonthreatening and, if possible, highly appealing candidate. The logic of this kind of campaign is to make the race into a referendum on the president's performance, hoping that enough people disapprove of it so as to consider making a change. The challenger's job is to give voters as little reason as possible not to select the challenger

**Table 1.1.   Presidential Reelection Results, 1956–2004 (ranked by margin of plurality victory)**

| President | Year | Plurality | Percent of Vote | Electoral College Score |
|-----------|------|-----------|-----------------|-------------------------|
| Nixon | 1972 | 23.2% | 61R-36D | 520-17 |
| Johnson | 1964 | 22.6% | 39R-61D | 486-52 |
| Reagan | 1984 | 18.2% | 59R-41D | 525-13 |
| Eisenhower | 1956 | 15.4% | 57R-42D | 457-73 |
| Clinton | 1996 | 8.5% | 41R-49D | 379-159 |
| **BUSH** | **2004** | **2.5%** | **51R-48D** | **286-251** |
| Ford | 1976 | −2.1% | 48R-50D | 240-297 |
| Bush | 1992 | −5.6% | 37R-43D | 168-370 |
| Carter | 1980 | −9.7% | 51R-41D | 49-489 |

*Sources:* For 2004 statistics, see *Dave Leip's Atlas of U.S. Presidential Elections,* available at uselectionatlas .org. For all other statistics, see Richard M. Scammon, Alice V. McGillivray, and Rhodes Cook, *America Votes 25: A Handbook of Contemporary American Election Statistics* (Washington D.C.: Congressional Quarterly Press, 2003).

as an alternative. This strategy was followed, roughly speaking, by Adlai Stevenson in 1956, Jimmy Carter in 1976, and, to a lesser extent, Walter Mondale in 1984 and Robert Dole in 1996. There are always differences of position between the two candidates, but the challenger makes a point of offering himself as a reasonable and safe alternative. The second strategy is for the opposition party to present "a choice not an echo," running a candidate who offers a bold alternative platform, sometimes remaking his own party in the process. This approach obviously runs the risk of repelling many voters, as they now may have a strong reason to vote against the challenger regardless of their assessment of the incumbent. But this strategy may also strongly energize the party's base, which otherwise might approach the campaign with little interest, and perhaps convert voters from the other side. This was the strategy embraced by Barry Goldwater in 1964, George McGovern in 1972, and Ronald Reagan in 1980, although Reagan also strove in that campaign to be broadly acceptable.

Political parties today are not, as they may once have been, entities that make rational calculations about which strategy will be most effective. No group of elders sits together in a smoke-filled room to consider all of the relevant factors. Rather, the nominee is determined in a complicated process in which candidates, voters, and groups press their views and interests on a whole series of grounds. In the end, the nation is presented with a result. Still, the question of the campaign strategy for the general election is not altogether absent as a consideration in the nomination race. The candidates signal their intentions about the kind of campaign they will run, and voters weigh this factor as one element in their large menu of items to think about. Democrats in 2004 faced a decision between an early front-runner, Howard Dean, who promised a version of a "choice" campaign, and a few other candidates—eventually, John Kerry emerged from among them—who were offering to run a campaign predicated on being "the other guy." Dean, who provocatively announced that he represented the "Democratic wing of the Democratic Party," advanced a plan to reshape the party and to find a majority in an enlarged and energized Democratic base. John Kerry, while moving closer to many of Howard Dean's positions during the nomination campaign, offered himself primarily as the "electable" candidate, emphasizing his record as a strong and tough leader, based in large part on his record in Vietnam, who could be trusted in conducting the war on terror. All in all, Kerry would offer a reasonable alternative for Americans to President Bush's policies.

Once nominated, this was exactly the strategy that the Kerry campaign sought to execute. John Kerry did his best—given his whole career record, the stand of many in his party, and some of the positions he had staked out during the nomination contest—to allow voters dissatisfied with President Bush to pull the lever for him. Always a bit aloof, Kerry never succeeded in generating very much enthusiasm for his candidacy; nor did his campaign ever show much boldness or originality. There was nothing, for example, like Bill Clinton's dramatic move in 1992 to pick a fight with the rap artist, Sister Souljah, to demonstrate his independence from the cultural Left. But Kerry carried forward the basic plan with steadiness and diligence. His bet was that lingering economic problems and especially the continuing difficulties in the conduct of the Iraq War had produced enough discontent—more than enough—to give him a victory. Appropriating Howard Dean's theme that Iraq was "the wrong war, in the wrong place, at the wrong time," and blaming Bush for a net loss of jobs, Kerry pounded away at the administration from his nomination in March through Election Day in November. The strategy came up short, although not by much. Did anyone, really, have a better idea?

The other factor that determines the character of an incumbent reelection campaign is the public's evaluation of the president's record. A strong record means that the president can dictate the terms of the campaign, no matter what the challenger tries to do. A number of the incumbents were in this position, and their challengers knew fairly early on that, barring some fatal error by the president or divine intervention, the prospects of victory were nil. Their duty was to carry the standard of their party, keeping its losses in other races to a minimum, or perhaps helping rebuild the party constituency for another day. Almost all of the previous incumbent victories were, at least by the final weeks of the campaign, foregone conclusions, due largely to favorable judgments of the presidents' records, although the margin of victory was clearly aided in 1964 and 1972 by worries about the extremism of the challenger. Some of the incumbent victories were glossy celebrations, like Ronald Reagan's "Morning Again in America" campaign of 1984 or Bill Clinton's "Bridge to the Future" in 1996. Three of these elections—1964, 1972, and 1984—rank among the great presidential landslides of American history.

These races bear no resemblance to 2004. George Bush's campaign was competitive and was much closer in spirit and tactics to the contests in which incumbents were defeated (1976, 1980, or 1992) than to those where the incumbent was the winner. The final results prove this point, if proof is needed. Bush's margin of victory was the narrowest of the six victorious incumbents, both in the popular vote and the electoral vote. (In fact, it is the narrowest incumbent victory in all American history, the next closest being Wilson's win by 3.2 percent in 1916.) President Bush, like President Ford, President Carter, and his father, had to run for his life. While many on his campaign team had hopes that the race might suddenly "break" into a comfortable lead, it was never really to be. After trailing in polls in the spring and summer, Bush appeared to gain a modest advantage following the Republican convention at the beginning of September, but it evaporated after the first presidential debate on September 30, in which John Kerry had the clear edge. For the final month of the campaign, the outcome of the race remained in doubt. Newspaper headlines in the last days tell the story: "Day Dawns with Unpredictability, Polls Show Tie" (*The Washington Post*, November 2) or "Swing States Lean to Kerry" (*USA Today*, November 1). The 2004 election was one in which the result was truly not known until the votes were counted. As the TV producers might say, it is the kind of election that does wonders for the ratings.

The competitiveness of the 2004 election was no surprise, at least not after the events of the first part of 2004. If the presidential election had been held in 2002, when George Bush was being hailed as the unifying leader after September 11, or in the spring of 2003, following the fall of Baghdad, everything would have been very different. During this period George Bush enjoyed widespread support among most Independents and many Democrats. But American presidents, unlike British prime ministers, do not have the luxury of deciding when elections take place. By 2004, the context was very different. True, the economy was showing steady improvement, although job growth always seemed to fall beneath the level "expected" by the anonymous group of experts. But the situation in Iraq was not the success that the Bush administration had hoped for a year earlier. Far from it. From the Kay report in January, indicating that there had been no weapons of mass destruction (WMDs) in Iraq, to the scandal of the mistreatment of Iraqi prisoners at Abu Ghraib prison that broke in late April, and above all to the continuing, deadly insurgency, the Iraq War had turned into a "hard slog." Support for the war among the American populace slid from nearly two-thirds after Saddam Hussein was captured in December (down already from the three-quarters after the fall of Baghdad) to slightly over half in June, where it leveled off.[5] The decline was especially steep among Democrats, turning the Iraq War into a partisan issue.

More generally, in the six months preceding the election, there was little in the news that could be considered as clearly positive for the president, with the exception of the elections held in Afghanistan and Australia, which received scant coverage. Some of the most "helpful" events to George Bush were—ironically—tinged with sadness: the four Florida hurricanes, which allowed the administration to show the efficacy of its disaster relief efforts; the death and funeral of Ronald Reagan, which reminded many of George Bush as Reagan's heir; and, finally, the grisly terrorist murder of hundreds of school children in Beslan, Russia, which reawakened the reality and fear of the terrorist threat. For the most part, however, as the election approached, the immediate news was unfavorable, even in the economic realm, where the stock market went into a downswing and oil prices reached all-time highs. To all this was added a massive shortage of flu vaccine, blamed by some on the administration. George Bush was running the 2004 campaign if not at the low point of his popularity as president, then very near it. His job approval hovered around 50 percent, and the percentage of Americans believing the country was on the wrong track was at or near its highest during his term. Although the various election models developed by political scientists mostly predicted a Bush win in 2004, these were of little solace to those in the president's campaign, if they were ever even noticed. The models had uniformly failed in their predictions in 2000, and none took account of foreign policy (or did so only through the indirect medium of presidential approval ratings).[6]

This was not a race, in short, in which George Bush could just show up, present his record, and do a victory lap. A real campaign had to be waged. All incumbents, even those in the enviable position of being able to anticipate victory, will take some steps to highlight differences with their opponents. But in competitive races the president's campaign must make serious efforts to draw a contrast, turning the race, at least in part, into a choice and not just a referendum. Reasons must be given to vote against the challenger as well as for the incumbent. Following the Democratic convention in July, a group of Vietnam veterans, calling themselves the

Swift Boat Veterans for Truth, launched a series of controversial but effective television ads questioning aspects of Kerry's Vietnam service and his subsequent antiwar activities. Kerry's strategy, which rested on a celebration of his biography as one of the keystones of the race (just as it had been in his critical victory in the Iowa caucuses), was upset, and this theme was largely dropped from the fall campaign. Beginning with the Republican convention, the Bush campaign turned its sights on Kerry's conflicting positions on the war in Iraq and also, by implication, his lack of steadfastness in the wider war on terror. The effort was to frame the choice between resoluteness and wavering. Borrowing a page from Howard Dean, who from the antiwar side introduced the theme of John Kerry as a "flip-flopper" on the Iraq War—Dean's campaign in Iowa tried to present Kerry with a pair of flip-flops as a Christmas present—the Bush team attacked John Kerry for his inconsistencies and for his record on defense and security issues. Contrasts with Kerry's liberal domestic record came later. Finally, as many noted, George Bush opened his campaign in a way that was redolent more of that of a challenger than a content incumbent. While Democrats spent much of the time at their convention touting John Kerry's personal status, George Bush offered an agenda for both domestic and foreign affairs that promised to change the status quo.

Election analysts agree that the greater part of the "persuasion" of voters, especially in an incumbent election contest, takes place before the actual campaign ever begins. Voters have before them the president's record about which they can make a judgment. The campaigns can try to interpret or spin that record, but they cannot change reality. Campaigns nevertheless can make the difference when the race is close, as it certainly was in 2004. By the "campaign" making a difference, two different things can be meant: the occurrence of a major external event during the campaign period that importantly affects the voters' assessment and the successful efforts undertaken by the candidates and their organizations (or supporters) to try to win votes. The 2004 campaign took place under a constant shadow of something happening that could shake up the whole race, such as a new terrorist incident, a major setback in Iraq, or a dramatic success in the War on Terror like the killing or capture of Osama bin Laden. These possibilities created an aura of great uncertainty in both camps. At any moment, a contingency could tip the election one way or the other. Perhaps the greatest surprise in the end was simply that there was no major October (or September) surprise. A last-minute videotape arrived from Osama bin Laden, but it hardly qualified as a decisive event.

This left the fate of the race to be determined by the efforts of the two campaign organizations. Neither one proved to be fatally flawed or committed a decisive error. There were mishaps on both sides, but there was nothing akin to the open bickering and incompetence of the Bush campaign team in 1992 or the disastrous performance of Al Gore in his first debate in 2000. Both campaigns were run competently. On the losing side, where criticisms are usually strongest, there was remarkably little recrimination for how John Kerry had waged the contest. The verdict pronounced by most pundits is the following: Republicans won the initial skirmish of the party conventions; John Kerry won the battle of the first (and most crucial) debate; and both sides did a remarkable job in turning out their supporters, but Republicans appeared to have a clear edge. Whether President Bush won *because* of the campaign—whether the Bush campaign succeeded in changing more minds than the Democrats or getting more voters to the polls—is impossible to know for certain, but Democratic strategists seem to have conceded the point, agreeing, in the words of their party chair, Terry McAuliffe, that Republicans "were much more sophisticated in their message delivery."[7] What can be said for certain is that the Bush campaign did enough to win under difficult circumstances, and in the end, that is what counts.

In light of George W. Bush's record, which was so open to interpretation, it was perhaps natural that many voters would revert to their primal red and blue instincts in making their judgments. This fact may help explain the otherwise surprising result that in spite of the massive changes that had taken place in the world during Bush's term—the terrorist attack of September 11, 2001, and the two wars that followed, and the end of the economic boom of the 1990s—the voting patterns of 2004 bore a strong resemblance to those of 2000. The 2000 election was one in which a historically high percentage of partisans (about 90 percent) voted for their parties' nominees. The same held true in 2004, even more so. The impression of resemblance between the contests of 2000 and 2004 was only strengthened by the experience of watching the returns on election eve. As the results began to roll in, the scene began to look eerily like a rerun of 2000. States that were red in 2000 began to fall obediently into the red column; those that were blue stayed blue. The stage seemed to be set for one of the big swing states—Florida, or perhaps this time Ohio—to decide the event, hopefully without the same trauma experienced in 2000.

The final result in 2004 was not, in fact, very far off from this scenario. After Florida went into President Bush's column, attention turned to Ohio where the tally was close enough that the result could not be called until the early hours of the next morning. John Kerry decided to sleep on what had happened. But the next day, unlike 2000, the race came to an end with the traditional phone call of congratulations to the winner and a public speech of concession. The rituals of peaceful democratic decision making had been restored. In all, just three states changed colors. New Hampshire crossed from red to blue, while Iowa and New Mexico went from blue to red—and in each of these states the net swing from 2000 was very small. Last time, Bush had barely won New Hampshire and barely lost Iowa and New Mexico; this time, it was the reverse. If anything, the switches rationalized the red-blue map of 2000, wiping out the one Republican island in New England and the one Democratic oasis between the Missouri River and the West Coast.

But resemblance is not the same thing as identity. Elections in a competitive situation are won at the margins, and it was at the margins that red clearly began to show through. Some fairly important changes occurred between 2000 and 2004. One of the most remarkable was the sheer size of the electorate itself. Some 17 million more citizens cast a vote in 2004 than in 2000, an increase of 16 percent, the largest such increase in the past half century (table 1.2). Because overall population is always increasing between elections—and not at a uniform rate—this measure is far from a perfect indicator of "real" growth. Election analysts make use of other measures of turnout, such as the number voting as a percent of the total voting age population (which is estimated for the years between the censuses) or the number voting as a percent of what some calculate to be the "eligible voters," which is the voting age population less the large number of noncitizen immigrants and felons. There are difficulties with each of these measures as well. But no matter which indicator is used, the rise in turnout in 2004 was of historic proportions. The full list of causes remains open to conjecture, but it certainly includes the troika of closeness, intensity, and mobilization. Voters in 2004 were aware that the race was up in the air (and remembered from 2000 that a few votes can make a difference); they perceived the greater importance of politics in wartime, and many had strong feelings, for or against President Bush; and, perhaps most important of all, both parties and their auxiliary organizations undertook unprecedented efforts to get their supporters to the polls.

Increased turnout is notable for two reasons that are unconnected to the partisan battle between red and blue. One relates to the charge, which has been favored by so many European commentators, that an anemic and generally declining voter turnout in America calls into question, perhaps even denies, the reality of American democracy. The 2004 result is a counter-indicator, although one unlikely to dampen many of these criticisms, which are often driven by ideological motives and designed to embarrass the United States. The other implication relates to a prominent academic thesis that contends that "negative campaigns," especially negative campaign ad-

**Table 1.2.    Voter Turnout in Presidential Elections, 1956–2004**

| Year | Change from Last Election | Voting Age Population | Voting Eligible Population |
|------|---------------------------|-----------------------|---------------------------|
| **2004** | **16.0%** | **55.3%** | **60.0%** |
| 2000 | 9.5% | 51.2% | 56.5% |
| 1996 | −7.8% | 49.0% | 53.4% |
| 1992 | 14.0% | 55.1% | 61.5% |
| 1988 | −1.1% | 50.3% | 54.7% |
| 1984 | 7.1% | 53.3% | 57.9% |
| 1980 | 6.1% | 52.8% | 55.1% |
| 1976 | 4.9% | 53.5% | N/A |
| 1972 | 6.2% | 55.2% | N/A |
| 1968 | 3.6% | 60.9% | N/A |
| 1964 | 2.6% | 61.9% | N/A |
| 1960 | 11.0% | 62.8% | N/A |
| 1956 | 0.4% | 59.3% | N/A |

*Sources:* For voting age population data from 1992 to 2000, see U.S. Bureau of the Census, *Statistical Abstract of the United States,* 2000, 120th ed., (2000), p. 273, 291 (downloaded July 5, 2001, from the U.S. Bureau of the Census website, www.census.gov/prof/www.statistical-abstract-us.html). Published in Paul R. Abramson, John H. Aldrich, and David W. Rohde, *Change and Continuity in the 2000 Elections* (Washington, D.C.: Congressional Quarterly Press, 2002), p. 75. For voting eligible population data from 1980 to 2000, see Michael P. McDonald, *U.S. State Turnout Rates for Eligible Voters, 1980–2000.* ICPSR Study No. 1248 available at webapp.icpsr.umich.edu/cocoon/ICPSR-STUDY/01248.xml. [Note that these archived data are not consistent with the new 1998–2002 estimates. These data are based on 1990 census population estimates, while data on this website are based on the 2000 census.] For voting age population and voting eligible population data for the 2004 election, see Michael P. McDonald, *United States Election Project.* Available from George Mason University at elections.gmu.edu/Voter_Turnout_2004_Primaries.htm.

vertisements, suppress voter turnout.[8] This argument, reminiscent of the theological notion that sin reaps its own just punishments in this world, has proven a favorite among a species of political moralists who like to preach against the evils of dirty campaigns. While the scientific measurements of negativity from 2004 are not yet in, very few commentators can be found who extolled this contest for being notably kind and gentle. Two young political scientists, Jacob Hacker and Paul Pierson—perhaps too young to recall 1964 or 1980—opined that the "GOP may well have waged the most negative campaign by an incumbent president in modern political history."[9] Some Republicans also complained of treatment in kind from the Democrats. For what it is worth, two-thirds of the voters thought Kerry unfairly attacked Bush, while 60 percent thought Bush unfairly attacked Kerry.[10] All this sounds suspiciously like politics. Yet turnout swelled nonetheless, leaving supporters of the "negativity thesis" with their work cut out for them.

It is the partisan implications of the increased turnout, however, that are of most interest. A general rule of thumb in electoral studies has been that, all things being equal, higher turnout tends to favor Democrats.[11] A related and partisan application of this finding has been the frequent charge that Republicans have followed a strategy of trying to suppress turnout, in order to increase their chances of winning. The 2004 results clearly challenge this view, at least if one is thinking about the future. Some may still claim that a greater turnout would result in Democratic gains. But many who were engaged in the process in 2004 have concluded that, as a practical matter, the turnout rate in many states approached the limit of what is feasible for the modern electorate. In addition, it is now far from clear whether identifiable demographic groups that have lower turnout—and could conceivably be brought to the polls in much larger numbers—hold more Democratic than Republican sympathizers. The belief in a massive, untapped reservoir of blue flowing beneath the surface may now be nearing its end. To listen to many Democratic strategists today, their hope for achieving a majority rests more with the growth of their "new" base among higher-income college graduates, a group that already votes at a very high rate, than with finding any large new advantage among nonvoters.[12]

Now that this intensive race for an edge in turning out partisan supporters has been launched, it is certain to continue and escalate in the future. Some of the methods and techniques pioneered by the parties, the best of which married high technology to huge efforts in old-style personal contacting, will be studied and adapted. The parties, of course, are not benevolent associations interested in increasing overall turnout, but organizations devoted to turning out the voters most likely to vote for them. If there is a public good in increased turnout, it results in large part from an invisible hand that rests on the self-interested activity of the two parties. Close observers on both sides agreed that the victory in the ground game went to the Republicans. As David Broder noted: "Democrats did a first-class job of mobilizing their supporters and bringing them to the polls. But Republicans did an even better job, and that is essentially why they won."[13] Evidence from the polls lends some credence to this verdict. More Republicans as a total share of the electorate voted this time than last (37 percent as opposed to 35 percent), and an even higher share of these Republicans (93 percent as opposed to 91 percent) voted for George Bush. Other factors could help account for these changes, but the Republican turnout effort would seem to be at the top of the list.

The most important shift to red in 2004 came in the gain in the share of the national vote, where George W. Bush went up from 47.9 percent of the vote in 2000 (a half point behind Al Gore) to 50.7 percent in 2004, making him the first president to be elected with a majority of the voters since his father's election in 1988. Although this increase was modest, it appears more significant when the *source* of national shares is considered. As judged by practical electoral analysts, a party's share of the vote represents its potential strength in any election, when it does not face competition from a "neighboring" third party. It is only by considering this number—which is always based on an estimate—that "real" gains and losses in national vote share can be calculated. Thus, in the two elections of 1992 and 1996 the Republican share of the vote was depressed (37.4 and 40.7 percent, respectively), due in large part to the size of the Perot vote (18.9 percent, in 1992 and 8.4 percent in 1996), which drew disproportionately from Republican-leaning groups.[14] Robert Dole's 3.3 percent gain over George Bush Sr. in 1996 looks in fact more like a loss when the size of the decline of the Perot vote is taken into consideration. George W. Bush's huge gain of 7 percent over Dole's score in 1996 is also less significant in light of the absence of a Perot candidacy in 2000. Meanwhile in 2000, the Democrats faced competition of their own from a neighboring party on the Left, Ralph Nader's Green Party, which won 2.7 percent of the vote. Combined, the "Left coalition" of Gore and Nader in 2000 won 51.1 percent of the vote, while the "Right coalition" of Bush and Pat Buchanan, who was scarcely a factor, garnered 48.3 percent. (The importance of the competition from Nader in 2000, which many Democrats held cost them the election, accounts for the extraordinary lengths Democrats went to in 2004 to keep him off of the ballot in many states.) The point to glean from this analysis for 2004 is that George Bush increased the Republican share of the vote from 2000 not by picking up support from a neighboring party, but by gaining absolutely against the Left coalition. Almost all of the 2.7-point increase for George Bush in 2004 represented a "real" gain.

When the policy reasons given for the voters' decision are analyzed, a rough picture emerges of what moved them. "Rough" is the word to stress because there is much less science to interpreting voter choice than many pollsters like to pretend. Not only are the poll questions often vague and confusing, but the actual line of causality can run in a different direction than many suppose: people often make a general overall decision about which individual they prefer, after which they embrace some policy explanations to justify that choice. Still, there is some utility to this line of analysis, as students of elections seek to interpret the "meaning" of the popular voice. Over the years, electoral analysts have identified four major policy dimensions: the economy, welfare issues (health, education, etc.), national security, and what has variously been called "social" or "moral" concerns.

During the three elections previous to 2004—1992, 1996, and 2000—the dimension of national security all but dropped out of consideration. With the Cold War over and no obvious threat looming in the international arena, foreign policy remained a concern of a few high-minded elites, but it scarcely seemed to occupy the general public. Tradition demanded that it be discussed during the presidential campaigns, but few people paid very much attention. From Clinton's theme in 1992 ("It's the economy, stupid!") to George Bush's "compassionate conservatism" in 2000, the focus of American politics was on domestic policy. The 2004 election appeared to be from another era. It saw the return of national security as a major dimension of voter concern. Its importance was also apparent from the character attributes that voters emphasized, where the qualities of firmness and leadership were, as they often had been during the Cold War, proxies for assessments of how the candidates would manage foreign affairs. Foreign affairs and national security, from at least the Reagan years onward, had been an area where Republicans held a distinct advantage, which is one reason why Democrats fared so well in the three elections when its role was insignificant.

The return of the national security issue in 2004 did help George Bush, although not unambiguously. Looking at the indicator of what voters selected as "the most important issue," Bush "won" with voters who framed the national security issue in the first instance in terms of the general war on terrorism, while he "lost" with voters who saw it in the first instance as the Iraq War. Since there were more of the former than the latter (and since Bush's margin of approval was greater within that group than was Kerry's on the Iraq War), it can be concluded that Bush in the end held the edge on the national security dimension. It was widely speculated that Bush's large gains among women voters from 2000 had much to do with this factor. A segment of the women voters, popularly dubbed "security moms," put terrorism first and apparently saw George Bush as the one best-suited to protecting their families. George Bush was perceived as the steadier or firmer candidate in keeping the nation safe from the threat of terror. It may even be that the negative character trait that the Kerry campaign identified to counter the Bush charge of Kerry as a flip-flopper—namely that Bush was "stubborn"—helped the president on the issue of fighting terrorism.

From the way questions are posed in the polls, it is difficult to establish a clear ranking of the relative importance of the four different dimensions of policy. But using the figures available, and sorting them by the different categories, national security concerns come out on top (and favored Bush), followed by economic issues (which helped Kerry), moral issues (strongly Bush), and finally welfare concerns (strongly Kerry). (See table 1.3.)

Given this ranking, how did it happen in the immediate aftermath of the election that a widespread view emerged, especially on the Left, that the moral dimension was the most important factor in the 2004 election?

Table 1.3. Most Important Issues for Voters in the 2004 Election

| Issues | Selected By | % for Bush | % for Kerry |
|---|---|---|---|
| National Security Issues | 34% | 58 | 42 |
| Iraq | 15% | 26 | 73 |
| Terrorism | 19% | 80 | 14 |
| Economic Issues | 25% | 26 | 74 |
| Economy/Jobs | 20% | 18 | 80 |
| Taxes | 5% | 57 | 43 |
| Moral Issues | 22% | 80 | 18 |
| Welfare Issues | 12% | 24 | 76 |
| Health Care | 8% | 23 | 77 |
| Education | 4% | 26 | 73 |

*Source:* CNN.com exit poll, available at www.CNN.com/ELECTION/2004/pages/results/states/US/P/00/epolls.0.html.

The explanation had something to do with a purely technical issue of how the poll questions were formulated, but even more with the psychological state of those seeking a justification for defeat. The technical issue was this: in asking the question about the most important issue, the national election poll supplied a list that broke the foreign policy dimension and economic dimension into subissues (e.g., terrorism and the Iraq War), so that the issue of "moral values" appeared as the single highest response. In addition, in looking back to this same question in the 2000 polls, the choice of "moral values" had not been offered, so that a superficial analysis might have concluded that it jumped from nowhere to the top. (In fact, other poll evidence from 2000 clearly shows that with the Clinton scandals so prominent, the dimension of "moral values" was of enormous importance in that election.) These technical issues, however, were only the backdrop to the psychological wish many had to believe that the election was determined by millions upon millions of evangelical voters who had turned out in a fit of primitive prejudice to express their fear of homosexual marriage. According to Garry Wills, writing in *The New York Times*, Bush mobilized those who believe "more fervently in the Virgin birth than in evolution" and was able to be reelected "precisely by being a divider, pitting the reddest aspects of the red states against the blue nearly half of the nation."[15] This view of the electorate was frightening to those who espoused it, but it was also consoling: it proved that defeat was at the hands of those whose votes had no moral, ethical, or intellectual worth.

In response to this highly polemical interpretation, a number of Republicans and conservatives understandably rushed to downplay the significance of the moral issue—perhaps too much so. They were correct to deny its primary importance, but the truth of the matter lies in an appreciation of degree. The "moral issue," although not the most important dimension in 2004, was nevertheless quite important, just as it had been in 2000. Nor was it synonymous with the issue of single-sex marriage. It spread across a whole range of ethical issues, including abortion, stem cell research, the character of schooling, and the tone of mass entertainment. These issues also turn out to be highly important not just to religious-minded voters (who are more apt to respond to the specific cue of "moral issues") but also to many strongly secular voters (who tend to hold opposite views and who apparently prefer to refer to these matters as "policy questions" rather than "moral issues"). Democrats no less than Republicans brought some of these questions into the campaign debate. The division on this set of questions shows up repeatedly in the connections between more religious Americans, who vote more strongly (but by no means exclusively) Republican, and more secular-minded Americans, who vote more strongly (but by no means exclusively) Democratic. There is clearly nothing new in this division.

It is a truism in the study of elections that the human mind must be able to keep more than one thing in mind at the same time. All along certain analysts condemned various Democratic and Republican strategists (Karl Rove, President Bush's political alter ego, was frequently mentioned) for plans to mobilize elements of their respective cultural bases, as if such plans were somehow both an error and a crime. The error was in thinking that this factor was the most important element of the election; the crime was that concerns of this kind are unworthy of mention in a national election and should be left to experts or to courts. But the truth in this instance is that plans to mobilize the cultural bases were adopted by leaders in both parties as one component of a larger campaign strategy. In every election, different groups of voters have different priorities, and election strategy always involves addressing a multiple set of concerns. Despite claims that moral issues should be excluded from partisan competition, many Americans persist in believing that they are germane to national elections. Elections can be one means for citizens to express a view about whether certain matters should or should not be decided by judicial judgments. Even if judges do not read the election results, politicians, including governors and state legislators, do. The "wall" between politicians and judges is not nearly as high as many suppose, and elections can be used to send signals from one set of elites to another. It is likely—former President Clinton suggested as much—that Democratic politicians will now begin to urge their colleagues on state courts to exercise greater caution in how they approach certain questions.[16]

The candidates as persons also send out general cultural signals, whether deliberately or unconsciously, and these form a part of the picture on which voters judge their characters. John Kerry knew all along that he faced a problem with American voters of appearing too elitist and "liberal." This problem stemmed from his Massachusetts base (a no-no in American politics since the campaign of Michael Dukakis), his enormous personal wealth, and even his strong intellectual propensities and capacity to see complexity, which can be mistrusted. If George Bush was intellectually challenged, as some claimed, John Kerry was culturally challenged. Kerry took many steps during the campaign to try to round out this image, in particular by emphasizing his manliness (the war record was important here) and his personal vigor. He deliberately used a few vulgarities, and he showed up famously near the end of the campaign in hunting gear, having bagged a goose. Every effort was taken to try to break the connection people might make between Kerry and Dukakis. Not all of Kerry's deficits were, in fact, the liability that many feared. His intellectual prowess was often a source of admiration, and his dominance in the first presidential debate was every bit as much a result of style—a cool and detached intellectual demeanor—as substance. But for all of his efforts to play down an elite cultural image, the campaign fell all too often into the trap of confirming some of the negative stereotypes. It was not just that John Kerry did not know how to pronounce the home field of the Green Bay Packers, nor that his wife, Teresa, appeared to disdain Laura Bush (falsely) for never having held a job; it was that John Kerry did not know how to vacation well. Bill Clinton commissioned polls to instruct him on where to spend his holidays to maximize the political effect. John Kerry showed up twice on vacation during the campaign, once on the ski slopes at Sun Valley snowboarding and a second time near Nantucket, off the coast of Massachusetts, windsurfing. A new and unwritten rule entered the American political playbook in 2004: if you are going to shift positions on some key issues, don't be videotaped windsurfing.

The terms "red" and "blue" have come to be used not just politically, to designate partisan leanings, but anthropologically, to describe cultural proclivities. This expansion of the metaphor, though it is suggestive in some ways, has had the unfortunate effect of conflating these two realms and of equating political divisions entirely with "cultural" divisions. The "cultural" component, which is only one part of the political equation (albeit, an important one), is wrongly taken to characterize the whole. In some presentations, the red-blue divide is evoked to express the idea of a radically polarized society split between two conflicting ways of life: a red America that is small-town, religious, and dominated by the church steeple, and a blue America that is secular, urban, and dominated by Thai restaurants. And in the most facile characterizations, everyone living in the first kind of area is imagined to vote Republican, while everyone in the second votes Democratic. It is as if Republicans and Democrats never meet, except perhaps in a chance encounter at an airport or a Division of Motor Vehicles. No one, of course, who has studied voting patterns would ever subscribe to such a view, although one ill effect of the color scheme is that it can contribute to this kind of dichotomous thinking. It was accordingly very helpful when a number of electoral analysts took up their pens to remind people that many of the geographic areas colored in red in 2000 (and now in 2004) only barely sided with President Bush (and other Republicans), and that the same was the case for the blue areas. Some clever cartographers followed, introducing different shades between the colors—purple or even fuchsia—reflecting their relative degree of support for Republicans and Democrats.

Geography, especially when it relies on units as large as states, is a fairly crude way to try to discuss the scope of cultural divisions in America. But since this theme was pursued so widely in these terms in 2000, it needs to be considered briefly for 2004. The results on this score may surprise many who have imbibed the notion that this election led to greater geographic "polarization." The opposite in fact was the case. George Bush's percentage share of the vote, as one might have expected, increased almost everywhere in the United States, the only exceptions being Vermont (a blue state, where he dropped by almost two points) and South Dakota (a red state, which Bush won by a landslide both times, dropping this time by a tiny fraction). But of the eight states in which Bush gained the most from 2000 (over five percentage points), five of them were blue states: Hawaii (7.8 percent), Rhode Island (6.8 percent), Connecticut (5.5 percent), New Jersey (5.9 percent), and New York (5.0 percent). Overall, the blue states moved in the direction of red by more than the national average as a whole. Geographically, the nation in 2004 was less, not more, polarized.

Looking ahead, Democrats have cast their eyes on states like Colorado and Virginia, where Kerry ran surprisingly well. The Democratic hope in these states rests on the demographic expansion of certain suburban areas that are filled with the kind of upper-middle-class professionals who tend increasingly to vote Democratic—areas like Fairfax and Albemarle counties in Virginia and Jefferson County in Colorado. Republicans rely on the demographic fact that Republican families, and now many of the red-state areas, are the fastest growing parts of the population. The long-term national outcome, in this view, boils down to a race between Republicans' efforts to produce more babies and Democrats' efforts to produce more lawyers and professors. Which group of partisans will derive the greater pleasure in this contest remains unknown.

Whether the nation became more polarized in 2004 depends on exactly what are the criteria of polarization. Only recently, race and minority divisions from the rest of the populace were singled out as the most worrisome source of polarization. By this standard, there was much less polarization in 2004. Race was largely absent from the 2004 campaign as an electoral theme, in contrast to 2000 when ads castigating Bush for opposing hate crimes legislation in Texas were a part of the campaign. While African Americans continued to vote overwhelmingly Democratic (88 percent), Bush gained some ground from 2000. Among Latino voters, the degree of polarization decreased dramatically. In what was one of the keys of Bush's victory, his share of the Latino vote rose from just a third in 2000 to 44 percent in 2004.[17] If gender is taken as the source of division, here again there was less polarization: the eleven-percentage-point difference between men and women in 2000, with women favoring Al Gore over George Bush, shrunk to just three points this time. Men and women are getting back together, a development likely to make members of both sexes more content. It may be, as some contend, that the reduction in the gaps between these demographic groups is being replaced by a common division on the basis of "cultural" beliefs that is cutting through all groups in the same way. The evidence here is not conclusive, but even if this were true, would the nation really be more polarized, or less?

## Realignment and the New System of 2004

While each election and race is distinct, the common denominator of political parties makes elections partly collective affairs. An election can be viewed as an event that confirms or denies a broader trend. Using 1979, the year before Ronald Reagan's election, as the base year, the general direction across the major elected offices — state as well as national — is clear (table 1.5). There have been ups and downs, and the presidency was already in play between the parties before this period, but there is no question that America has become more Republican.

There are other ways of indicating the same point. One is to look at the party with which voters themselves claim to identify. Following the 1992 election, the Gallup poll found 25 percent of the electorate identifying itself

**Table 1.4.    Polarization: Voting Cleavages in the American Electorate 2004**

| Category | %Bush | %Kerry | 2004 Gap | 2000 Gap | Change |
|---|---|---|---|---|---|
| African American | 11 | 88 | Kerry +77% | Gore +82% | −5% |
| Hispanic/Latino | 44 | 53 | Kerry +9% | Gore +36% | −27% |
| Men | 55 | 44 | Bush +11% | Bush +16% | −5% |
| Women | 48 | 51 | Kerry +3% | Gore +11% | −8% |
| Jews | 25 | 74 | Kerry +49% | Gore +60% | −11% |

*Sources:* For 2004 election data, see: CNN.com exit poll, available at www.CNN.com/ELECTION/2004/ pages/results/states/US/P/00/epolls.0.html. For 2000 election data, see James W. Ceaser and Andrew E. Busch, *The Perfect Tie: The Story of the 2000 Presidential Election* (Lanham, Md.: Rowman & Littlefield Publishers, Inc, 2001), p. 163.

as Republican as against 35 percent Democrat and 40 percent independent; following the 2004 election, Republicans had gained the lead with 38 percent, while Democrats were at 35 percent and independents at 27 percent.[18] Of course, self-described party identification can jump around, and it is not always a reliable indicator of actual voting practices. This has led some scholars to calculate a general index of party strength based on the actual voting results for the six major institutions in American politics (the presidency, the two houses of Congress, the governor, and the two state legislative chambers). The effort here is to devise a single and comparable figure at two-year intervals to indicate the relative strength of the two parties—a kind of Dow Jones average of American party strength. Since 1992, when Democrats held a slight lead nationally, Republicans have been gaining and are now in front.[19]

The 2004 election marks a decisive point in this development, less because of the magnitude of the Republican gains in this election than because of the significance of crossing a critical political threshold. For the first time since 1952, Republicans won a recognizable majority in all three of the elected institutions of the national government, which after all is the

**Table 1.5.    Change in Party Strength 1979 and 2004, Number and Affiliation of Elected Officials**

| Year | President | Senate | House | Governors | State Legislatures* |
|---|---|---|---|---|---|
| 1979 | D | D 58 | D 277 | D 32 | D 68 |
|  |  | R 41 | R 158 | R 18 | R 28 |
|  |  | I 1 |  |  | Tie 2 |
| **2004** | **R** | **D 44** | **D 201** | **D 22** | **D 47** |
|  |  | **R 55** | **R 232** | **R 28** | **R 49** |
|  |  | **I 1** | **I 1** |  | **Tie 2** |

*Note:* * Total number of state legislative chambers controlled by either party. Nebraska has a nonpartisan legislature.

main political prize associated with being a majority party. In 2000 Republicans managed to attain unified control of the federal government, but without really winning that election. They backed into the position, electing a president who trailed in the plurality vote, dropping two seats in the House (while retaining a razor-thin majority of 221-212), and losing four seats in the Senate (leaving that chamber in a 50-50 tie, broken only by Vice President Dick Cheney's vote). Another such "victory" and the Republicans would have been undone. By contrast, the Republican victories in 2004 were real, even if not huge, allowing Republicans to be able to claim the status of being, for the moment at least, the majority party.

This change in the relative strength of the two parties over the last generation is the most notable fact in the electoral history of our time. By what name should it be called? The simplest and most descriptive term, it would seem, is "realignment," and a few analysts, including a handful of Democrats, have not hesitated to employ this word. But most political scientists have resisted doing so, not necessarily because of a partisan aversion to placing this crown on the head of the Republican Party, but because they have concluded the term itself should be retired. The reason is that it has been tied in the literature of political science to a grand theory of electoral and political change that most have come to believe is false. According to the "classic" theory, realignment is a great event that respects the dramatic unities of time, place, and action; it is the electoral version of an exploding nova star, generating in a single moment (one national election or at most two) a massive amount of energy that reshapes all political matter for the next era. The introduction of this energy into the political system, which generally follows in the wake of a national crisis, produces three effects: (1) a decisive shift in the relative electoral strength of the parties, accompanied by internal changes in the character of the parties' internal coalition, in which the previous minority party (or a new party) sometimes takes over as the majority party; (2) a change in the agenda of national politics and in the dominant ideas governing public life, corresponding to the program or the public philosophy of the majority party; and (3) a change in the way politics is conducted and in how political information is transferred and received in society. To top it all off, realignments come with a predictable regularity, occurring roughly every thirty-two to thirty-six years.

This remarkable, not to say fantastic, theory was developed largely by Walter Dean Burnham, a professor of political science who began his career at Kenyon College before going on to teach at MIT and the University of Texas, from which he recently retired. Part statistician, part seer, Burnham not only claimed to have discovered this pattern historically, but he has also never been shy about insisting, beginning as early as 1968, that the phenomenon still applies to our own era. Mesmerized by the richness of this analysis, many scholars spent much of their careers awaiting the next realignment, only to grow impatient with its tardiness in arriving before finally beginning to entertain doubts about the validity of the concept itself. The misgivings were recently cataloged and given systematic expression by David Mayhew, one of the nation's leading political scientists. Mayhew put the theory under a clinical microscope and judged it to be inaccurate or wanting in almost every particular. He recommended abandoning the term, concluding that the "realignment perspective" is "too slippery, too binary, too apocalyptic, and it has come to be too much of a dead end."[20] There Mayhew ends his little book, having demolished an edifice but without having put anything else in its place.

For those left with the task of trying to situate the 2004 election in some historical perspective, there seems to be no alternative for the time being other than to try to combine the best of Burnham and the best of Mayhew. This act of forced union can be accomplished, first, by setting forth a minimal definition of a realignment that, in the spirit of Mayhew's critique, divorces the concept from the grand theoretical claims made on its behalf; but second, by drawing on Burnham, by treating the imaginative claims linked to realignment theory as questions or hypotheses, which can be analyzed to see what light, if any, they shed on the current situation. This approach is not offered as a new theory of electoral change, but simply as a way to consider the larger implications of this particular election.

Relaxing, then, Burnham's dramatic assumptions about the great unities of time, place, and action, a realignment can be conceived simply as a major change in the underlying strength of the two parties during a specified period of time. By this definition, a realignment has already taken place in the time period between the 1960s or 1979, when the Democratic Party was in the clear majority, and today, when the Republican Party holds an edge. (How long the Republican advantage will hold, no one can know for certain.) Distinguishing this change from the change posited in a "pure" realignment in the classic theory, it is clear that in the current case not all of the energy for the transformation has flowed from a single explosion. It has taken twenty-four years to achieve the "equivalent" of what was supposedly achieved in a single election, such as 1800, 1860, or 1932. This rolling realignment nevertheless possesses a kind of unity, as the three most important Republican victories during this period—1980, 1994, and 2004—are all slightly different versions of the new conservatism inaugurated in 1980. It took one initial explosion and two secondary ones to generate the energy sufficient for Republicans to reach the critical threshold of majority status.

Where does this account leave the 2004 election? It is not, clearly, the election that launched the process. Burnham, who has always been more eclectic in the application of "theory" than some make out, has aptly characterized 2004 as the election that "consolidates" the realignment. For those still wedded to the classic theory, Burnham has divined a likely future of Republican dominance: "If Republicans keep playing the religious card along with the terrorism card, this could last a long time." He has referred to 2004 as perhaps "the most important election of [his] lifetime." At seventy-five, he could presumably be including 1932 in the comparison, although even the precocious Burnham may not have been charting electoral patterns when he was three.[21] If this realignment has been consolidated, it should now be possible to look back on this period as one event and to ask what are some of its distinctive properties. The time may have arrived to begin speaking of a "system of 2004" that is different in important respects from the system of 1932. The new system, which emerged with a gradual but clear shift in party strength and a reorientation in the internal party coalitions, is characterized by an increase in partisan consistency, the ascendance of a new set of political ideas supported by a new kind of intellectual infrastructure, and the advent of a new mode of political communication. America is living in a new political universe.

A realignment in the classic theory is said to provoke a major change in the internal coalition of the parties. This hypothesis clearly holds true of the two parties in the current period, although it is a much more difficult task to describe internal coalitional changes over a long period than in a single moment. In a pure realignment, when everything happens suddenly, the changes take place in the same electorate; what one side loses, the other side gains (or picks up from existing nonvoters). Over a longer period, many changes that occur are unrelated to the energy released by the realignment—for example, in the current realignment, the emergence of Latino voters, who hardly existed a generation ago, or the shrinking proportion of blue-collar workers, who were previously a much larger contingent in the Democratic Party. Nevertheless, many of the recent changes have been realignment-driven. The Republican Party a generation ago was chiefly a coalition of small business owners and entrepreneurs, mainline Protestants of the middle and upper classes, plus a large set of partially disgruntled Democrats, among labor and throughout the South, who often supported Republican presidential candidates but not Republicans for other offices. The geographical base of the party was in the Midwest and, for a time, the Northeast. By 2004, the party still holds its business and entrepreneurial part, but it has added an important new element: the religious voters, found either in the new Protestant evangelical sects or among the more orthodox of Catholics, Jews, and older Protestant sects.

As the foundation of American politics is still geographical, the most important changes are tied to geography. Here the most notable feature of American politics in this realigning period has been a massive regional shift. The South has become the major geographical base of the Republican Party, while New England—a much smaller region—has become a bastion of the Democratic Party. The change in the South, which was already well under way in voting behavior at the presidential level before 1980, has since steadily worked its way down to other offices, with the final level, not yet reached in all of the southern states, being the state legislatures (table 1.6). Today, in the eleven states of the Old South, 85 percent of the senators from the region and 63 percent of the members of the House are Republican. Meanwhile, an opposite, although less complete, change has been taking place in New England. In 1976, when Jimmy Carter was elected president, Gerald Ford won four of six New England states. In 2000, Al Gore carried five of the six—it was his strongest region by percentage—and John Kerry this time won all six. Beneath the presidential level, Republicans in New England still fare quite well in many statewide elections. But the briefest look at House and state legislative contests in Massachusetts, for example, shows a situation resembling nothing so much as the kind of one-party politics that were found in Mississippi a half-century ago: Democrats win almost every position, with Republican opposition being either token or nonexistent.

A consequence of this re-sorting process—and a feature of the new system of 2004—is stronger and more consistent partisanship. In the system of 1932, partisanship was relatively weak, and each party contained a powerful dissident wing to which the other party's dominant wing could appeal in trying to form cross-partisan coalitions. Southern Democrats often combined with most Republicans, while liberal or progressive Republicans sometimes made common cause with the dominant New Deal/Great Society Democrats. While the northeastern liberal Republican is not unheard of today, it is an endangered species; likewise, most conservative southern Democrats have by now become Republicans. The actual shift of Vermont Senator James Jeffords from a Republican to an Independent who aligns himself with Democrats, and the virtual shift of Georgia Senator Zell Miller as a Democrat who ended up giving the most fiery speech at the 2004 Republican National Convention, was a metaphor for this entire process. Increased partisanship can be seen today in much higher partisan unity in congressional floor voting, a decline in split-ticket voting in the electorate, smaller postconvention "bounces" for the candidates, campaigns that seek

**Table 1.6.  Regional Party Strength, 1976–1978 and 2004, Percentage of Two-Party Presidential Vote and Number of Elected Officials**

| Region | President | House | Senate | Governors | State Legislatures |
|--------|-----------|-------|--------|-----------|--------------------|
| | | 1976–1978 | | | |
| New England | D 53.0 | D 18 | D 7 | D 5 | D 7 |
| | R 47.0 | R 7 | R 5 | R 1 | R 4 |
| | | | | | Tie 1 |
| South | D 54.8 | D 77 | D 15 | D 8 | D 22 |
| | R 45.2 | R 31 | R 6 | R 3 | R 0 |
| | | | I 1 | | |
| | | *2004* | | | |
| **New England** | **D 58.6** | **D 16** | **D 6** | **D 2** | **D 10** |
| | **R 41.4** | **R 5** | **R 5** | **R 4** | **R 2** |
| | | **I 1** | **I 1** | | |
| **South** | **D 42.8** | **D 49** | **D 4** | **D 3** | **D 11** |
| | **R 57.2** | **R 82** | **R 18** | **R 8** | **R 11** |

*New England:* Connecticut, Maine, Massachusetts, New Hampshire, Rhode Island, and Vermont
*South:* Alabama, Arkansas, Florida, Georgia, Louisiana, Mississippi, North Carolina, South Carolina, Tennessee, Texas, and Virginia

to rally the partisan base as much as to appeal to swing voters, and the reemergence of unified government. The outlines of the new system now suggest that, in the broad scope of American history, the system of 1932 was the aberration in its relatively relaxed partisanship.

The second effect of realignment posited in the classic theory is a change in the dominant set of ideas that governs the nation and sets the national agenda. This part of the theory also has application to the current realignment, but again with similar difficulties in applying the idea neatly to a change that has taken place over so long a period of time. The main lines are nevertheless clear. A nation that once was best described as being guided by liberalism (under Lyndon Johnson) or at least progressivism (under Jimmy Carter) is now better described as being strongly influenced by conservatism. Of course the meaning of both liberalism and conservatism has shifted and altered somewhat, in part as each has responded to the other. The liberalism of Bill Clinton, if it was that, became much more centrist or "third way" in the aftermath of the Reagan years and the Republican victory in 1994, while the conservatism of George Bush became more centrist (or compassionate) in response to Bill Clinton's reelection in 1996 and Republican reversals in Congress in 1998. But in the end, after all of the swings of the pendulum, it is conservatism in one form or another that has gained enormous ground.

It is a conservatism deeply different from that found in Europe, which is often statist, elitist, and paternalistic. Rather, since Goldwater, Republican conservatism has aimed at the preservation of limited government, though not as limited as libertarians would prefer; a defense of social and moral traditionalism; the maintenance of a strong and autonomous civil society; and a kind of nationalist globalism, eschewing both isolationism and liberal internationalism, increasingly grounded in a foundationalism looking to the natural rights doctrine of the Declaration of Independence. These ideas have advanced with the assistance of extensive infrastructure that conservatives have built over the last generation. Conservative columnists like William F. Buckley, George Will, and David Brooks have attained mainstream prestige; magazines and journals like the *National Review*, *Weekly Standard*, *Commentary*, *National Interest*, and *Public Interest* both make the public case for conservative ideas and help organize the thinking of conservatives themselves. Think tanks like the Heritage Foundation, the American Enterprise Institute, and dozens of local imitators affect the policy agenda and policy outcomes. Even inside academia, conservative voices are heard more frequently—and are better organized—than they were a generation ago. A fundamental shift of political power—a realignment—cannot take place or be sustained in the absence of a change in key sectors of the civil society. Not since the Progressive era has there been a comparable kind of intellectual institution building, and it is a model that liberals are now trying to emulate.

In comparison to the ideological underpinnings of the New Deal, the ideas of the 2004 system operate to a greater extent independently of material interests. As John Micklethwait and Adrian Wooldridge, the authors of the highly acclaimed book *The Right Nation*, point out, "In no other country is the Right defined so much by values rather than by class."[22] The political cleavages in America reflect the battle of ideas more than the struggle among economic classes. The distribution of the vote across classes is remarkably even. If the class midpoint in America is defined as a family income of $50,000, close to as many below the line voted for Bush (43 percent) as did those above the line (56 percent). In the realm of voting behavior, America is approaching the Marxian utopia of the perfect communism of a classless electorate.

The third and final effect in realignment theory is a change in how political campaigning is conducted and how political information is processed and transmitted. The examples cited here from the past include, following the realignments of 1800 and 1832, the creation (and re-creation) of political parties as the instruments for organizing and conducting elections and the development of the popular press, which was launched by the parties and was partisan in character. Other examples include the change in 1896 from the drill-style campaign to the advertisement and educational campaign that was pioneered by Mark Hanna for the campaign of William McKinley. In the current realigning period, a change of this sort is also taking place, and when all is said and done, it may constitute one of the major transformative events of American political history. Campaign methodology has been changed by Internet fund-raising, recruiting, and communication, which have facilitated the formation of new kinds of voter mobilization machines. We now have Boss Tweed armed with a Blackberry. Above all, however, there has been a steady replacement of what many have dubbed the "old" media by the "new." This transformation has been both a cause and a consequence of the political shift in the last generation, so much so that it is difficult to imagine that the current realignment could have fully been realized in its absence.

The terms "old" and "new" media appear to suggest changes related chiefly to technological developments, but this characterization captures only a small part of the transformation underway. Prior to the realignment, in the era dominated by old media, the prevailing system consisted not just of a particular method of communicating information, but also of an underlying conception of the nature of information itself. Information was transmitted under the aegis of what was known as "news," where news was understood to be a nonpartisan and objective account of events and affairs. News was gathered and conveyed by what were called journalists, a group that claimed to possess professional standards that assured impartiality. During the middle part of the twentieth century, both the prestige and remuneration of this group, especially its national pacesetters, increased enormously. The national elite of this group, in part because of technological reasons, were a relatively small number of hands, coming from a few prestigious newspapers (chiefly the *New York Times* and later the *Washington Post*), the major news weeklies (*Time* and *Newsweek*), and, once television was developed, the chief journalists of the three television networks, ABC, CBS, and NBC. As time went on, television came to have the greatest direct impact, with its network news anchors receiving the greatest remuneration, although these broadcast journalists usually relied on print journalists for their interpretive schemes. All combined, the journalists and the organizations for which they worked came to be called, in titles that are suggestive of their enormous power and responsibility, the "fourth estate" or more simply "the media."

Wherever and whenever in this period a particular politician or group felt injured or harmed by the media, there might be attempts to question its objectivity or assert bias. Complaints on this score could be heard from politicians on both the Left and the Right. But a deeper and more serious charge emerged in the 1960s, during and after the Vietnam War. It was that the media, in line with a movement of opinion within the intelligentsia, was systematically biased in favor of a liberal viewpoint. The bias was so great and deep-seated that it was just as likely to be unconscious as conscious. This charge was widely accepted by conservatives, and President Nixon went so far as to adopt a highly developed strategy deigned to combat the influence of the media. He did so by sowing seeds of suspicion about the network news, sending his vice president, Spiro Agnew, to ask, in a famous speech in Des Moines "whether a form of censorship already exists when the news that 40 million Americans receive each night is determined by a handful of men . . . who admit to their own set of biases."[23] Nixon went on to try to work around the national media and speak directly to the American people—a strategy which, because it abandoned the media altogether, was bound to be limited in its success. Nixon himself eventually discredited that strategy. In his forced resignation, in which the media played such an important and constructive role, many journalists found not just revenge but vindication. Never again would a president be so impertinent as to take on—frontally—the elite media.

Yet, a different line of conservative action began in the 1980s and is still unfolding. Instead of merely complaining about the character of the media, conservatives (chiefly) began to develop alternative channels of mass communication. The first and still probably the most important was the rehabilitation of an older medium, the radio, in the form of national talk radio programs.[24] Although this medium was open to all, it was in fact developed almost exclusively by conservatives (it still is) who were highly conscious of, and who continually harped upon, their antagonism to the old media. The pioneers of talk radio were offering an alternative channel of mass communication, far friendlier to Republicans. The second change depended initially on the development of cable TV, which opened the door to more television channels and thus eventually to other networks, including those specializing completely in news and public affairs, beginning with CNN. Again, as CNN shows, there was nothing intrinsically liberal or conservative in this development. But it did make possible an alternative to the monopoly of the old media. The Fox cable news channel stepped into the newly created space with a clear intent to counter the perceived biases of the other networks. A final change, more recent still, was the opening up of the Internet and the development of blogs. The rise of the blogosphere, which as a technological development has no particular bias, has cut further into the already diminishing influence of the old media. Insofar as the old media possessed its alleged liberal bias, the blogosphere has functioned temporarily to open up channels of communication more hospitable to conservatism.

A number of symbolic events in the challenge of the old media by the new media occurred during the 2004 campaign. The first was the television rating victory of Fox News in the coverage of the Republican convention, where for the first time a cable news channel bested all of the "old" networks in the number of Americans watching the convention. Given that Republicans are more partial to Fox and more apt to follow the Republican convention, and that the networks have downplayed their coverage of conventions, this "first" was perhaps less important than many made out. But it did indicate a changing of the guards. The second event was more significant. It came in the form of a major news story in September by CBS attacking President Bush's National Guard Service during the Vietnam War. The story featured a thirty-year-old memo from Bush's commanding officer at the time, the validity of which was vouched for by CBS and its longtime anchor, Dan Rather. The memo was a forgery—an evident one at that—and this discovery was first proven within the blogosphere. One of the most venerable institutions of the old media went toe-to-toe with the amateurs of the new media and blinked. Instead of the blogs citing the old media, it ended up that the old media—or parts of it—had to cite the blogs. What looked to be the clear partisan intent of the CBS report only served to confirm for conservatives their long-held view of the systematic liberal bias of the old media. Similarly, when ABC News chief Mark Halperin issued an internal memo urging his reporters to hold Bush more accountable than Kerry for distortions in the campaign, it made its way almost instantly into the blogosphere before leaping to talk radio.

The most important aspect of the transformation in the communication system that is now underway, however, lies not in any shift in bias of the news coverage, but rather in the demise, pure and simple, of the previous conception of news. People today tend to select the channels they watch and the publications they read on the basis of their existing preconceptions and of which source they believe that they can trust. Technology has made possible a greater number of choices, but it is a change of underlying views about the character of information that is leading many to seek out the new options. The "average" conservative no more accords a presumption of impartiality to the *New York Times* than does the "average" liberal to the Fox News Network. The motto of the *Times*—"all the news that is fit to print"—is dismissed just as quickly by conservatives as is the Fox News motto—"fair and balanced"—by liberals. For his final television program on PBS, Bill Moyers selected what he called "the biggest story of our time:

how the right-wing media has become a propaganda arm of the Republican National Committee."[25] For years, this is just how conservatives viewed Moyers and PBS, only with the left arm reaching out to the Democratic National Committee. The larger point in these mutual recriminations is again not who is right or wrong, but the fact that we are witnessing an end of the concept of news as we have known it. The transmission of information in the nation is now in many respects closer to the system found during the middle of the nineteenth century, when information was garnered through partisan newspapers, than the system found in the middle of the twentieth century, when the conveyance of information was purportedly neutral. This change, too, is part and parcel of the realignment of our time.

One of David Mayhew's most trenchant critiques of classic realignment theory is that it posited an inevitability to affairs that is simply not appropriate in a world defined by contingency. Who, after all, would have predicted September 11? That something resembling a realignment system can be observed is no prediction that it will endure and no guarantee that the process that brought it about is closer to its beginning than to its end. The future, if it can be seen at all, is best left to prophets.

## Notes

1. Niccolò Machiavelli, *History of Florence* (book 2, chapter 6) available at www.online-literature.com/machiavelli/florence_italy/11/ (accessed January 5, 2005).

2. See, for example, "Red vs. Blue: A Spectrumological Reversal of Symbolisms," available at www.upwithbeauty.org/2004/09/ (accessed January 5, 2005). Of course, had the colors been reversed, some complaints would undoubtedly have been heard that Democrats were tainted by being assigned red, the color of socialism. Other interesting musings on the color scheme can be found at answers.google.com/answers/threadview?id=415905.

3. *Federalist 72*, available at federalistpapers.com/federalist72.htm (accessed January 5, 2005).

4. The number is nine if one includes Lyndon Johnson in 1968, who withdrew from the race during the nomination phase. It is worth noting as well that two of the presidents on this list ran as incumbents without themselves having been previously elected as president: Lyndon Johnson in 1964 and Gerald Ford in 1976. Ford was not even elected as vice president, but was selected under the procedures of the Twenty-fifth Amendment in 1973, following the resignation of Spiro Agnew.

5. Pew Research Center Survey. The question posed was "Do you think the United States made the right decision or the wrong decision in using military force against Iraq?" The results can be found at www.pollingreport.com/iraq.htm (accessed January 5, 2005).

6. *PS: Politics and Political Science*, September 2004.

7. Thomas Edsall and James Grimaldi, "GOP Got More Bang for Its Billion," *Washington Post*, December 30, 2004, p. A1.

8. For a statement of the position in favor of the thesis that negative campaigning decreases turnout, see Stephen Ansolabehere and Shanto Iyengar, *Going Negative: How Political Ads Shrink and Polarize the Electorate* (New York: Free Press, 1995). For a response see the writings of Steven Finkel, Paul Freedman, and Ken Goldstein. Among them: Steven Finkel and Paul Freedman, "The Half-Hearted Rise: Voter Turnout in the 2000 Elections," in *Models of Voting in Presidential Elections: The 2000 Elections*, ed. Herbert Weisberg and Clyde Wilcox (Stanford, Cal.: Stanford University Press, 2003); Ken Goldstein and Paul Freedman, "Campaign Advertising and Voter Turnout: New Evidence for a Stimulation Effect," *Journal of Politics* 64(3):721–40; and Steven Finkel and John G. Geer, "A Spot Check: Casting Doubt on the Demobilizing Effect of Attack Advertising," *American Journal of Political Science* 42:573–95, 2002.

9. Jacob Hacker and Paul Pierson, "Popular Fiction," The New Republic On Line, November 8, 2004, available www.truthout.org/docs_04/110904W.shtml (accessed January 5, 2005).

10. All poll figures unless otherwise indicated are from the news network exit poll, which is available on the CNN.com website.

11. The best review of what is known about turnout is found in Paul Abramson, John Aldrich, and David Rhode, *Change and Continuity in the 2000 Elections* (Washington, D.C.: Congressional Quarterly Press, 2002), chapter 4.

12. See Gerard Alexander, "The Long View," *The Weekly Standard*, November 22, 2004.

13. David Broder, "A National Pledge of Party Allegiance," *Washington Post*, December 5, 2004, p. B7.

14. Exit polls in 1992 showed that Perot voters were split roughly evenly between Bush and Clinton for their second choice, but they were clearly drawn primarily from the ranks of disaffected Republicans and Republican-leaning independents.

15. Garry Wills, "The Day the Enlightenment Went Out," *New York Times*, November 4, 2004.

16. William Schneider, "On This, Clinton and Rove Agree," *National Journal*, November 20, 2004.

17. Some Democrats have questioned the exit poll accuracy of the figures on Latino voting, but the *Los Angeles Times* exit poll shows a similar jump.

18. Jeffrey Jones, "Country Tilts Republican in Post-Election," December 14, 2004, The Gallup Organization. Available at the Gallup Organization website. Measurements taken after the election often seem to inflate the strength of the victorious party.

19. In this index, 50 is the break-even point, with a figure below that number indicating a Democratic advantage and a figure above it a Republican advantage. The index was at 48.6 in 1992 and 54.0 in 2004. The index is calculated by a complicated weighting formula, explained in James Ceaser and Andrew Busch, *The Perfect Tie* (Lanham, Md.: Rowman & Littlefield, 2001).

20. David Mayhew, *Electoral Realignments: A Critique of an American Genre* (New Haven, Conn.: Yale University Press, 2002), p. 165. The major work of Walter Dean Burnham is *Critical Elections and the Mainsprings of American Politics* (New York: Norton, 1970).

21. Fred Barnes, "Realignment, Now More than Ever," *Weekly Standard*, November 22, 2004.

22. John Micklethwait and Adrian Wooldridge, *The Right Nation: Conservative Power in America* (New York: The Penguin Press, 2004), p. 12.

23. Speech delivered, November 13, 1969, in Des Moines, Iowa. The text is available at www.americanrhetoric.com/speeches/spiroagnew.htm (accessed January 5, 2005).

24. The rise of conservative talk radio is traced by many observers to a 1987 Reagan administration decision to abolish the so-called "Fairness Doctrine," a Federal Communications Commission rule requiring equal time for political commentary on the airwaves. See David Frum, "Men, Not Machines," *National Review*, October 11, 2004, p. 23.

25. "Moyers prepares for Friday's 'Now' Farewell," *Charlottesville Daily Progress*, December 11, 2004, p.A11.

# Chapter Two

# The Bush Presidency

When George W. Bush was sworn in as the forty-third president of the United States on January 20, 2001, he assumed the executive office of what political analyst Michael Barone called the "49 percent nation." He was the third consecutive presidential victor to win with less than 50 percent of the popular vote. Not since the 1880s had the nation been poised so perfectly on the political fence, with the two parties so closely balanced. Tensions between the parties were also very great. The polarization of the Clinton years—the one-vote congressional margin for Clinton's economic program in 1993, the two government shutdowns in 1995–1996, Republican obstruction of judicial appointments, and Clinton's scandals, impeachment, and trial—left deep scars.

Bush's election itself mightily exacerbated these tensions. A decisive moment that helped shape Bush's presidency came one month after the murky results of the November 7 election. Between December 3 and December 8, events in Florida were moving quickly toward what looked to be a relatively clean conclusion to the bitter election controversy. The U.S. Supreme Court had issued a thinly veiled caution to its Florida counterpart, Gore was turned down in his attempt to contest the state-certified election results in the courtroom of Judge N. Sanders Sauls, and Democrats lost last-ditch lawsuits challenging the absentee ballots from two Republican counties. Only one piece remained. Gore quickly appealed Sauls's decision to the Florida Supreme Court, which, given its long-standing tradition of upholding trial court decisions on findings of fact, it was widely expected to deny. Democratic elites edged closer to accepting a Bush victory, and the nation began to heave a collective sigh of relief that the ordeal was nearly over.

Then everything was upended. On the evening of December 8, the Florida Supreme Court by a majority of four to three overturned Sauls's decision and imposed a remedy so radical that not even Al Gore had asked for it. The court ordered an immediate statewide recount of all "undervotes"—or ballots on which no discernible vote had been made for president. In his dissent, Chief Justice Charles Wells declared the decision likely to incite a "constitutional crisis" that would "do damage to our country, our state, and this court as an institution." Florida's election machinery creaked back into gear, and recounts—the third for some counties—began the next day. Democratic hopes revived. Most Democrats (and many Republicans) expected the result would give Gore the lead. Republicans prepared for action by asking the Florida legislature to choose an alternate set of presidential electors, whose votes would be sent to a Republican-controlled Congress. The next day, the U.S. Supreme Court issued an order to halt the recounts. Three days later, by a 7-2 vote, the Supreme Court held that the Florida recount was unconstitutional, and by a 5-4 vote that time had run out for a remedy. The dissents were passionate. Justice John Paul Stevens argued that "preventing the recount from being completed will inevitably cast a cloud on the legitimacy of the election." Al Gore conceded the next day. The next four years would be deeply affected by the intense feelings engendered during these four days from December 8 to December 12, 2000.

In the short term, the Gallup polls showed that 83 percent of Americans considered Bush's victory legitimate. A year after the election, a consortium of media organizations examined the uncounted Florida ballots and concluded that under almost all of the conditions used for recounting the votes, George Bush would have won both a statewide recount of all undervotes and a full recount of the four counties Gore had insisted upon.[1] Yet Democrats were outraged, believing that partisan justices snatched a victory that had been within their grasp. To his opponents, George W. Bush became the "accidental president," a figure whose legitimacy, already in question due to his loss of the national popular vote, was crippled by his reliance on a friendly Supreme Court. Like the election of 1824, this election had been "stolen." For their part, Republicans nursed a quiet grudge of their own, but it was masked by the satisfaction of victory and generally overlooked. They would not forget the way that Democrats had tried to win the election with lawyers, friendly county election boards, judicial legerdemain, and sheer force of will. The postelection fight was arguably a seminal moment in the emotional mobilization of Republicans and their allies in the "new media," and contributed to a redoubling of their efforts in 2002 and 2004.

## Before September 11

Bush entered office fully anticipating a domestic presidency. Only 12 percent of voters in 2000 identified foreign policy or national security as the most important issue and, apart from an important program for missile defense, Bush's agenda was to focus on politics at home. Bush's vision, and that of his chief strategist Karl Rove, was to create a new Republican majority by transforming the Republican Party. The new GOP would step away from the image of harder-edged conservatism of the 1990s Gingrich revolution and toward a "compassionate conservatism" defined by its willingness to expand as well as contract government. The litmus test would not be limited government but government that "empowered" individuals through tax cuts combined with enhanced choices in education, health care, and social service provision. At the same time, Bush would tilt toward social conservatism but do his best to straddle hot issues, such as gay rights.

Critics (and more than a few allies) wondered whether "compassionate conservatism" was a political philosophy, a governing strategy, or an electoral tactic. It may have been all three, but it clearly aimed to bridge the gender gap, appeal to moderates, and bring into the Republican coalition more black and (especially) Hispanic voters, who were identified as a pivotal group. Bush seemed deeply committed to compassionate conservatism, but he had not devoted the years and effort to it that, say, Reagan had given to the development and propagation of his brand of conservatism. The first national test of compassionate conservatism, the election of 2000, could not be rated a success. In the primaries, Bush had relied upon a more traditional conservatism to win, and in the general election he had not been able to close the sale. Unable to forge the transformation he sought at the ballot box, he would have to try again as president, when he could deal in the realm of actions rather than words.

Bush proved himself an adept manager and received plaudits for the efficiency of his truncated transition.[2] His cabinet appointments were mostly uncontroversial, and he relied heavily on old Republican hands while including a large number of women and racial minorities, a combination which sought both to calm concerns about his inexperience and to reach out beyond the standard GOP constituency.

Bush's "first" presidency, his term prior to September 11, went through three distinct periods. In the first period, lasting roughly from January 20 to June 1, he surprised many observers by vigorously promoting parts of his conservative legislative agenda, including his number one legislative priority of a broad tax cut. The surprise here derived from the fact that, in the wake of his contentious victory, many Democrats and experienced Washington hands were promoting the notion that George Bush should function as the head of a kind of grand coalition government, advocating only measures that met the approval of leaders in both political parties. This idea was floated with such frequency, and met with such widespread admiration, that it was widely taken to represent the "reality" of American politics.

Yet George Bush clearly was of another mind. He had no intention, despite the circumstances of his election, of placing his presidency into a kind of receivership. Following the general strategic model of Ronald Reagan, Bush limited his legislative agenda to a few big items. Besides his income tax cut proposal, his other top priority was an education bill (No Child Left Behind), which could expect broad bipartisan support. Bush also had a short list of secondary priorities, including an energy bill and federal support for faith-based initiatives, which, like education reform, was central to his campaign for "compassionate conservatism" and which aimed to bring together white evangelicals, Catholics, and inner-city ministers. While Bush did not back off of his agenda, he made a concerted effort in the first months of his presidency to redeem his promise to restore civility to Washington politics. He courted several Democrats, and Senator Ted Kennedy became a guest of the Bushes at the White House. One key House Democrat declared, "It's strange to have a president who knows his manners." As loyal as Democrats had been to Bill Clinton during his impeachment travails, many had tired of the scandals and embarrassments, and their relief on this count contributed to a positive atmosphere in Washington. In spite of everything, the spring of 2001 brought what many never expected: a Bush honeymoon with the Congress.

The early months of the Bush presidency also brought a vast change in perceptions of the nation's economic situation. As January turned into February and March, it became increasingly clear that the economic expansion of the 1990s was grinding to a halt. Early warning signs had appeared throughout 2000 but went largely unheeded. The stock market experienced a precipitous decline, peaking in January 2000 and losing one-seventh of its value by October 2000, before recovering slightly at the end of the year; manufacturing employment contracted by 59,000 jobs in 2000; and the economy was extremely sluggish in the second half of 2000, actually shrinking slightly in the third quarter. In the first quarter of 2001, the American economy entered a recession, though it was not officially recognized as such until the fall. Bush had campaigned for tax cuts in 2000 as a political and even moral imperative, a means of preserving limited government by making it impossible for Washington to spend the whole projected surplus. Now, he could argue for them as economically necessary, too.

His original proposal to provide $1.6 trillion in tax relief over ten years was whittled to $1.35 trillion, and a number of other changes were introduced by both Democrats and Republicans. Still, it was Bush's plan in inspiration and grand outline. The legislation remained highly controversial, above all on the perennial issue of fairness. Democrats attacked the bill for giving the biggest aggregate tax cuts in dollar amount to the wealthy, while Republicans pointed out that it was taxpayers at the bottom of the income distribution who received the largest percentage cuts, with several million being removed from the tax rolls altogether. From a statistical standpoint, both were right. In the end Bush won: 240-154 in the House, 58-33 in the Senate, with 28 House Democrats and 12 Senate Democrats joining a unified GOP (only two Republicans, both in the Senate, voted no). While the tax cut received most of the attention, other Bush priorities quietly advanced, including his No Child Left Behind education program.

Bush was also widely praised for his patient but firm response to a crisis that erupted on March 31 when a Chinese fighter jet collided with an American reconnaissance plane, forcing the American plane into an emergency landing on Chinese soil. China held the American plane and the twenty-four crew members as virtual hostages until Bush issued the apology demanded as a price for their release. Once the crew was safely home, Bush promptly resumed spy plane missions, agreed to sell some advanced weapons to Taiwan (though not all of what the island had requested), and announced his determination to defend Taiwan if it was ever attacked by Beijing, a de facto rejection of the policy of "strategic ambiguity" in place since the Carter administration. Americans got a glimpse of Bush under pressure: methodical rather than impulsive, determined but measured.

Then, at the end of May, disaster struck for the Republicans, and the second period of Bush's pre-September 11 presidency began. Third-term Republican Senator James Jeffords of Vermont announced that he was going to leave the GOP to become an independent who would vote with the Democratic caucus. Jeffords had long been a maverick on the left edge of the Republican Party and was the only GOP senator to endorse the Clinton health plan in 1994. Republicans accused him of acting in a fit of pique over dairy subsidies and a variety of petty snubs, while Democrats depicted his move as the rejection by a Republican statesman of high principle of his own party's ideological rigidity. Whatever the reality, Jeffords's shift meant that the Senate majority had changed hands. Trent Lott was out as majority leader, as were all of the Republican committee chairs, and Tom Daschle and the Democrats were in as majority leaders.

The Republicans' brief moment of "unified government," for which they had waited almost a half-century, was over. So, too, was the honeymoon.

The change broke Bush's momentum and cast doubt on his leadership. Columnist Michael Kelly argued that Jeffords's defection called "seriously into question the vaunted reputation of the Bush White House for competence."[3] Some Republicans agreed; Nebraska Senator Chuck Hegel warned Bush that "if he is wise, he will see there is a crack here that is very dangerous to his presidency."[4] Bush's other legislation stalled, and he seemed uncertain what to do next. Democrats began talking of Bush as a lame duck president only five months into his term. As a *Washington Post* editorial pointed out, the dominant "story line" for the Bush administration had changed from one of "exceeding expectations" to one in which, "through arrogance and ineptitude, the Bush people have lost control of the Senate and the agenda."[5] Such analyses were bolstered by early summer polls showing Bush's public standing slipping across a range of issues.[6]

Yet before anyone had time to get used to this idea, the roller coaster took another turn. A second wind propelled the Bush presidency into the final stage of the pre-September 11 period. He found a way, using the Republican House as the instrument, at least to regain the political initiative. Just before Congress adjourned for its summer recess, the House passed showdown votes on Bush's faith-based initiatives bill; his energy bill, including a controversial provision allowing oil exploration in the Arctic National Wildlife Refuge; and his preferred version of HMO reform. Of course, there was still the Senate, but at least the administration was not stymied. A *New York Times* editorial declared that "even Mr. Bush's opponents would have to acknowledge he is on a winning streak. . . . He has shown far more skill in handling Congress than many people expected."[7] Bush also gave a serious speech on embryonic stem cell research, then opened his campaign to add Hispanic votes to the coalition of "compassionate conservatism" by proposing an extensive guest worker program for illegal Mexican immigrants, a plan that brought groans from some of Bush's conservative supporters who saw it as amnesty but that also reaffirmed his independence from them.

After seven months in the White House, Bush had achieved his largest legislative goal, regained his balance after losing control of the Senate, and discovered the utility of using the Republican House as the opening wedge of any legislative drive. He had also come face-to-face with the stalemate engendered by an opposition Senate and a lukewarm public. The 49 percent nation was still very much alive, as was the small-bore politics of the 1990s. The summer was consumed by tabloid speculation about the relationship of Congressman Gary Condit and his missing intern Chandra

Levy. On September 10, Congress, having returned from its recess, engrossed itself in debate over the Social Security "lockbox," a piece of technocratic jargon left over from the 2000 campaign which would within hours slip into both obsolescence and obscurity.

## After September 11

On the morning of Tuesday, September 11, 2001, the president of the United States was in a classroom in Sarasota, Florida, reading to schoolchildren when Karl Rove slipped him a disturbing note. A few minutes later, White House chief of staff Andrew Card whispered into his right ear what much of the rest of the nation knew because it was watching it live: the United States was under coordinated attack from unknown terrorist enemies. First one commercial jetliner, then another, were deliberately crashed into the two towers of the World Trade Center in New York City. Moments later, a third plane crashed into the side of the Pentagon. A fourth plane, bound for another target in Washington, D.C., fell into a Pennsylvania field. Amid fears that the president himself might be targeted, Bush flew to Air Force bases in Louisiana and then Nebraska, before returning to the White House on the evening of September 11.

With nearly three thousand people dead, it was not the bloodiest day in American history—the battle of Antietam still held that grisly record—but it may well have been the most terrifying. The terror was compounded by a strange combination of clarity and haze. Modern communications technology allowed viewers to watch, over and over, the planes crashing into the towers; the rush of humanity seeking escape, some by hurling themselves off of the towers, choosing certain death over fire; the fall of the towers, as their tons of concrete and steel fell across lower Manhattan; and, in the end, the desolate scene of the collapse, as smoke and dust and human ashes mixed together and wafted skyward. Horror has rarely been more clearly visible to the naked eye. These events had no detachment of time and place, but were happening here and now while a nation and the world watched.

Uncertainty gripped the nation. Gas lines formed as Americans filled up to prepare for the unexpected. Wild rumors flew throughout the day: a car bomb had exploded outside the State Department; other planes were still unaccounted for in the skies. After the rumors were quelled came the questions: Who did this? Why? How would the attack affect our polity and our economy? How should we respond? And perhaps most to the point: What would happen next? Was the attack merely a prelude to something even worse? Was another shoe about to drop? On the evening of September 11, no one knew the answers. Americans could only reflect on the questions in the eerie silence afforded by the clearing of all commercial air traffic from the skies. The only sound came from U.S. Air Force F-16s conducting combat air patrols over major American cities. In a period of twenty-four hours, a threshold was crossed. September 11, 2001, was a pivotal moment in national history that could only be made sense of by dividing time into "before" and "after."

George W. Bush faced a moment that he, like most Americans, could never have expected. He would later recall what he thought when Card broke the news to him: "They had declared war on us, and I made up my mind at that moment that we were going to war."[8] Minutes later, he told his staff on Air Force One, and then Vice President Dick Cheney, "We're at war."[9] The following morning, in a September 12 statement, Bush shared this view with the country, saying, "The deliberate and deadly attacks which were carried out yesterday against our country were more than acts of terror. They were acts of war"—albeit a somewhat new and different kind of war. Treating the terrorist attacks as a war was, for Bush, first instinct, but it was also a decision that had profound political and policy consequences. There were other ways of thinking about it, perhaps other options, and Bush exerted considerable force of will to impose the language of war on the situation.

With few exceptions, American policy for the two previous decades had treated terrorism as an intelligence and law enforcement challenge rather than as a military or paramilitary engagement. When terrorist acts occurred, they were treated as isolated instances to be dealt with by the arrest and prosecution of the guilty parties. State sponsorship of terrorism was played down as an issue. But September 11 was too big, too immediate. It *looked* too much like a war, with small pieces of Manhattan and northern Virginia standing in for London during the blitzkrieg of 1940. And the remorseless hatred of America's enemies glowed too hot to be mistaken for mere mischief. Few doubted that those enemies would have killed 30,000 or 300,000 on that day, had they possessed the means.

Thus began Bush's odyssey as a wartime president. It was a role he grew into, not one for which he was naturally prepared. His first appearances on television, two short statements during the day of September 11 and then an address to the nation at night after returning to Washington, were shaken and halting. His words were right: "Terrorism against our nation will not stand. . . . The resolve of our great nation is being tested. But make no mistake: We will show the world that we will pass this test. . . . America has stood down enemies before, and we will do so this time." And in his Oval Office address, he staked out what would become a centerpiece of his antiterrorism policy: "We will make no distinction between the terrorists who committed these acts and those who harbor them." But his demeanor was that of a stricken observer rather than a forceful leader.

Not until September 14, the date chosen as a national day of prayer and remembrance, did Bush fully find his voice. First, at a nationally televised service at the National Cathedral in Washington, Bush spoke in measured tones of comfort, purpose, and resolve. Drawing on his faith, he quoted Scripture, saying that nothing "can separate us from God's love." Then, with steel in his voice, he told the nation that "war has been waged against us by stealth and deceit and murder. This nation is peaceful, but fierce when stirred to anger. This conflict was begun on the timing and terms of others. It will end in a way and at an hour of our choosing."

Later that afternoon, visiting Ground Zero in New York, Bush achieved what almost all agreed was the defining moment of his early presidency. In an impromptu move, he climbed atop a pile of rubble and began to speak to a crowd of rescue workers, using a small megaphone. One of the workers from the crowd yelled, "We can't hear you." Bush found the perfect response, shouting: "I hear you, the rest of the world hears you, and the people who knocked these buildings down will hear all of us soon." His relationship with the American people would never be the same.

On September 20, nine days after the attack, Bush's transformation was completed. Before a joint session of Congress, Bush gave an address outlining the threat ("a fringe movement that perverts the peaceful teachings of Islam"), identifying Osama bin Laden's group Al Qaeda as the chief suspect, and demanding that the Taliban hand over bin Laden and other Al Qaeda leaders, close terrorist training camps, and allow the United States to inspect the camps. "These demands," Bush said, "are not open to negotiation or discussion. The Taliban must act and act immediately. They will hand over the terrorists, or they will share in their fate." Bush also declared that the United States would wage a broad war against terror groups, not limited to Al Qaeda. The time for equivocation toward, and toleration of, terror was over. To the nations of the world, he said, "Either you are with us, or you are with the terrorists. From this day forward, any nation that continues to harbor or support terrorism will be regarded by the United States as a hostile regime." In the end, he said, "Freedom and fear, justice and cruelty have always been at war, and we know that God is not neutral between them." Bush framed the issue in starkly moral terms as a fight against evil and evildoers. Not since Reagan had an American president spoken so forcefully in moral terms, discussing evil as a tangible object.

During the years of the Cold War, Americans concerned with the character of their leaders hoped for a steadiness and fortitude that could easily be associated with personal integrity (though the correspondence might not be complete). In the 1990s, when no major crises appeared to threaten, character in this sense became a lesser concern, and the qualities Americans sought shifted to compassion or empathy, soft rather than hard virtues. After September 11, the old model of character made a comeback, and Bush was now well-positioned to benefit. He was coming into his own as a president who symbolized uncompromising resolve and moral clarity. Bush's "deep distaste for the necessary insincerities of political life" brought him some trouble in the early months of his presidency—as when he officially buried a Kyoto Protocol that was already long dead politically—but Americans appreciated the straightforwardness of their wartime president.[10]

Consistent with the long-standing "rally effect" in public opinion, Bush's approval rating began climbing on September 11, reaching 78 percent before he had uttered a word. In the aftermath of his September 20 address, he reached a record approval rating in the Gallup poll of 90 percent. Thus began the biggest and longest-lasting rally effect ever recorded in the public opinion polls. That rating had much to do with the dire circumstances; within days, an outpouring of patriotic unity swept over the country. Flag manufacturers could not keep up with demand, as a *Newsweek* survey found that four out of every five Americans had flown the flag in the days after September 11. Contributions poured into innumerable ad hoc relief funds set up to aid attack survivors and the families of the dead. As the political symbol of American nationhood, Bush gained as a matter of course. But no small part was owed to Bush's decisive and multifaceted, yet measured, response to the attack.

That response included issuing new security regulations in airports, backed up by uniformed and armed soldiers; freezing the financial assets of terrorist groups and their supporters; creating an Office of Homeland Security to coordinate the relevant pieces of the federal bureaucracy; and proposing new legislation—the Patriot Act—aimed at enhancing the capacity of law enforcement authorities to track and intercept terrorists. The act passed 98-1 in the Senate and 357-66 in the House, although it quickly became controversial among civil libertarians. At the same time Bush took steps to dampen anti-Muslim feelings in the United States, appearing at a mosque, inviting an Islamic cleric to participate in the memorial service at the National Cathedral, and speaking out forcefully against anti-Muslim violence. Partly under pressure from those concerned with compromising civil liberties, the administration even discouraged extra scrutiny of young Arab males at airports; grandmothers and small children were being searched, along with former Vice President Al Gore.

After three weeks of anticipation, during which Bush repeatedly counseled national patience, the hammer finally fell on the Taliban and Al Qaeda. According to the accounts of insiders, the president was first presented with an old-fashioned military plan calling for massive air strikes. Unsatisfied, he demanded innovation. That innovation was provided by George Tenet and Donald Rumsfeld. Tenet, director of the CIA, offered a plan that relied heavily on CIA covert and paramilitary operations, not just in Afghanistan but in upwards of eighty countries where terrorism was an issue. Bush responded by exclaiming, "Great job!" and giving Tenet the go-ahead to start operations in Afghanistan.[11] Rumsfeld, an old Republican pro who was now Bush's Pentagon chief, had already tangled with the Pentagon bureaucracy over his desire to emphasize the development of lighter and more mobile forces better suited to irregular warfare far from easy logistical support. The Afghan War that Bush approved was Tenet's and Rumsfeld's kind of war, heavily dependent on the CIA, Special Forces, airborne and Marine units, precision air strikes, and local allies who would bear much of the burden of fighting.

In the meantime, Bush had to overcome two challenges. One was logistical: Afghanistan was a landlocked country. The other was political: Remembering the terrible fate that befell the Soviet army in Afghanistan just a decade earlier, many commentators expressed skepticism about the prospects for military success. The logistical detail was ironed out when diplomatic efforts succeeded (with Russia's blessing) in convincing Uzbekistan and Tajikistan, on Afghanistan's northern border, to allow the United States to base operations there. To the south, in perhaps the most important American diplomatic coup of the early days of the war on terror, Pakistan's Pervez Musharraf was turned from genuine ambivalence to giving as much support for the United States as his difficult position allowed. The Taliban had in many ways been a creature of Pakistan's intelligence service, so Musharraf's condemnation of the September 11 attacks and his willingness to allow U.S. overflights of Pakistani territory was a major turning point. The political problem could only be met head-on, by proving the skeptics wrong.

One last ultimatum was issued to the Taliban, and ignored. On Sunday, October 7, the president announced that "on my orders the United States military has begun strikes against Al Qaeda terrorist training camps and military installations of the Taliban regime in Afghanistan. . . . Our military action is also designed to clear the way for sustained, comprehensive, and relentless operations to drive them out and bring them to justice."

Crowds that had gathered in football stadiums across America stopped for a moment of silence, or, in some cases, a cascading roar of approval. The innocent dead would not go unavenged.

The intensity of these times was captured by one commentator who referred to the Autumn of Fear. Within days of September 11, the economy, already in recession, was sent reeling. The stock market lost 13 percent of its value in one week; in the first 120 days after the terrorist attacks, nearly a million jobs were lost. On October 4, a new wave of terrorism riveted the country when media personalities and public officials began receiving envelopes containing anthrax, a deadly biological agent. Under the right conditions, a large anthrax attack could kill tens of thousands. Delivered in small doses by U.S. mail, it actually did infect eighteen and kill five. The White House, CIA, and Supreme Court mail rooms had to be closed for decontamination; the Hart Senate Office Building was also closed; the Capitol itself was briefly evacuated. Some of the letters containing anthrax were mailed not far from where some of the September 11 hijackers had lived, and one included the phrases "Death to America" and "Allah is great." Many experts thought this letter to be most likely a cover for a domestic group or individual, and the FBI shortly turned most of its attention to domestic suspects. (To this day, the source remains unknown.) At the same time, the Justice Department declared that Al Qaeda terrorists had considered plots involving the use of commercial semi trucks and the retrofitting of crop dusters for chemical or biological agents. Americans began to confront the potential of "sleeper cells" in their own neighborhoods, and some began to stockpile gas masks as well as antidotes for anthrax and radiological poisoning. In December, Richard Reid, a British convert to Islam with ties to Al Qaeda, tried to blow up an American Airlines flight from Paris to Miami with a shoe bomb, but failed because his sweaty feet had spoiled the ignition fuse. He was wrestled to the floor by passengers and crew. Throughout much of the fall, Vice President Dick Cheney was kept at an "undisclosed secure location" to maintain continuity of government in the event Bush was killed.

Yet fear was only one component of the response. There was a tremendous stirring of religious faith, as churches and synagogues across America filled up in the days and weeks after September 11. Fear was also accompanied by a sense of resolve, strengthened by reflection on the passengers of American Airlines Flight 93, who had stormed the cockpit and forced the hijackers to crash the plane short of its target, most likely the Capitol building in Washington. And once American forces engaged the enemy in Afghanistan, martial pride took hold. Polls taken on October

7 showed that 90 percent of Americans approved of the war; a month later the figure was steady at 86 percent.

The Afghan campaign will likely go down in military history as a textbook example of the principle of economy of force, using the minimum resources to gain the maximum benefit. Though some after two weeks began to declare the operation stalled—the *New York Times* columnist Johnny Apple suggested it had become a "quagmire"—more sober heads were not discouraged.[12] Rumsfeld became a folk hero for blunt talk at his regular press briefings. Day by day, the U.S. bombing campaign eroded the communications, command, and control of the Taliban, while weakening their defenses. The CIA and U.S. Special Forces organized and prepared the Northern Alliance, the Afghan forces that had been fighting the Taliban for five years, for a decisive offensive. On October 19, Army Rangers parachuted into Kandahar, the home base of the Taliban, collecting intelligence and killing a number of Taliban soldiers. An intense air bombardment broke a hole in the Taliban line blocking the crucial northern crossroads of Mazar-i-Sharif, and the Northern Alliance, aided by Special Forces on horseback, flooded through. The city fell on November 9, followed less than a week by the fall of Kabul, and then, with the aid of the Marines, Kandahar itself. The enemy was broken and fled to the Afghan mountains, the rough-and-tumble borderlands of Pakistan, or west to Iran. Some reached Iraq, including the wounded terrorist leader Abu Musab al-Zarqawi, who received medical treatment in Baghdad. In early December, U.S. troops and their Afghan allies surrounded an enclave of the enemy in the mountains at Tora Bora, where rumors had bin Laden located. An offensive was launched, but the escape route was not fully blocked, and many fighters made their way to the relative safety of Pakistan. If bin Laden was there—and he may or may not have been—he, too, escaped. Critics, including John Kerry, would later claim that Tora Bora demonstrated the downside of Rumsfeld's strategy of using a minimal skeleton of American troops in combination with local forces, although field commanders rejected that interpretation.

During the entire Autumn of Fear, normal politics was at a standstill. In one way, Bush was tremendously aided by the suspension of partisanship since the maintenance of his high approval ratings depended in no small part on the almost total lack of criticism directed at him. On the other hand, Bush was also constrained from taking full political advantage of his high public standing. Among other things, he refrained from campaigning for the Republican candidates in the odd-year elections held on November 8. There were only three races of note. Republicans won the mayorship of New York and lost the governorship of New Jersey—badly. In the Virginia governor's race, where Bush might have made a difference had he campaigned, Democrat Mark Warner won by a tight 52-47 percent margin. Afterward, Democratic National Committee chairman Terry McAuliffe predicted that in 2002 Bush would "be of no benefit to any Republican candidate in the country."[13] McAuliffe and other Democrats may well have misread the results, distorting their party's strategy in 2002.

The bipartisan spirit spilled over into the domestic realm, as Bush accepted certain legislative deals with Democrats, sometimes more or less on their terms. In December, Congress finally approved Bush's trademark education bill, the No Child Left Behind Act, giving him a victory in his second primary legislative priority of 2001. But the price of passage in the Senate was steep: Ted Kennedy wrote significant portions of the final bill, and vouchers were stripped out, as were provisions allowing added state flexibility in spending federal dollars. To many conservatives, the bill ended up looking like another expansion of the federal government into state and local educational affairs. On final House passage, more Democrats than Republicans voted for the bill. However, Bush was able in a single stroke to erase much of the disadvantage his party had suffered for years in popular perceptions on education issues. The president also acceded to Democratic demands to create a new federal bureaucracy—the Transportation Safety Administration—to oversee airport security tasks like passenger and baggage screening. Finally, in March 2002, after half a decade of struggle, Congress enacted the McCain-Feingold campaign finance reform bill (now called the Bipartisan Campaign Reform Act, or BCRA) with mostly Democratic votes. BCRA contained several provisions Bush disliked (a ban on individual soft money contributions and a ban on issue advertising by groups within sixty days of a general election) and omitted some that he wanted (especially a paycheck protection measure to limit political use of union dues). The bill was made more palatable to some opponents by increasing the maximum amount that individuals could contribute from $1,000 to $2,000 per candidate per election. Perhaps hoping to continue the bipartisanship of the fall, and to avoid the political fallout of a break with Senator John McCain, Bush signed the bill. (He may also have hoped the Supreme Court would void parts of the bill to which he objected, but it did not.)

Substantial fighting continued sporadically in Afghanistan, including a major U.S. offensive labeled Operation Anaconda as late as March. Bush also dispatched troops to places as far-flung as former Soviet Georgia and the Philippines to fight Al Qaeda affiliates. Delivering a forceful State of the Union address in January, Bush identified national security and the war on terror as the administration's—and the nation's—number one priority for the foreseeable future. There was no question that compassionate conservatism had been supplanted by a war presidency. Nevertheless, the Autumn of Fear gradually gave way to a winter, spring, and summer characterized by a lull. Slowly, the shock induced by September 11 wore off and politics began to return to normal patterns. At some point in early 2002, the bipartisan consensus broke down. Although Senate Democrats had quietly stalled Bush's proposed economic response to September 11, conflict broke into the open on January 4, 2002, when Tom Daschle harshly attacked Bush for presiding over the return of federal deficits. (Bush's response was, "Not over my dead body will they raise your taxes.") Political sniping also revolved around the new issue of homeland security, including the question of whether to establish a new cabinet-level department. Democrats politicized homeland security first, but Republicans in the end reaped the larger political benefit.

## The Midterm Elections of 2002

The U.S. Constitution requires that elections be held for the House of Representatives and one-third of the Senate every two years, in rain or shine, peace or war. The smattering of odd-year elections in 2001 might have been conducted in an atmosphere of muted partisanship, but too much was at stake in the 2002 elections for them to be similarly immune to tough political combat.

The Republican edge in the House was so small that a net Democratic gain of six seats would catapult Richard Gephardt into the speaker's chair. The Democratic edge in the Senate was owed to Jeffords's defection and could be reversed by a net Republican gain of one seat. It was clear that the shifting of even a few thousand votes in the right races could maintain the stalemate, force George W. Bush to face a completely hostile Congress, give Bush a Republican majority in both houses, or even trade a Democratic House for a Republican Senate. For both parties, the 2002 elections were also a preparation for 2004. Democrats would test-drive December 8 rage in the Florida governor's race, where incumbent Jeb Bush, the president's brother, had to run for reelection. Republicans would try out a new beefed-up organization and the use of national security as an electoral issue.

Democrats could hope that the focus on national security was lessening, leaving room for the elections to be decided on their preferred domestic turf. They saw that Bush's popularity had not automatically translated into Republican wins in November 2001. House Republicans had lost seats in three elections in a row. And, with only two exceptions in the previous hundred years, the president's party had always lost seats in the House in a midterm year. Even in years dominated by war and national security, like 1898, 1918, 1942, 1950, and 1966, the president's opposition made significant gains.

Four factors would prove crucial to the outcome.

First, there were structural factors. As the Constitution requires, the decennial census was performed in 2000 and House seats were reallocated accordingly. Bush had won seven of the eight states that gained seats, Gore six of the ten states that lost seats. In total, the "red" states of 2000 made a net gain of seven seats at the expense of the "blue" states. In the view of most observers, the redistricting process would likely net the Republicans somewhere between three and nine seats, all other things being equal. Gerrymandering and incumbent advantage meant that analysts saw no more than thirty to forty-five House seats that were even potentially competitive, meaning that there was little room for much movement in either direction unless an overwhelming party tide developed, which hardly anyone predicted. The theories developed by political scientists to explain why the president's party usually loses seats in midterm elections also tended to indicate that Republicans were in a strong position to hold their own in 2002.[14] On the Senate side, an important factor was the distribution and location of the seats that were up for election in 2002. Of the thirty-four seats in play, twenty were held by Republicans, giving something of an advantage to Democrats, who would not have to defend as much territory. In addition, all four of the open seats were held by Republicans. However, a number of the Democratic seats were in "red" states like South Dakota, North Carolina, Louisiana, Missouri, and Georgia, where Democratic candidates often did their best to associate themselves with Bush.[15]

Second, there were the parties. The GOP had been whipped at the turnout game in 2000, and it had almost cost Bush the presidency. They were determined to not let it happen again and put together an unprecedented "seventy-two-hour program" for voter turnout centered on battalions of volunteers armed with voter lists and cell phones. Republicans, with the White House taking the lead, assiduously cultivated the new media in the form of talk radio. Because of BCRA, 2002 was also the last year the parties could raise and spend large quantities of "soft money."

Third, there was the president. More than any president in recent times, Bush staked everything on his party's midterm election performance, playing a key role in every stage of the campaign. As scholar Michael Nelson observed, Bush "threw himself into the midterm election earlier and more energetically than any president in history."[16] He helped recruit a number of top-drawer Senate candidates, including John Thune in South Dakota, Elizabeth Dole in North Carolina, Norm Coleman in Minnesota, and Saxby Chambliss in Georgia, as well as House candidates in a few crucial districts. A prolific fund-raiser for his own campaign in 2000, Bush also raised large sums for Republican candidates and the Republican Party. He appeared at seventy fund-raising events, raising at least $140 million, shattering Bill Clinton's 1998 midterm fund-raising record of $105 million. Consequently, at the beginning of October, the Republican National Committee had $30 million on hand to finish out the campaign, while the Democratic National Committee had only $5 million. Bush actively campaigned for Republican candidates across the country, making ninety visits to key Senate and House races. In the last five days of the campaign, he traveled 10,000 miles to seventeen cities in fifteen states. He made the midterm contest his campaign.

Finally, there were the issues. Two issues dominated: the state of the economy, which was still shaky, and national security, which was parceled among the three components of terrorism, homeland security, and the freshly activated issue of Iraq. The economy was the preferred fighting ground of Democrats, both because Bush and the Republicans were perceived to be weaker on this issue and because it was less risky to criticize Bush on domestic policy than on national security in wartime. Anxiety remained high, and some economists spoke darkly about the impending threat of a deflationary spiral leading to depression. But Democrats were unable to gain much traction on the economy. For one thing, despite the recession, conditions were not so bad. Unemployment, although higher than in 2000, was still at modest levels; economic growth and personal income growth resumed in 2002; and lower interest rates helped millions who were buying or refinancing houses or cars. The Dow Jones Industrial Average slipped to around 7,000 at the end of September, but regained 1,500 points in the last month and a half of the campaign. For another, Bush refused to be painted as unconcerned or inactive, as his father had been during the economic slowdown of the early 1990s. He pushed a second round of tax cuts to offset post-September 11 sluggishness and went through the symbolic motion of convening an "economic summit" to hear concerns from citizens.

Democrats received a gift when Enron, a Texas-based energy firm whose CEO had close ties to Bush, went bankrupt in December 2001 amid indications of severe financial impropriety. A number of other corporate scandals soon came to light, and House Minority Leader Richard Gephardt predicted that Democrats might gain thirty to forty seats in the House on the basis of the scandals. But a number of developments combined to limit the damage to Republicans. It turned out that most of the corporate misconduct began in the late 1990s, and some Democratic-leaning firms (like Global

Crossing) stood accused along with Enron. When the Senate brought up a financial reform measure, Bush endorsed it, and it passed 97-0. There was little opportunity for Democrats to turn the issue into a clear dividing line between themselves and Republicans.

Under Bush's prodding, the GOP also neutralized most other domestic issues that traditionally serve as the staple of Democratic campaigns. The passage of the No Child Left Behind Act gave Republicans new credibility in the area of education; the House passed a prescription drug benefit for seniors; and Republican candidates denied interest in "privatizing" Social Security, preferring "personal accounts" instead. Bush signed a bloated farm bill rather than force farm state Republicans to defend a presidential veto, and with an eye firmly planted on states like West Virginia and Pennsylvania, he imposed heavy steel tariffs (though as a quid pro quo he won a renewal of presidential "fast track" trade authority). For their part, Republicans in the area of domestic politics began to point to Democratic obstructionism. From the energy bill to a number of judicial nominations, the Democrats who had controlled the Senate since June 2001 were blocking action, and Republicans in red states began to make hay.

All that was left was national security. Karl Rove had suggested as early as December 2001 that Republican candidates "run on the war." Republicans started from a position of strength, and then cleverly trapped Democrats who had sought to gain ground on this issue.

Much of 2002 was dominated by Bush's efforts to formulate a coherent long-term national strategy to fight terrorism. As the administration response filled out over time, not unlike the development of the policy of containment from 1946 to 1950, two broad pillars formed the basis of the policy. Both rested on the assumption, established by Bush within minutes of the towers being hit, that the language of war was not merely metaphorical, but represented the actual reality of America's situation. The first pillar was that the best defense is a good offense. Intelligence and law enforcement would be enhanced, but passive defense alone was doomed to failure. It was, after all, what had been tried prior to September 11. Instead, the United States would take the fight to where the enemy was, striking (as in Afghanistan) in his home so he could not strike in ours.

Two corollaries flowed from this determination. One was that the United States would consider those regimes that harbor terrorists as responsible as the terrorists themselves. Within days of the September 11 attacks, Pentagon sources disclosed that "target packages" were "all ready" for invasions of up to ten countries implicated in terrorism.[17] The other was that the United States would consider preemptive wars against rogue states developing weapons of mass destruction rather than allow large threats to reach their full potential. Bush implied as much in his 2002 State of the Union address, when, naming Iraq, Iran, and North Korea, he declared:

> States like these, and their terrorist allies, constitute an axis of evil, arming to threaten the peace of the world. By seeking weapons of mass destruction, these regimes pose a grave and growing danger. They could provide these arms to terrorists, giving them the means to match their hatred. . . . We'll be deliberate, yet time is not on our side. I will not wait on events, while dangers gather. I will not stand by, as peril draws closer and closer. The United States of America will not permit the world's most dangerous regimes to threaten us with the world's most destructive weapons.

This warning was followed up by a speech at West Point in June, when Bush declared that "if we wait for threats to fully materialize, we will have waited too long." In September, a National Security Strategy Report formalized this idea into what became known as the doctrine of preemption. In one sense, the offensive basis of potential preemption against state allies of terrorism was broadly consistent with the contours of U.S. strategic design since at least the 1820s. But the bold and explicit statement of the position was new. It had the advantage of making things clear, putting enemies on notice, and preparing the American public for what was shortly to be asked of the nation. It had the disadvantage of galvanizing opposition, both abroad and at home, to what was called a unilateralist and militarist approach.

The second pillar consisted of a long-term strategy to deal with the "roots" of terror. While some instinctively considered those roots to be economic in nature—poverty and consequent hopelessness breed terrorism— Bush rejected this view, at least in its simple form. Osama bin Laden had hailed from a wealthy family, and most of the hijackers were relatively affluent. The problem was not poverty per se but fanaticism cultivated in a closed atmosphere of political tyranny. Bush gradually developed a doctrine of promoting the democratization of the Middle East. It was not clear that the objective was attainable, but Bush believed that if the terrorist culture of the Middle East was not broken up somehow—if the region did not join the modern world—greater catastrophe would only be a matter of time. The same insight was also applied to Mideast peace negotiations between Israel and the Palestinians, when the Palestinians were told in June 2002 to reform themselves and select democratically legitimate leaders as the precondition for serious American support for negotiations. In this policy, Bush drew on the foundational principle of natural rights in the Declaration of Independence, which he introduced with an assuredness and conviction reminiscent of the rhetoric of Ronald Reagan: "Freedom is not America's gift to the world; it is the Almighty God's gift to every man and woman in this world." The goal of democratization, combined with the policy of offense, meant that the United States was in theory committed to regime replacement or regime transformation of a broad swath of countries serving as incubators of the terrorist threat.

The administration's evolving strategic framework explained part of the growing partisan division in 2002. It was perhaps inevitable that when attention was turned to the next phase of the war on terror, disagreements would emerge on what to do next and how broadly to cast the net. Both pillars were highly controversial, especially among American liberals and among Europeans who resisted Bush's natural rights grounding and his high-risk, high-payoff tendency to go to the source of problems rather than simply managing them. Administration critics often attributed both pillars, but especially the notion of democratization, to the influence of "neoconservatives," who came under attack from Left and Right as "democratic imperialists."[18]

It was, however, more mundane issues of homeland security that became the focal point of political struggle for much of the year. It was here that national security was first politicized, as Democrats early in 2002 demanded hearings on September 11. Those hearings demonstrated that the U.S. government before September 11 was in possession of a variety of clues that might have pointed to the attack, but that poor communication and complacency had combined to keep anyone from "connecting the dots," as it was often put. At one point, Senator Hillary Clinton used the pregnant phrase that launched the downfall of Richard Nixon, asking on the floor of the Senate, "What did the President know? When did he know it?" To show their own commitment to security, Democrats called for the creation of a Cabinet-level Department of Homeland Security possessing full power to coordinate the tangle of disconnected bureaucracies responsible for different parts of the defense of the country against future terrorist attack. The ad hoc Office of Homeland Security, headed by former Pennsylvania Governor Tom Ridge, had been hampered by Ridge's lack of formal authority. A Cabinet department would give him that authority, but would add another layer of bureaucracy. Skeptical of the benefit and unwilling to be pushed by congressional Democrats, Bush was reluctant to endorse a department, which made him a target of Democratic criticism. Partisan pressure was given greater force by the vocal insistence of many families of September 11 victims, who had become an organized group. Democrats thus broke the taboo on trying to turn September 11 to overt political advantage, and for weeks they scored points off of Bush's opposition.

Then, in June, Bush reversed himself, embracing the creation of a Homeland Security Department that would consolidate twenty-two federal agencies, forming one of the four largest federal departments. He wanted it, however, on his terms, which included exempting a large percentage of the workforce from normal civil service rules. Bush argued that the mission of the department required greater personnel flexibility than the civil service system allowed, but he also knew that his demand put Democrats in a politically difficult position. If they refused, they could be blamed for the failure of the department; if they accepted, they would infuriate their allies in organized labor. For their part, Democrats accused Bush of undermining workers' rights and establishing a beachhead for massive presidential patronage; they understood their political dilemma and were unwilling to alienate labor. In this fight, Bush held the high cards. By September, homeland security had become a defining issue between the parties, with Republicans framing the conflict as Democratic obstructionism carried into the national security field. As Republicans portrayed it, in a choice between national safety and paying off their union friends, Democrats had chosen the unions. Bush ratcheted up the rhetoric, charging that "the Senate is more interested in special interests in Washington, and not interested in the security of the American people." Senate Majority Leader Tom Daschle responded angrily, demanding an apology from the president. The Democrats had started a fight on homeland security that they could not win.

The issue of Iraq also now began to be debated in earnest. In one sense, it was a new issue, only starting to come into focus once major combat in Afghanistan wound down. In another sense, it was a very old issue, dating back to the Iraqi invasion of Kuwait on August 1, 1990. The United States and an unprecedented coalition had driven Saddam Hussein out of Kuwait in March 1991, but what followed was at best an uneasy truce—or a state of low-intensity warfare. The United States settled into a policy of containing Saddam, which required the permanent stationing of troops, planes, and equipment in Saudi Arabia, home of the Muslim holy sites of Mecca and Medina, as well as a commitment to the permanent maintenance of economic sanctions against Iraq. On occasion, the low-intensity war threatened to flare, as when Saddam's intelligence service tried to assassinate former President George H. W. Bush in 1993 or when he massed troops on the border of Kuwait in October 1994. American and foreign intelligence services were convinced that Saddam had continued a covert biological, chemical, and perhaps even nuclear weapons program after the Gulf War, and that he had failed to completely dismantle the stockpiles he had possessed before the war. In December 1998, after Iraq made it impossible for United Nations (UN) weapons inspectors to continue their work, President Clinton ordered Operation Desert Fox, an intensive bombing campaign of suspected Iraqi weapons facilities, saying, "Saddam Hussein must not be allowed to threaten his neighbors or the world with nuclear arms, poison gas, or biological weapons. . . . I have no doubt today, that left unchecked, Saddam Hussein will use these terrible weapons again."

By this time, many came to think that containment was not an option that could be pursued indefinitely. France and Russia were actively agitating for the end of sanctions; Saddam was defying the UN; the anti-Saddam coalition had effectively shrunk to the United States, Britain, and Kuwait; and the heavy American presence in Saudi Arabia was increasingly problematic. In 1998, Osama bin Laden issued a *fatwa*, or religious decree, declaring holy war on the United States, citing as grounds the American defilement of Muslim holy places and its ongoing campaign against Iraq. That summer, Al Qaeda carried out bombings of U.S. embassies in Tanzania and Kenya, killing 263 people and injuring more than five thousand. Concerned about links between Al Qaeda and Iraq's VX poison gas program, Clinton ordered the bombing of a Sudanese factory thought to be a joint center for producing this weapon. In October 1998, Congress passed and Clinton signed the Iraq Liberation Act, committing the United States to a policy of removing Saddam Hussein through aid to his Iraqi opponents; the United States officially abandoned containment in favor of "regime change."

Immediately after September 11, eyes turned to Iraq. Could Saddam have been behind it? He was the only leader in the world to have issued a statement of rejoicing rather than regret after the attack. Furthermore, some investigators contended that evidence pointed to possible complicity by Iraq with the first World Trade Center bombing in 1993.[19] After concluding that no evidence indicated direct responsibility by Iraq for September 11, Bush focused on Afghanistan. Once the task of vanquishing the Taliban was accomplished, Bush revisited Iraq. His view was that September 11 cast Iraq in a new light. Another attack using VX gas or a nuclear bomb rather than jetliners could kill tens or even hundreds of thousands in a single stroke, and Saddam's connections with a wide range of terrorist groups were well-known.[20] For those in the administration favoring action against Iraq, the potentially deadly mix of terrorism and weapons of mass destruction might be stirred by a dictator whose ability to calculate risks—and hence to be deterred—had often proven faulty.

By mid-2002, the administration began the push for war. At first Bush asserted that his authority as commander-in-chief left the decision in his hands and brushed off Democratic demands for a congressional vote. He also considered relying on the legal authority of the congressional resolution authorizing war in 1991. Aside from protecting the prerogatives of the legislative branch, Democrats also calculated that an early vote on a resolution could clear the issue out of the way so that they could refocus the fall campaigns on domestic issues. Finally, under enormous pressure from members of Congress from both parties, Bush reversed his position, and a vote was scheduled for early October. The debate on the resolution guaranteed that national security would be front and center right before the election, and the timing made opposition risky. Much of the Democratic leadership, including House Minority Leader Gephardt, signed on, and a resolution authorizing the use of force passed overwhelmingly, 296-133 in the House and 77-23 in the Senate. Almost half of Democrats voted for it in the House and more than half in the Senate. But the episode embittered some of those who voted yes, including John Kerry, who complained about "the timing, the cynicism of it, the raw political exploitation of it."[21] The problem here for Democrats was that they had demanded a vote on this resolution. It was a classic case of the injunction to be careful what you ask for, as you might get it.

Hovering over both homeland security and Iraq was the specter of terrorism. In the spring, an Al Qaeda cell was broken up in Buffalo, New York, and an Al Qaeda operative (Jose Padilla) was arrested for involvement in a plot to carry out a radiological bomb attack in a major American city. In the fall, an Al Qaeda terrorist bombed a crowded club in Bali, killing 188, and Chechen terrorists took over a Moscow theater, leading to scores of deaths. (It would not be the last time that Chechen Islamicists would inadvertently influence an American election.) There were other, subtle ways that September 11 dominated the 2002 elections. Public sentiment placed a premium on the smooth operation of government in crisis, militating against a "throw out the bums," anti-incumbent mood. September 11 also produced a more politically conservative environment, characterized by increased religiosity and patriotism and a more hardheaded stance on a variety of issues. This included increased public calls for tighter border controls (a sentiment which forced the Bush administration to retreat from its plans for immigration liberalization). When the administration backed out of the Anti-Ballistic Missile treaty of 1972, hardly a whisper was raised in protest.

When the votes were counted, Republicans won a historic victory. In the House, the GOP gained six seats, doubling the size of its majority. The Republican share of the national House vote increased from about 49 percent in 1996, 1998, and 2000 to 52 percent in 2002. In the Senate, the real battleground of 2002, Republicans gained a net of two seats, enough to win a narrow 51-48-1 majority. Incumbents Jean Carnahan of Missouri and Max Cleland of Georgia went down, as did Walter Mondale in Minnesota, who was nominated to step in as the Democratic nominee at the last minute after the death of incumbent Senator Paul Wellstone in a plane crash. It was only the second time since 1934 that a president's party had gained House seats in a midterm election, and the first time since 1934 that a president's party had gained seats in both houses. Democrats picked up a handful of governorships, but Republicans gained about 225 state legislative seats (compared to an average midterm loss of about 350 for the president's party) and took a 21-16 lead in state legislatures. The president's brother, Jeb, who Democrats implicated in the "stolen election" of 2000, swamped his Democratic challenger 56 to 43 percent in Florida.

Local factors played a role, as always, but the election this time was to an unusual degree a national event, driven by national trends. The national Republican turnout effort was a great success, and the Republican message was clear; conversely, Democrats were divided on whether they supported or opposed Bush's tax policy and the war in Iraq. National security was the decisive factor in the vote. Gallup polls had shown national security leading the economy for most of 2002, except for a brief moment in July at the height of the corporate scandals. The Gallup postelection poll showed that, by a 57-34 percent margin, Americans thought Democrats were "too weak" on terrorism, while a 64-27 percent verdict held Republicans to be "tough enough."[22] At least two Democratic senators—Carnahan and Cleland— went down to defeat due to the homeland security issue. Democrats were particularly bitter at the defeat of Cleland, a Vietnam triple amputee whom Republicans in Georgia tagged as soft on defense. Pre- and postelection surveys also shed some light on who voted for whom. The "gender gap" seemed to narrow, as women voters began to see national security as a domestic, and even a family, issue in the light of September 11. The GOP may also have cut its deficit among Catholics, Hispanics, and union households.[23] Regionally, Republicans made their biggest gains in the Midwest. Notably, the number of House districts voting for a congressman of one party after having voted for a presidential candidate of the other party fell to its lowest level in the fifty years for which such data is available.[24] The increasing partisanship of the electorate, a signal feature of the "system of '04," was on full display.

Overall, analysts from both parties agreed that national security dominated the campaign and the vote. Liberals decried that development, accusing Bush and Republican strategists of demagogically manipulating the issue. Columnist E. J. Dionne called the homeland security debate "one of the sorriest episodes in the history of partisanship. . . . By turning domestic security into a divisive and partisan issue, President Bush helped his party win an election."[25] Conservatives and many moderate Democrats like Al From countered that the Democrats needed to "get serious about national security." Some academics argued that national security helped the GOP for the simple reason that Republicans have long maintained an edge as the tough party on defense and security issues; as the focus shifted to those concerns, they naturally gained.[26] The election results were widely read as a mandate for Bush's security policies, including an aggressive posture toward Iraq, and it also seemed, for a moment, that Bush's victory by proxy had given him a measure of legitimacy that had eluded him in 2000.[27] Bush had taken the politically risky step of putting his prestige on the line, and it had paid off.

Midterm elections have often presaged the outcome of the next presidential election, and two of the most important policy revolutions in the twentieth century—the New Deal era and the New Frontier/Great Society era—were profoundly intertwined with exceptional midterm years in which the President's party broke the antiadministration pattern (1934 and 1962).[28] Michael Barone compared 2002 to 1962, when Kennedy's Democrats won a surprise victory, and declared, "No more 49 percent nation."[29] In the aftermath of the election, veteran political correspondent David Broder cautioned Democrats that 2002 "could be a prelude to long-term Republican dominance." Broder saw parallels between the national scene and what Bush had done in Texas, where he "started from a narrow win in his first race for governor and, step by step, converted it into a broader and more lasting victory for the Republican Party."[30] The real test, however, lay ahead, and would depend on the outcome of events, not just on the skill of Bush and his strategists.

## War in Iraq

The Republican victory had immediate consequences, starting with leadership changes in Congress. Disgraced by the results, House minority leader Gephardt stepped down (as Newt Gingrich had done in 1998), and House Democrats took a sharp turn to the left, selecting Nancy Pelosi of San Francisco as his replacement. In the Senate, majority leader-to-be Trent Lott was forced to step down after lamenting Strom Thurmond's 1948 presidential defeat at Thurmond's one-hundredth birthday party. He was replaced by Bill Frist of Tennessee, a favorite of President Bush whose ascent promised close cooperation between the White House and the Senate. In terms of policy, Senate Democrats released their hold on some of the judicial nominees they had been delaying and immediately capitulated on homeland security, giving Bush the bill he wanted. And in the UN, the Security Council on November 8 overwhelmingly approved a new resolution, Resolution 1441, demanding a return to Iraq of weapons inspectors and a complete accounting of Iraq's WMD stockpiles and programs.

From November 2 until March 19, news was dominated by the buildup for war with Iraq. In December, Iraq produced a 12,000-page report on its arms program that virtually no one found acceptable because it did not effectively account for either the location or destruction of its previous arsenal. Saddam allowed inspectors to return, but continued acting evasively. On occasion, inspectors would stumble across prohibited items, like unmanned air drones, long-range rockets, or a stash of chemical artillery shells. Meanwhile, debate raged in the United States and around the world. Should the inspections be allowed to continue longer? Should the UN declare Iraq in material breach of its obligations? Should the United States be willing to act without the blessing of the UN? Was a preemptive war justified by the circumstances? Or should military operations against Iraq be considered the continuation and conclusion of an old war rather than the start of a new one?

Bush focused on Iraq in his 2003 State of the Union address, preparing the case for preemptive action: "Some have said that we should not act until the threat is imminent. Since when have terrorists and tyrants announced their intentions, politely putting us on notice before they strike? If this threat is permitted to fully and suddenly emerge, all actions, all words, and all recriminations would come too late. Trusting in the sanity and restraint of Saddam Hussein is not a strategy, and it is not an option. . . . We will consult. But let there be no misunderstanding: If Saddam Hussein does not fully disarm, for the safety of our people and for the peace of the world, we will lead a coalition to disarm him."

By mid-March, Bush had reached the point of decision. The inspections were inconclusive, and given the intelligence at his disposal, he believed they had failed. (According to an account by *Washington Post* reporter Bob Woodward, CIA Director George Tenet told Bush twice that the evidence for Iraqi WMD was a "slam dunk.") Tens of thousands of troops were massed in Kuwait, awaiting orders. Peak readiness could not be maintained indefinitely, and the economy was suffering from uncertainty about war. France, Germany, and Russia remained opposed to military action, and the French had begun to signal that they would support war under no conceivable circumstances. Thus, no UN resolution explicitly authorizing force would be forthcoming, now or in the future. In the administration's view, if the inspections concluded without new discoveries, pressure would mount to give Iraq a clean bill of health and end the sanctions. In their eyes, the status quo was collapsing. Dealing with Saddam was a now or never proposition. Bush chose now.

The manner in which Bush went to war—both the justifications he offered and the process he used—became key issues in the 2004 election. Bush was attacked for his "unilateralism," by which critics meant acting without final approval from the UN or a broader international consensus. But he had received congressional authorization and claimed to have sufficient justification under different UN resolutions. He had also constructed a "coalition of the willing" of thirty countries, including such traditional allies as Britain and Australia and newer ones like Poland and Bulgaria. On March 17, Bush addressed the nation and the world, giving Saddam and his sons Uday and Qusay forty-eight hours to leave Iraq. On Wednesday, March 19, before the deadline had even passed, Bush pulled the trigger. Presented with intelligence indicating Saddam's whereabouts, he agreed to a surprise air strike on that location. Saddam survived, and the war went on. Embedded reporters gave live reports by satellite hookup. Americans, accustomed to instant everything, grew concerned when the war was not over after two weeks. Yet, by historical standards, the Iraq campaign has to be considered a marvel of military planning and execution. Much of the Iraqi military simply melted away, having no desire to interpose itself between the U.S. Army and Saddam Hussein; those who stood to fight were demolished. By April 5, the army and Marines were on the outskirts of Baghdad. On April 9, the Baathist regime crumbled and fled. Photos were beamed around the world showing giant statues of Saddam pulled down and trampled on by Americans and Iraqis alike. On May 1, at the urging of military commander Tommy Franks, George W. Bush declared major combat in Iraq to be over. To commemorate the moment, Bush landed on the aircraft carrier U.S.S. *Lincoln* and spoke under a banner proclaiming "Mission Accomplished."

In one sense, the mission was accomplished. In the space of six weeks, coalition forces had overrun an enemy country the size of the state of California. Saddam was no longer in power, no longer free to pursue WMD or to harbor, nurture, or subsidize terrorists. In response, Bush's approval rating reached 71 percent, 13 points above its already-high level before the war. Again, Bush had taken a risk, and, at least in the short term, it had paid off. Bush immediately used his standing to push through a new tax cut in May, his third major tax cut in as many years.

## Bush's Decline and Stabilization

Yet in another sense, the mission was just beginning. If Iraq slipped back into anarchy or tyranny, the effort would have been in vain. Many former regime leaders remained on the loose, including Saddam and his sons. Rebuilding Iraq was as important as conquering it. The difficulty of that task became apparent immediately, as looting broke out in Baghdad and other cities. American forces which were numerous enough to win the war were stretched too thin to keep the peace. They were to be liberators, not conquerors, and there was a natural reluctance on their part to enforce order. Initial reports of looting proved highly exaggerated, but there is no question that the breakdown of order got the coalition occupation off to a bad start. If the war was well-planned, the same could not be said of the occupation. Bickering between the State Department and Defense Department interfered with progress. Nor did the friends of the old Iraq take defeat quietly. A collection of Baathists and foreign and domestic jihadists carried on the fight, and attacks on coalition forces slowly increased. In July, Uday and Qusay, who were presumed to be directing some of the insurgency, were killed in a firefight with American troops, leading to hopes that attacks would decline. It was not to be. In November, Americans were jolted by the deaths of eighty-two Americans in Iraq, a figure that had jumped from thirty in September and forty-three in October.

In addition, no WMD stockpiles had yet been found, and the likelihood of finding any was diminishing daily, although evidence was discovered of prohibited missile programs. One of the justifications for war was called into question. Those questions were thrown into sharp relief by a sixteen-word phrase in Bush's 2003 State of the Union address where he referred to a British intelligence report claiming that Saddam was trying to procure uranium in Africa. Former diplomat Joseph Wilson had been sent to Niger to investigate and concluded there was nothing to the report, and he told the CIA so—before January 2003. Wilson launched a campaign against the administration in the summer of 2003, complaining that Bush had wrongly repeated the charge anyway. The imbroglio became a cover story in *Time*. Trying in vain to quiet the firestorm, the original phrase was repudiated. CIA Director George Tenet said the information "did not rise to the level of certainty which should be required for presidential speeches."[31]

The Wilson charges may not have been the tipping point, but sometime over the summer of 2003 Bush lost the protective coating that had spared him from really severe criticism since the September 11 terrorist attacks. Looking to Iraq, some opponents began whispering the word "quagmire," while others began to shout the word "lie." Bush came under increasing fire from the crowded Democratic field and from liberal groups organized around the goal of preventing his reelection.[32] For the first time since September 11, Democrats began to sense real weakness in the president. As the vulnerability became more apparent, the pent-up anger left over from Florida began to show itself. It was all the more intense for being so long and so involuntarily bottled up. It was no coincidence that the momentum on the Democratic side was enjoyed by Howard Dean, the most stridently anti-Bush of the serious candidates.

That times had changed could be seen in the intensity with which Congress fought over an $87 billion supplemental appropriations bill for military operations and civil rebuilding in Iraq and Afghanistan in October. While the bill ultimately passed comfortably, the wide final margins belied a growing opposition. The appropriations debate presented the increasingly antiwar Democrats with a dilemma, especially those Democratic members of Congress who intended to seek the presidency. Ultimately, Kerry and Edwards voted "no," Lieberman and Gephardt "yes." Problems in Iraq, as well as lagging job creation, contributed to a slow but steady decline in Bush's approval until it reached 50 percent in the November 14–16 Gallup poll.

Yet just when it appeared that Bush's fortunes were caught in a downward spiral, events helped to stabilize his standing. Economic data showed the economy growing at a sizzling rate of 8.2 percent in the third quarter of 2003. A curious pattern was at work throughout the Bush administration in which bad economic news was balanced by good news abroad, and bad news abroad was balanced by better news at home. In May 2003, it looked as if the president would be able to run on Iraq and hope that it was more important to voters than the economy; in November, it now looked like bad news from Iraq might have to be overcome by the accelerating economic recovery. In Iraq, too, the situation seemed to improve. On Thanksgiving, the president made a surprise visit to U.S. troops in Baghdad to boost their morale, and on December 13, troops of the 101st Airborne Division dragged Saddam Hussein out of a hole, bedraggled and without resistance. Hopes again soared that the insurgency might be at an end.

On the domestic front, the president's top remaining domestic priority finally wended its way through the legislative labyrinth. The administration's Medicare prescription drug program, estimated to cost $400 billion over ten years (soon upped to $500 billion), was enacted with the crucial support of AARP. In the House, the Republican leadership was forced to strong-arm reluctant members, but the measure finally passed 216-215.

(Around this time, many conservatives began to argue that Bush's domestic presidency, sans tax cuts, had been disconcertingly centrist, or even liberal.) The combination of Saddam's capture, the economic uptick, and the big legislative victory ended, for the moment, the president's slide. He moved back up to 63 percent in the mid-December Gallup poll. He appeared to end the year—the crucial penultimate year of his presidency— with real momentum.

## Looking Back, Looking Ahead

Every incumbent's reelection effort turns largely into a referendum on his performance in office. As 2003 shaded into 2004, it was not clear how Bush's tenure would be judged. Jobs had been lost in the first two years, as recession and September 11 took their toll, but the economic picture was never as gloomy as it had been in 1992 or 1980, years other incumbents had lost.[33] No one could forget Bush's leadership after September 11 or his vigor in chasing down terrorists, but difficulties in Iraq posed a potential danger to his national security accomplishments. There had been no attacks on American soil since September 11, although nobody could say how long that would last or how much credit Bush would be given for a nonevent. Bush had achieved far more than most observers in January 2001 predicted: three tax cuts in as many years, major education reform, a prescription drug benefit, a major reorganization of the federal government for homeland security, a reorientation of U.S. strategic doctrine toward missile defense and preemption and democratization, a stunning midterm election success, and military victory in two wars. He had never slipped below a 50-percent approval rating and spent much of his first three years in the approval rating ether. Throughout, he had taken maximum advantage of the leverage offered by his presidential position, and he had run a focused and disciplined administration.[34]

Yet Bush never really achieved a political breakthrough of his own. Once the rally effect from September 11 had finally run its course in mid-2003, he was largely back where he was on September 10, 2001. Although his position and his party's position had improved in 2002, a dramatic new coalition of "compassionate conservatism" had not emerged. Bush had, perhaps, reinvigorated the Reagan coalition, but had not fundamentally transformed it. Even with his success in the midterm elections and consistently high popularity, Bush had still failed to win his energy bill, his faith-based initiatives bill, and a number of his judicial appointments; Social Security reform, a centerpiece of his 2000 campaign, had fallen off the agenda, derailed by the tepid stock market and Enron's 401k shenanigans. Despite Bush's stated desire to unify rather than divide, despite the genuine ambiguity and centrism of much of his legislative record, despite the momentary national consensus on terrorism, Bush faced 2004 as a deeply divisive figure, loved by many but despised by a large and growing contingent.

Throughout his term, Bush lived in the complicated shadows of his three predecessors. Although he was straightforward in his style, he was an enigma to many who studied his presidency. Some made the case that Bush was another Ronald Reagan, someone who was "radical" rather than "conservative" in the Burkean sense. In this view, Reagan served as Bush's inspiration in style (focusing on a few high priorities), rhetoric (like the "axis of evil"), and policy (tax cuts, opposition to abortion, missile defense, and going on the offensive and promoting democracy as the best way to break an intolerable deadlock against enemies). Both men tried to stifle the growth of government by limiting revenue, and both found their political grounding in the natural rights of the Declaration of Independence. Like Reagan, Bush thought big. Early in Bush's administration, long-time conservative activist Grover Norquist enthused that Bush was even "more conservative than Ronald Reagan," a sentiment that was echoed in alarm by a number of liberal commentators. He deliberately modeled himself after Reagan more than after his own father, who had raised taxes, paid little heed to mounting economic difficulties, let his base among social conservatives deteriorate, and stopped the Gulf War short of total victory. Many in Bush's inner circle, including Cheney, were haunted by the question of whether they should have gone all the way to Baghdad in 1991. More generally, Bush often seemed driven by the desire to avoid repetition of his father's mistakes. In early 2003, in a *New York Times Magazine* essay, Bill Keller called Bush "Reagan's Son," enumerated a multitude of parallels between the two, and concluded that if Bush succeeded in his aims, "he will move us toward an America Ronald Reagan would have been happy to call his own."[35] No wonder he was known by some as the "little Gipper."

Yet, a case could also be made that, whatever his intentions, Bush in fact resembled his father more than he resembled Reagan. Stylistically, he sometimes shared his father's aversion to laying a foundation for policy through persistent public argument, a problem exacerbated by his relatively inarticulate persona. Even his often strained communications skills seemed to prove that the apple does not fall far from the tree. And, like his father, Bush was often uncomfortable fighting the culture wars; if he wound up taking conservative positions on affirmative action or gay marriage, it was because courts had taken up the subjects and left him little

choice. Substantively, the arguments he made on domestic policy more often echoed his father's hope for a "kinder, gentler America" than Reagan's
clarion call for a return to a constitutionalism of limited government and
federalism. Indeed, Bush endorsed the first major entitlement program
since Lyndon Johnson in the form of the prescription drug program for
seniors, and he proposed a liberalized immigration policy, a major federal
intrusion into education, and more spending on AIDS and alternative fuels
than any president in history. Bush oversaw the biggest rise in discre-
tionary domestic spending since the 1960s, signed a campaign finance reform bill supported primarily by liberals, and twice agreed to liberal calls
for an expanded federal bureaucracy in homeland security. He imposed
steep steel tariffs (later rescinded), signed an expensive farm bill, and
failed to veto a single congressional appropriation despite a burgeoning
federal deficit. On many of these dimensions, George W. Bush had the
most progovernment administration since LBJ's, which led some to re-
mark on a resemblance to the administration of Richard Nixon, another
Republican who received little credit from Democrats for his moves in
their direction. And although few wished to make the comparison, he also
enacted parts of Bill Clinton's unfinished agenda. Bush provided more
funding for education than Clinton dared to ask for. In the absence of war,
it was not difficult to imagine Bush facing a Republican primary challenger attacking him from the right.

In fact, there is a view that argues that Bush initiated a new domestic
governing philosophy of "big government" conservatism, the aim of which
is to use the power of the federal government to promote conservative
ends. His administration began a velvet revolution in the conservative approach to power that had not yet been put into effect or fully articulated.

These observations also point to the complexity of Bush's relationship
to Bill Clinton. Bush came to office by arguing subtly but effectively that
he was not another Clinton. Yet the two came to share a similar handicap:
a significant portion of the population professed to despise and hate them.
Like Clinton, Bush was hated for his political audacity and prowess. His
willingness to act forcefully on his campaign promises despite his contentious election, and his success in using national security as a bludgeon
against Democrats in 2002, engendered great animosity.[36] Like Clinton,
Bush was also hated, quite simply, for who he was. For many Americans,
Clinton was a cultural anathema: a marijuana-smoking, draft-dodging
hippie from the 1960s whose legendary self-indulgence and postmodern
disregard for truth found new outlets in the White House. For many other
Americans, it was Bush who was the anathema: an inhabitant of an alien
land (Texas) not quite part of their America and an evangelical Protestant

whose religion suggested to them narrow-mindedness and bigotry. To many of these secular fundamentalists, it was Bush's faith, which was the source of his moral certainty; his rejection of postmodernist relativism; and his embrace of the old verity of natural rights as a gift from the Creator to each individual, that grated most on their sensibilities. It was not a coincidence that many of Bush's most vehement critics were European intellectuals, who had long imbibed the moral skepticism of the age, and those Americans who hoped to make their country as much like Europe as possible.[37]

As he faced the election of 2004, Bush had a number of things working in his favor. Eschewing the federal campaign finance regime, as he had done in 2000, Bush raised a record $84 million by October 1, 2003. Electoral College math had changed to Bush's benefit: because of population shifts from blue states to red states, if he won exactly the same states as in 2000, he would gain seven more electoral votes. The midterm elections of 2002 pointed the way toward a formula for Republican success in message (national security) and mechanics (heavy emphasis on local organization). Indeed, Bush's strategists had been at work throughout 2003, laying the groundwork for a massive organizational effort modeled on 2002. Whatever Bush's problems, he was obviously not (yet) in as difficult a position as Jimmy Carter had been in 1980. No president seeking reelection in wartime had ever been defeated, although Truman and Johnson had withdrawn from consideration during their wartime primaries. And no president had been defeated since 1932 unless he faced a primary challenger in his own party; Bush faced no such challenge. To the contrary, Bush enjoyed unprecedented levels of support among Republicans, which had proved crucial in the 2002 elections. On the other hand, no president who had gained power in such a contentious election as 2000 had ever been reelected; John Quincy Adams, Rutherford B. Hayes, and Benjamin Harrison had not returned to office. The shadow of December 8 hung over Bush still.

All that remained was to discover the identity of the president's Democratic opponent, almost sure to be determined in the first three months of 2004.

## Notes

1. See Dan Keating and Dan Balz, "Florida Recounts Would Have Favored Bush," *Washington Post*, November 12, 2001, p. A1.

2. John P. Burke, "The Bush Transition," in *Considering the Bush Presidency*, ed. Gary L. Gregg II and Mark J. Rozell (New York: Oxford University Press, 2003), pp. 21–68; James P. Pfiffner, "Introduction: Assessing the Bush Presidency."

3. Michael Kelly, "Bush's Blunders," *Washington Post*, May 30, 2001, p. A19.

4. David S. Broder, "A Crack in Bush's Governance," *Washington Post*, May 27, 2001, p. B7.

5, "The First 162 Days," *Washington Post*, July 1, 2001, p. B6. See also "Mr. Bush's Fumble," *New York Times*, May 25, 2001.

6, See Richard L. Berke and Janet Elder, "Bush Loses Favor Despite Tax Cut and Overseas Trip," *New York Times*, June 21, 2001.

7. "Mr. Bush and Congress," *New York Times*, August 4, 2001.

8. Bob Woodward, *Bush at War* (New York: Simon & Schuster, 2002), p. 15.

9. Woodward, *Bush at War*, p. 15; David Frum, *The Right Man: The Surprise Presidency of George W. Bush* (New York: Random House, 2003), pp. 140–41.

10. Frum, *The Right Man*, p. 150.

11. See Woodward, *Bush at W*ar, pp. 75–78.

12. R. W. Apple Jr., " A Military Quagmire Remembered: Afghanistan as Vietnam," *New York Times*, October 31, 2001.

13. Dan Freedman, "Top Demo Sees Bush Loss in '04; McAuliffe Says Economy Is Key to Victory," *San Antonio Express-News*, November 10, 2001, p. 21A.

14. Those theories stress either current national conditions (including presidential popularity), which were largely favorable to Republicans in 2002, or are based on the observation that the better presidents do when they are elected, the more their party suffers in the next midterm election, which serves as a kind of political boomerang. Since Bush and Republicans did barely well enough to attain power in 2000, the boomerang was likely to have little force behind it. See Andrew E. Busch, "On the Edge: The Electoral Career of George W. Bush," in *Considering the Bush Presidency*, ed. Gary L. Gregg II and Mark J. Rozell (New York: Oxford Press, 2003).

15. See Kate O'Beirne, "They're All Bushies Now?" *National Review*, November 11, 2002, pp. 20–22.

16. Michael Nelson, "George W. Bush and Congress: The Electoral Connection," in *Considering the Bush Presidency*, ed. Gary L. Gregg II and Mark J. Rozell (New York: Oxford University Press, 2003), p. 151.

17. "Under Seige," *U.S. News & World Report,* September 24, 2001, p. 10.

18. See, for example, Ivo H. Dalder and James M. Lindsay, "Bush's Foreign Policy Revolution," in *The George W. Bush Presidency: An Early Assessment*, ed. Fred I. Greenstein (Baltimore: Johns Hopkins Press, 2003), p. 129.

19. See Laurie Mylroie, *The War against America: Saddam Hussein and the World Trade Center Attacks* (New York: Regan Books/HarperCollins, 2001).

20. Some of the facts, as they were assessed at the time, were these: The Iraqi intelligence service was itself in many respects a wide-ranging terrorist organization, and the notorious terrorists Abu Nidal and Abu Abbas had been given refuge in Iraq, as had Abu Musab al-Zarqawi when he fled Afghanistan. Saddam boasted of subsidizing Hamas suicide bombers and their families to the tune of $35 million, while an Al Qaeda–affiliated group called Ansar al-Islam, with six hundred terrorists, was operating in northern Iraq against Saddam's Kurdish enemies.

21. Joan Vennochi, "Kerry Walks a Fine Line," *Boston Globe*, November 19, 2002, p. A23.

22. A Richard Wirthlin survey showed voters placing national security ahead of the economy by a 41-17 percent margin. A survey conducted by Democrat Stanley Green-

berg and Republican Bill McInturf contained a twist. In their poll, a plurality of voters thought the economy was the biggest concern facing the country, but more respondents said that their own vote was based on national security and Bush's response to terrorism.

23. Steven Thomma, "Survey Tells How GOP Triumphed," *Denver Post*, November 14, 2002, p. A1.

24. See Gary C. Jacobson, "The Bush Presidency and the American Electorate," in *The George W. Bush Presidency: An Early Assessment*, ed. Fred I. Greenstein (Baltimore: Johns Hopkins Press, 2003), p. 207.

25. E. J. Dionne, "Brilliant Politics, At a Price," *Washington Post*, November 22, 2002, p. A41.

26. See Donald Green and Eric Schickler, "Winning a Battle, Not a War," *New York Times*, November 12, 2002, p. A31.

27. See Nelson, "George W. Bush and Congress," pp. 153–54.

28. In 1934, Democrats gained seats in both the House and Senate; in 1962, they gained seats in the Senate and lost only four in the House, claiming a moral victory that the press widely acknowledged and compared to 1934.

29. Michael Barone, "No More 49 Percent Nation," *U.S. News & World Report*, November 18, 2002, p. 33; Michael Barone, "Party Like It's 1962," *Wall Street Journal Opinion Journal*, November 9, 2002, www.opinionjournal.com/editorial/feature.html?id=110002599 (accessed November 2002).

30. David Broder, "Dems Should Take Hard Look at Bush's Political Career," *Denver Post*, November 17, 2002, p. 4E.

31. A year later, two separate reports, a U.S. Senate Intelligence Committee report and the British Butler Report, verified the original British claim.

32. These groups operated under section 527 of the federal tax code and reported to the IRS, a novel way around the stringent limitations of the 2002 campaign finance reform. Republicans had a choice of either doing the same thing or trying to stop the 527s altogether by appealing to the courts to curb the 527s. They followed the second strategy and lost, leaving the field dominated by groups like MoveOn.org, which at one point put two advertisements on its website comparing Bush to Adolf Hitler.

33. See Lydia Saad and Frank Newport, "Bush Not Reliving His Father's Economic Nightmare," Gallup News Service, May 5, 2003; www.gallup.com/poll/releases/pr030505.asp?Version=p.

34. Charles O. Jones, "Capitalizing on Position in a Perfect Tie," in *The George W. Bush Presidency: An Early Assessment*, ed. Fred I. Greenstein (Baltimore: Johns Hopkins Press, 2003), chapter 7.

35. Bill Keller, "Reagan's Son," *New York Times Magazine*, January 26, 2003, pp. 26–31, 42–44, 62.

36. John C. Fortier and Norman J. Ornstein, "President Bush: Legislative Strategist," in *The George W. Bush Presidency: An Early Assessment*, ed. Fred I. Greenstein (Baltimore: Johns Hopkins Press, 2003), p. 171.

37. While the War on Terrorism contributed to international antipathy to Bush, polls showed he was already disliked by the European public before September 11. See Michael A. Dimock, "Bush and Public Opinion," in *Considering the Bush Presidency*, ed. Gary L. Gregg II and Mark J. Rozell (New York: Oxford University Press, 2003), p. 84.

# Chapter Three

# The Democratic Nomination Contest

Imagine a script in which the lead character appears briefly at the beginning, all but vanishes for the middle, and then reappears dramatically at the end to walk off with the prize. This, in a nutshell, was the plot line for Senator John Kerry's march to the Democratic nomination in 2004.

John Kerry entered the race early, at the end of 2002, with a strategy of shock and awe designed to create an aura of invincibility about his candidacy. The plan envisaged relying on his personal reputation—his senatorial stature, appeal as a New Englander, and war hero status—to lock up the major sources of funding in the party and to establish an insurmountable lead in the first primary state of New Hampshire. The only serious competition that then loomed, on paper at any rate, came from Senator Joe Lieberman, who was running first in the national polls among the Democratic contenders. Kerry's strategists were convinced, however, that Lieberman's ranking was built on little more than the name recognition he had acquired from his vice-presidential candidacy in 2000. Lieberman, they reasoned, was either too conservative or too nice a guy (or both) to appeal to most Democrats.

Columnist Robert Novak previewed the race on the day Al Gore announced his decision not to run (December 15, 2002):

> The immediate leader in the polls now that Gore is gone is expected to be Joe Lieberman, who is eager to run now that he does not have to honor his pledge to make way for his former running mate. Nevertheless, few party insiders are interested in Lieberman. . . . The clear choice of the party establishment is Senator John Kerry of Massachusetts. He is smart, good-looking, the richest man in the Senate (thanks to his second wife's wealth), and a battle-hardened campaigner. This New Englander is fortunate that the first big primary election is in neighboring New Hampshire, where polls have shown him running just behind Gore.[1]

Kerry's battle plan began auspiciously enough. He raised more funds than any of the other candidates in early 2003, and the early polls taken in New Hampshire showed him to be safely in the lead.[2] But by the summer John Kerry began to slip, and when he made his official announcement in September, his campaign was in free fall. By early December, the situation ranged from bleak to hopeless. Kerry was down to single digits in the national polls and was trailing dismally in New Hampshire; the campaign was virtually out of cash; there were major problems in the campaign organization (the campaign manager, Jim Jordan, had just been fired); and no major endorsements were in the offing. Journalists had all but written off Kerry's candidacy, barely bothering even to cover his campaign. The "establishment," such as it was, was betting on a new candidate to carry the day: Wesley Clark.

Yet less than a month before the first real test by voters, the Kerry campaign miraculously came back to life. Throwing caution to the wind—perhaps he had no choice—Kerry literally bet the house, mortgaging his share of the Beacon Hill townhouse, owned jointly with his wife, Teresa, and injecting all of the desperately needed cash into an improbable contest in Iowa. Kerry won a stunning victory, picking up 38 percent of the delegates' caucus goers and besting his nearest competitor John Edwards (who himself had experienced a near-miraculous turnaround) by 6 percent. The two odds-on favorites in Iowa—Howard Dean and Richard Gephardt—lagged far behind, winning 18 and 11 percent, respectively. Gephardt withdrew from the nomination race. A week later in New Hampshire, Kerry won a convincing victory over Howard Dean (39 percent to 26 percent). After that, it was blitzkrieg. Kerry wracked up victory after victory in the tightly packed schedule of primaries and caucuses over the next three weeks, losing races only in South Carolina (to John Edwards) and Oklahoma (to Wesley Clark). Three other major candidates quit the race—Lieberman, Clark, and Dean—leaving only one real competitor, John Edwards, who appeared to many to be running for the vice-presidential nomination (the post he eventually received). Kerry dispatched Edwards on Super Tuesday (March 2), and the race was over. Kerry became the nominee before he ever had the chance to be declared the front-runner.

So much for the story line of the leading character.

When the full script of the 2004 nomination race is examined, however, its most memorable moments will be found in the middle acts, in the rise and fall of the campaign's most compelling figure, Howard Dean. A short spark plug of a man who was largely invisible in national Democratic politics when the campaign began, Dean rose from asterisk status in the polls in early 2003 to become the central figure in the Democratic Party by the year's end. Coming from the position of an ex-governor of a small state (Vermont), Dean's ascent reminded many of Jimmy Carter in 1976, the man for whom Dean had worked when he first entered politics, only Dean began his quest without being as well-known or as highly regarded. Dean's presence in the race began to be noticed in the spring of 2003, when he surpassed all other candidates in fund-raising and became the clear favorite of the new and burgeoning Internet constituency. By late summer, Dean had scored a twofer—being featured in the same week on the covers of both *Time* and *Newsweek*, where he was touted as the front-runner. By December his nomination began to look inevitable. Ahead in all of the polls, in possession of an organization widely regarded as the most innovative in decades, flush with money, the recipient of endorsements from such respected party figures as Bill Bradley, Al Gore, Tom Harkin, and Jimmy Carter—who could possibly stop him?

But then—to use the hackneyed sports metaphor reserved for American political campaigns—just as Dean's horse was rounding the corner to the homestretch, furlongs ahead of the rest of the pack, it just . . . collapsed. Or, if one wishes to switch metaphors to a sport that more Americans (though fewer Dean supporters) follow, Dean's race car entered into the victory lap and the wheels fell off. Almost the day after his crushing third-place finish in Iowa, a campaign that had raised so much money was discovered to be virtually out of cash; the vaunted campaign organization was in shambles, with its slightly offbeat but innovative manager (Joe Trippi) about to be fired; and the candidate himself, widely regarded just a day before as both tenacious and formidable, delivered his famous concession speech, quickly dubbed "the primal scream," that made him the butt of ridicule. Dean fell into that most unfortunate of traps that menaces any presidential candidate: confirming the negative stereotype that his critics had crafted. For the previous six months, Dean's rivals had depicted him as angry, out-of-control, and unpresidential. The videotape of the scream, played repeatedly on every news channel for a week, showed just that. The inevitable followed: Dean began a rapid and relentless slide in the polls from which he could not recover. Following his loss in New Hampshire, he hung on for an agonizingly long three-week period, suffering one primary defeat after another. Even many of Dean's supporters prayed for his withdrawal, hoping to spare him (and themselves) further humiliation. Finally, after making a last stand in the friendly state of Wisconsin on February 17, where he managed only a weak third-place finish and—more ignominiously still—lost the university town of Madison, Howard Dean pulled out of the race. Dean had risen from obscurity only to return to oblivion. Redemption, however, would come, as Howard Dean reemerged in 2005 to be selected as the new chair of the Democratic National Committee.

No observer of American politics can fail to be intrigued by two great questions: how did Howard Dean get to a point where he seemed to have the Democratic nomination all but locked up? And, having gotten there, how did he manage to let it slip away?

A curious fact about Dean's campaign is that, when judged by his performance in electoral competition, his candidacy would hardly seem to warrant more than a passing reference. To a modern-day Rip van Winkle who had watched Howard Dean file his campaign papers on December 3, 2002, and who then fell asleep until January 19, 2004 (the day of the Iowa caucuses), nothing much would seem to have happened. Dean ended roughly where one might have predicted. During the active phase of his campaign, Dean never managed anything near a victory, finishing (after New Hampshire) no better than third place in the next nine primaries and receiving 10 percent or less of the vote in six of the contests. Dean's sole victory came in a sympathy vote in his home state of Vermont, two weeks after he had withdrawn. To put his record in a comparative perspective, Howard Dean performed far worse in the official votes than Paul Tsongas or Jerry Brown in 1992, also-rans who are hardly remembered as presidential candidates by anyone who is not a political junkie.

But while he left hardly a statistical trace on the 2004 race, Howard Dean etched a deep mark on the campaign itself and perhaps—although it remains to be seen—on the future of the Democratic Party. He drove the Democratic Party to an antiwar position, enunciating what would eventually become John Kerry's central position in the fall campaign, that President Bush had "launched the war in the wrong way, at the wrong time, with inadequate planning" (simplified by Kerry to the "the wrong war, in the wrong place, at the wrong time").[3] Dean also anticipated the main line of attack of the Bush campaign against Kerry, when he declared, all the way back in March of 2003, "To this day I don't know what John Kerry's position [on the war] is. . . . If you agree with the war, then say so, but don't try to wobble around in between."[4] Karl Rove, with additional material to work with, expanded the wobble into the full-blown flip-flop.

Howard Dean was the first candidate since 1972 to have headed up a genuine movement in the Democratic Party. His candidacy was larger than the candidate himself, with huge numbers of deeply anti-Bush citizens, some already attached to nascent organizations like MoveOn.org, flocking to his standard. His campaign was also just picking up steam when the small but vocal and well-organized antiwar movement found itself unoccupied. Thus, Dean tapped into a stream—some might say a raging torrent—of anger directed at President Bush and presided over the revival of the peace wing of the party, although Dean was always careful to distance himself from charges of being a pacifist and made a point of reminding people of his support of the invasion of Afghanistan. Even though (or more likely because) the movement was as important as the candidate, Howard Dean inspired great enthusiasm and devotion among his followers, many of whom were young, highly idealistic, and Internet-savvy. The Dean campaign made use of cyberspace not only to raise large amounts of cash—an innovation pioneered by John McCain in 2000—but also to arrange for "meetups" and recruit campaign volunteers. The avant-garde of the movement became known as "Deaniacs." No other candidate could match this kind of appeal; there were no Edwardians or Kerryites. As the leader of a movement, Dean spoke of remaking the Democratic Party, borrowing a phrase from the late Senator Paul Wellstone promising to revive "the Democratic wing of the Democratic Party." And he often referred, with thinly veiled contempt, to Democratic moderates as the "Republican wing of the Democratic Party." Behind this rhetoric lay a plan, which gained credibility with many experts over the year, for reshaping the Democratic Party into a majority party by purging moderates and by energizing and expanding the base of "real" Democrats. When Dean left the race, he uttered phrases that in other cases would be considered mere platitudes, but which in his case had a more genuine ring: "We have led this party back to considering what its heart and soul is, although there is a lot of work left to do."

There was a third great participant in the Democratic nomination drama of 2004, only it was not a person. It was the goddess of fate—what the ancient Greeks called *Moira*. To an unprecedented degree, external events—chiefly the ups and downs and changing assessments of the Iraq War—drove the nomination race. Other issues and themes were important, including health care, jobs, trade pacts, and education, which at times registered as being of greater concern to Democratic votes. But none of them differentiated the candidates to the same degree or affected as much the candidates' standing with Democratic voters.[5] The Iraq War was regularly invoked as the "test" of a Democrat's fitness to be president. As Howard Dean told Larry King, "If you're a Democrat and did support the Iraq War, it calls into question your judgment in one of the most serious questions or actions any president will have to take."[6] If the war had ended neatly in the spring of 2003, when George Bush swept down from the sky to appear on the aircraft carrier *Abraham Lincoln* and announced that "the major combat operations in Iraq have ended," Howard Dean might still have had some success, but it is difficult to imagine that he would have reached the heights that he did. John Kerry and John Edwards would have been mildly prowar candidates, pointing to their vote in favor of the Iraq War. And Joe Lieberman and Richard Gephardt would have used their strong support of the war as a powerful reason to support their nomination. But with the growth of the insurgency in Iraq in the summer and the growing doubts that weapons of mass destruction would be found, the shape of the race shifted. Opposition to the war began to mount among Democrats, and Dean's candidacy became more potent. Two other major candidates entered the race on the basis of their opposition to the war: Senator Bob Graham and former General Wesley Clark. (Graham withdrew early, finding himself unable to compete with Howard Dean for the antiwar constituency.) Kerry and Edwards began their steady drift to the antiwar position, leading to their fateful decision in October to oppose the administration's request for further funds to continue operations in Iraq. Any chance of nominating Joe Lieberman or Richard Gephardt began to fade.

The war in Iraq in 2003 nevertheless retained considerable support among Democrats, and many were sensitive to the views of the rest of the populace, which remained in favor of the decision. A candidate opposing the war could accordingly go too far and risk appearing unelectable to the Democrats. Moira, the goddess of fate, now intervened in the Democratic race for a second time. The run-up to the initial contest in Iowa occurred during an uptick of support for the war that followed the capture of Saddam Hussein on December 13, 2003. Americans across the board experienced a feeling of national euphoria, akin to that which followed the fall of Baghdad. Many thought this event marked the beginning of the end, if not the end itself. Howard Dean was put immediately on the defensive, and opponents leaped on his comment that "the capture of Saddam Hussein has not made America safer" as definitive proof of his lack of judgment.[7] Kerry observed that "those who believe today that we are not safer with his capture, don't have the judgment to be president or the credibility to be elected president."[8] Mainline commentators jumped in. In a blistering editorial entitled "Beyond the Mainstream," the *Washington Post* called Dean's comments "not just unfounded but ludicrous."[9] As much as any single event, the attack at this time on Dean's preparedness for the presidency began to raise doubts about whether he should be anointed as the party's nominee.

It is interesting to speculate on the possible effect of the Iraq War on the Democratic contest if the primary season had begun a bit later or had proceeded at a much slower pace. By March, opinion on the war in Iraq was again shifting, rather dramatically, against the war, as the effects of the Kay report's findings that there were no weapons of mass destruction began to sink in and the insurgency grew stronger. Under these conditions—primal scream or not—Howard Dean might have appeared a far more convincing candidate. Instead, he was back home in Vermont, eating the ice cream sundae that the local Ben and Jerry's had named for him: "Maple-Powered Howard."

## The Nomination System and the Rules

In every nomination race since 1972, important changes have taken place in the structure or rules governing the nomination process. Over the past few elections, the main changes have involved the scheduling of the delegate selection contests, specifically the tendency of states to move their primaries or caucuses toward the beginning of the campaign season. This process is known as front-loading. To give a simple indication of what has occurred, the date on which the nomination campaign started in 1972—the first Tuesday after the first Monday in March, when New Hampshire held the first primary—was the date on which the nomination race ended in 2004. Even the formality of waiting for the party convention to do the nominating has all but gone by the wayside. President Bush telephoned John Kerry on the eve of March 2 to congratulate him on his victory and to wish him a good campaign.

Since 1988, when front-loading in earnest began as a movement of Democrats in southern states to create a de facto early regional primary

**Table 3.1. Important Moments in the 2004 Democratic Nomination Contest**

| | |
|---|---|
| December 2002 | Al Gore announces he will not seek the presidency in 2004. |
| **2003** | |
| June | Coming off a successful second quarter of fund-raising, Howard Dean emerges as the clear Democratic front-runner. |
| September | Wesley Clark enters the race. |
| October | Bob Graham exits the contest. |
| **2004** | |
| January 19 | Kerry surges to a surprisingly comfortable victory in the Iowa caucuses. |
| January 20 | Following a poor showing in Iowa, Gephardt drops out. |
| February 3 | Lieberman drops out after failing to win any delegates in the February 3 primaries. |
| February 11 | Clark exits the race after third-place finishes in two key southern primaries—Tennessee and Virginia. |
| February 18 | Dean leaves the race after finishing third in Wisconsin. |
| March 2 | Kerry sweeps Super Tuesday; Edwards quits the race. |
| | Kerry receives a congratulatory phone call from President Bush. |
| March 11 | Kerry officially secures enough delegates to win the Democratic nomination. |

("Super Tuesday"), officials in both national parties, along with most commentators, have considered front-loading undesirable. They objected not only to the loss of an established tradition, in which the contest unfolded leisurely over a long period, but also to a decision that was reached so quickly, a method that seemed to reduce options and to make the process less deliberative. Even those guilty of perpetrating the crime—the state party leaders and legislators in the various states—generally agreed with this assessment. They pleaded as their excuse that their own state or region should not be asked to pay the price of sacrificing all influence by holding a primary after the outcome had already been decided. Here was a classic instance of what social scientists call a collective action problem: no individual actor can solve the general predicament, and each only makes matters worse by following his own best interest.

The leaders of the national parties took some steps to discourage or reverse the process. There was much talk of a joint strategy to combat front-loading, but given their different approaches to national party rule making since 1972, in which Democrats have taken a more "directive" approach with the states than Republicans, agreement on a single plan proved impossible. Each party adopted its own approach. Democrats passed a national party rule for the 2000 race that prohibited primaries and caucuses—except in Iowa and New Hampshire—before the first Tuesday in March. Republicans tried the kinder and gentler method of offering bonus delegates to states that agreed to keep their primaries further back (a method that had little impact). The result of these disparate approaches in 2000 was an unprecedented disjunction between the two parties in the scheduling of primaries, which have traditionally taken place in each state on the same day. During the period between February 1 and March 7, Republicans held six primaries and two caucus contests, while Democrats were largely left to cool their heels. The practical consequence was that, following the New Hampshire contest in which Al Gore won a narrow victory over Bill Bradley, the Democratic contest dropped from the national radar screen, and national attention for the next month focused almost exclusively on the Republican race between George Bush and John McCain. Many Democrats concluded that this was a disaster, placing the party, as DNC party chair Terry McAuliffe put it, at "a competitive disadvantage."[10]

McAuliffe was determined to change the Democratic Party rules, and in January of 2002, the DNC approved a new rule that eliminated the blackout period and allowed states to schedule their contests any time after New Hampshire. (Holding the first two slots for Iowa and New Hampshire has become a tradition that these two states now jealously guard.) The obvious and anticipated effect of this new rule was not only that Democrats would now join Republicans in states in which Republicans were already holding primaries in February, but also that additional states, undeterred by the existence of a Democratic rule, would move their primaries closer to the beginning. The rush for the front was once again on, and the 2004 schedule became the most front-loaded process to date, by a large margin. Super Tuesday, which in 1988 began the move to the front, now effectively became the closing event.

Whatever reasons induced the national parties to try to limit front-loading, that effort stalled in 2004. Instead of trying to "beat" front-loading, the parties decided to join it. Making a virtue of necessity, many Democrats preached the advantages of a highly front-loaded arrangement, emphasizing the benefits of getting the race over early and thus allowing time for a healing of party wounds, ending the difficulties of trying to use national party rules to dictate the setting of primary dates, and—though the point was rarely avowed in public—helping a front-runner establishment candidate (the type of candidate commonly thought to benefit most from this schedule) to win the nomination.

The outcome of the 2004 Democratic contest raised major questions about the adequacy of the traditional analysis of the effects of front-loading. Conventional wisdom has contended that front-loading boosts the chances of the early front-runner. As a former DNC chair Don Fowler put it, "Front-loading favors well-known, well-financed candidates," who are also, of course, establishment figures—someone, for example, like John Kerry.[11] Since well-known and potentially well-financed candidates are likely, almost by definition, to be favorites under any popular system, it is difficult to measure the added advantage front-loading provides them. Still, this argument seems to build on observations that have been made about the current system, which has already proven to be quite friendly to the front-runner and a tough nut for insurgents to crack. Political scientists have shown that the candidate who wins the so-called "invisible primary," meaning the contest that occurs before the actual voting begins, wins the nomination. Winning the invisible primary has been defined as raising the most money and coming in first in the national polls. The more formal-minded among political scientists have sought to express this relationship in the form of a regression equation that "predicts" or "forecasts" nomination campaign performance on the basis of these two factors. More money and higher poll ratings "predict" better performance in winning primary votes and delegates.

Formulas of this kind state a relationship, but they obviously do nothing to flesh out a concrete explanation of how the process actually works. The explanations offered have referred to two different scenarios. According to the first, or perfect, scenario, a front-runner scoops up most of the money during the invisible primary phase (perhaps deterring other potential candidates from entering) and comes into the actual campaign season with everything working in his favor: a lead in the polls, a strong organization, and the aura of inevitability. The knockout is swift and convincing. The problem with the "perfect scenario" is that it has not generally fit the facts. Recent nominees have often lost early contests in Iowa and New Hampshire and have seemed to lose momentum temporarily and to be hanging on the ropes. Such was the case most recently in 2000 with George W. Bush after he was defeated by John McCain in New Hampshire. Electoral experts generally agree that while the front-runner profits from many of the material advantages of being first, the actual position of being in front brings along with it some notable liabilities. The front-runner becomes a target of relentless scrutiny by the media and the foe of all of the other candidates, who share a temporary interest in trying to bring him down.

The explanation of why the regression equation works has turned accordingly to a second scenario. Here, the front-runner can suffer an upset early on, but he is in an excellent position to recover, using his superior resources and the organization he has built to withstand the onslaught. As William Mayer has written: "Front-runners are a good deal more resilient than they are frequently portrayed in the media. A front-runner who loses early can—and usually does—come back."[12] Front-loading is understood to add to the prospects of such a recovery. The insurgent candidate cannot raise funds rapidly enough to capitalize on his early success, as everything happens too quickly, and he cannot build an organization to compete in the large number of contests that immediately follow. The front-runner's comeback is swift and decisive. As David Broder puts it, "Political scientists say that the whole 'drama' of the primaries is a fraud—that the opposition party almost invariably nominates the candidate who raises the most money in the pre-election year and leads the field in the final polls of the year."[13]

These two scenarios explain the reasons why it has been thought that a front-loaded process adds to the already considerable advantage of the front-runner, establishment candidate. Their logic nevertheless admits of a third, if somewhat unlikely, possibility—what can be labeled the "nightmare scenario." In this instance, an insurgent manages to defeat the front-runner in Iowa or New Hampshire, and then catches a huge wave of momentum that puts him over the top before voters have the time to reflect on their decision or examine the insurgent candidate very closely. The front-runner is never able to recover.

These scenarios shed more light on the reasoning behind some of the normative judgments that have been made about a front-loaded system. For those who favor front-loading, its strong suit is that it helps the establishment candidate, perhaps the candidate approved by a powerful national chair. The objections to front-loading are based on two different grounds. One is that front-loading is simply *too* oriented toward the establishment candidate and too susceptible to the influence of money. In the words of the *New York Times* editorial page: "The nation is moving toward the worst possible scenario—one big, diffuse presidential primary held in the dead of winter, where only the candidates with large amounts of ready cash need apply."[14] The other objection focuses on the possibility of the nightmare scenario. Elaine Kamark of the Kennedy School at Harvard, who has played an influential role in Democratic Party rule-making processes, argued in 2001 for "a more rational spreading out" of big state contests on the grounds that a front-loaded process "allows for very little self-correction."[15] This position argues for greater deliberation, which is supposedly afforded by a longer process.

The 2004 Democratic nomination contest has wrought havoc in this line of analysis, not only in its outcome but also by revealing the inadequacy of the categories used to discuss these issues. By the strict definition of the scholarly studies, the result of the 2004 nomination contest clearly disconfirms the "prediction" of the regression equation. Howard Dean was the front-runner, having met the criteria of raising the most money and being in the lead in the polls when the selection of delegates began. He was the clear winner of the "invisible primary." But Dean, defeated in Iowa, was never able to mount a comeback. Meanwhile, continuing with the technical analysis, an underdog or insurgent candidate, John Kerry, seized the initiative and went on to win the nomination with little difficulty. Almost overnight he was transformed from Mr. Unelectable to Mr. Inevitable. The result appeared to follow the line of the third or "nightmare scenario."

The only problem in describing the race in these terms is that the technical labels do not fit common sense. Howard Dean, by most reasonable criteria, was viewed as the insurgent, only his insurgency occurred before a single delegate selection contest ever took place. Dean was a new kind of beast, at once front-runner and insurgent. As *The Economist* aptly observed at the beginning of January 2004, "Insurgent candidates have won the nomination before . . . but no insurgent has become a prohibitive favorite before a vote has been cast."[16] In such a case, it might be surmised, though it cannot be proven, that the "laws" of front-runner status operate differently: once the aura of the insurgent's inevitability is broken, he would have much more difficulty than the "typical" front-runner in making a recovery. By the same token, it hardly seems appropriate to describe John Kerry as a typical insurgent; he looked more like a front-runner turned underdog, perhaps like Ed Muskie after New Hampshire in 1972. He might have boasted, like Bill Clinton, about being the comeback kid, but no insurgent could ever walk or talk with the gravitas of a John Kerry.

The problem with the technical analysis is the assumption, understandable in light of previous experience, that an insurgent can take the upper hand only after the official process of selecting delegates has begun. Perhaps the likes of 2004 will never be seen again. It may also be the case, however, that in the event of another powerful insurgency (which in any case is a rarity), a repeat of the 2004 result is not out of the question. In one sense, the 2004 campaign followed the script of the second scenario, only with everything pushed back one stage: the establishment candidate was upset in an early phase of the contest (at the outset of the invisible primary), but then made his comeback early in the delegate selection contest. This occurrence may appear less of an aberration when one considers that the entire race, in particular the invisible primary, has changed as the process has become more front-loaded. Political activists, contributors, and commentators all now realize that the decisions will be happening much earlier, and they have adjusted their actions to take this into account. The invisible primary is far less invisible than it once was. There is of course no substitute for the "real" event of voters selecting delegates, so it would be incorrect to say that *everything* has moved back. But much has, including the timing of formal candidate debates. The categories of scholarly analyses of the campaign must change accordingly.

There is at least one point, however, on which the concerns expressed over the nightmare scenario may still provide some insight into the 2004 events. John Kerry was surely no traditional insurgent, but his rapid emergence enabled him to escape much of the critical scrutiny that a front-runner usually endures. Although this experience is almost always painful for the candidate and can sometimes prove fatal, it does have the benefit of getting certain things "out" before the public. The collective judgment of the media and the American people has been that, in the case at least of personal or biographical matters, a candidate should have to submit to such an ordeal only once. After that, the candidate can dismiss the recycling of such matters as "old news." John Kerry completed his nomination campaign with very little of this kind of examination, and it is fair to wonder whether, had he been a genuine front-runner, the charges and questions later raised about his Vietnam service and subsequent antiwar activities would have been aired during the nomination contest. "Pay me now or pay me later," as the expression goes. John Kerry might have been helped if he had paid this price in February rather than August.

A second important element in the nomination system is the method of campaign financing. Although the McCain-Feingold reform bill passed in 2002 and introduced a few new wrinkles into financing rules at this stage, these are of interest mostly to the expanding array of experts in this field. None was really revolutionary in its implications for the nomination process. What did change in 2004, however, was something much more important than the law. The moral backing of the whole regime of public campaign financing collapsed.

Until this election, it had been an article of faith among Democrats to accept public financing during the primary season. Doing so was not just in the interest of most of the candidates, but it was proof of their faith in the democratic spirit and of their support for reform. (The public financing option at the nomination stage is based on a formula of matching public funds for certain private donations; in 2004, it would have placed a cap on spending for any candidate of $45 million, of which a maximum of $18.7 million would have come from the federal government.) To reject public funding for Democrats was to sell out in some way to big money. Only Republican candidates had ever done so. No one had been a stronger supporter of public financing than Howard Dean. In March he promised to make an issue of any Democrat—John Kerry was who he had in mind—who opted out of public financing: "It will be a huge issue. . . . Campaign finance reform is just something I believe in."[17]

But it was Dean who changed positions and eliminated—probably forever—the taboo on declining public funding. He had reasons for doing so, not the least being that he was now in a position to be able to raise much more than the $45 million allowed under the law. In addition, the Dean campaign was already bumping up against the state spending limits—also a part of the campaign finance law—in Iowa and New Hampshire. There remained, however, the delicate problem of justifying this dramatic departure from Democratic orthodoxy. Dean's approach was a masterstroke of tactical maneuver. He posed the issue initially as a move that was directed entirely at George W. Bush, not his Democratic rivals. Dean had no choice: "The unabashed actions of [Mr. Bush] to thwart our democratic process with a flood of special-interest money have forced us to abandon a broken system."[18] This argument, judged disingenuous by his rivals, may also have shown Dean's growing confidence in winning the nomination. Its logic was addressed to the interregnum phase of the campaign, from March to September, when—as we will explain momentarily—the Democratic candidate would need the freedom to raise funds to compete with the huge amounts that the president's campaign was readying to spend in the spring. Dean also noted that he was opting out of public financing in a populist, not an oligarchic, fashion, by raising much of his money in small chunks: "Our campaign has not been talk of campaign-finance reform; it has been actual reform. . . . Over 200,000 people have given an average of $77 to bring us here, and they have now overwhelmingly refused to be intimidated by George Bush and his cronies."[19] Finally, in a gambit taken straight from Ross Perot's playbook, Dean refused to take so controversial a step on his own authority, but gave the decision to the "people," meaning the 600,000 supporters on his list. He held a plebiscite, which was conducted, naturally, mostly on the Internet: "I am putting this decision in your hands. . . . The next president will be beholden to only the people. . . . It is for the people to change the system for themselves."[20] And lo, the people decided! The much anticipated result, as reported by the campaign (with no election observers), showed that over 85 percent endorsed the move.

Dean's abandonment of public financing prompted exactly the kind of protests from the other candidates that one might have expected. Gephardt mocked the anti-Bush excuse, complaining that the real target was the other Democrats. Kerry was the most severe: "Three months ago, Governor Dean was saying what a Democratic principle it is to have campaign-finance reform and what a big issue it would be if someone stepped outside. That's when he wasn't raising a lot of money. Now, Mr. Change-Your-Opinion-for-Expediency is saying, 'Oh, I'm now able to raise money. Maybe we should get out of the system.' I think somewhere along the line, fundamental principles are important."[21] Having been given the chance to register his indignation, righteously, against Howard Dean, John Kerry was not nearly as disappointed as he appeared because Dean had just handed him the lifeline that would help to save his candidacy. Kerry's campaign at the time was in dire financial straits, with little prospect of being able to raise significant funds from other contributors. Some of the big money opposing Howard Dean was now being soaked up by Wesley Clark. Kerry had only one source left: his "personal" wealth, which was the wealth, indirectly, of his wife Teresa Heinz Kerry. For just this reason, Kerry probably could never have opted out of the system on his own. He now had cover, and he did not even need to hold a vote of his followers: "He [Dean] changed the rules of this race—and anyone with a real shot at the nomination must now play by those rules."[22] Although Dean's campaign took the expected shot against Kerry—"It's a lot easier to ask one person to write a $10 million check than it is to ask two million for $100"[23]—the complaint obviously had little effect. The moral injunction of Democrats against opting out of public financing had been destroyed. Perhaps it was never that powerful in the first place.

Experts will debate whether Howard Dean's decision was, from a tactical standpoint, a wise one. It doubtless helped John Kerry to keep his campaign afloat, although by this time Dean no longer counted John Kerry as his main competition, if he still considered him a rival at all. Furthermore, at the end of the day, Dean's collapse in Iowa came not just from a surge by John Kerry, let alone a surge that can be attributed to large spending. John Edwards also beat Dean handily in Iowa while remaining under the public finance regime. One point is clear, however: Howard Dean's decision clearly helped John Kerry in his campaign against George Bush by forcing him out of the public financing system at this stage. Following the election, Howard Dean's campaign manager, Joe Trippi, in the time-honored practice of losing contenders piling on a defeated nominee, claimed this credit for Howard Dean—and even more so for himself—for rescuing a meek and hapless John Kerry: "It was the risk-taking Dean campaign that forced the risk-adverse Kerry campaign to opt out of the public financing system. Had that decision not been forced on Mr. Kerry, he would have been badly out-spent by George Bush . . . throughout the long summer of 2004."[24] What Trippi was referring to is the provision of the current law that dictates that a candidate who accepts public funding in the nomination phase must also accept spending limits until the fall campaign begins.

Perhaps, too, someone will someday be able to assign Howard Dean the further credit of providing Democrats the political maneuvering room to join with Republicans in revisiting this part of the campaign finance law, which is so clearly flawed. Apart from George Bush's decision in 2004 to opt out of public financing during the nomination phase, allowing him to raise huge amounts of money in this period, this part of the campaign finance system had already proven itself in the past to create an unfair advantage for the incumbent. Ronald Reagan in 1984 and Bill Clinton in 1996 both accepted public funding in the nomination phase. Facing no opposition for the nomination, they were able to save this money and spend it in the spring and summer against their opponents, Walter Mondale and Bob Dole, who had used all of their public funding for its intended purpose of waging a nomination contest. Reformers have, so far, been unable or un-willing to find a solution to what has amounted to a legally imposed penalty on the party that has had a competitive nomination contest. This penalty has proven in the past to be less of a disaster than it might have been, but only because the parties managed to find ways to "work around" some of the spending limits. By refusing public financing in 2004 and by availing himself of other means—chiefly the fund-raising activities by the so-called 527 committees—John Kerry was able to equal the spending of President Bush from March to September. There was rough parity in spending, but it came in spite of, not because of, the legal provisions of the system.

## The Democratic Party

Nearly all of the internal debate among Democratic strategists that followed the 2000 election turned out to have only limited relevance to the 2004 nomination race. One reason was that this debate focused on the party's position on domestic politics and had little to say about national security, which in the end proved so important to the outcome. The pre-September 11 debate nevertheless supplied the template for Democratic strategists in their thinking about their party. As is usual after a defeat, many analysts sought to draw lessons from the last campaign. According to one line of argument, put forth most vigorously by some in the Democratic Leadership Council (DLC), Al Gore's defeat in 2000 resulted from his decision to abandon a moderate campaign based on defending the record of economic growth of the Clinton administration and to run instead on a populist appeal, pitting the "people" against the "interests." This decision cost him the election. With the economy in such good shape and the American people so content, the Democrats should have won easily, even with a few scandals in the White House. According to another line of argument, there was nothing unsound in Gore's strategy—indeed, he began to pull ahead in the 2000 race at the very moment that he adopted his populist line. And in the end he still won a plurality of the votes. The problem with the Gore campaign was not strategic, but tactical; his performance in the debates raised questions about his personal fitness for office, costing him his lead. Gore lost for one reason and one reason alone: he was Al Gore.

The DLC argument, whatever its merits, pointed to an interesting dilemma for Democrats in their nomination process. The 2000 results demonstrated that Al Gore did a remarkable job of holding the base of the Democratic Party, including the growing segment of wealthier and professional Democrats who now make up such a large part of the Democratic Party in its urban and suburban bastions. Gore's campaign of economic populism evidently did not disturb these upper-class and professional Democrats, who love to cheer these populist arguments, even if a few of them might balk at too extreme a version. What, then, was the basis for the DLC complaint against his strategy? The answer was this: Gore lost by failing to attract an *additional* slice of the wealthier and professional segment of the electorate that was, or could have been, his, if only he had pursued a more moderate line. As Joe Lieberman put this case in 2002, slightly criticizing the 2000 campaign strategy, some of the campaign rhetoric about "the people vs. the powerful" sent the wrong message and "ultimately hurt": "It was not the pro-growth approach, and it ultimately made it more difficult for us to gain the support of some of the middle class, independent voters who don't see America as 'us vs. them,' but more in Kennedy's terms of a rising tide lifts all boats."[25]

The DLC argument contained another element, which was echoed in a widely read primer published in 2002 by John Judis and Ruy Teixiera, *The Emerging Democratic Majority*. One implication of this book—although few Democrats openly admit the point—is that the appeal of economic populism to the working class is not as important to the Democratic Party as many suppose. The manufacturing working class, or what one might call "Old Labor," is a shrinking segment of the electorate; its support of Democrats is important, but it cannot be the foundation of any effort on which to rebuild a majority. (Richard Gephardt's poor showing in the Iowa caucus in 2004, where he based his entire campaign on the appeal to the traditional working class voter, was a strong indication of the validity of this argument.) Furthermore, the appeal of *economic* populism is often not as important to members of the working class as the appeal to *cultural* populism—morality, religion, and traditional values. Here, Republicans have had the edge. Realists in the Democratic Party have accordingly concluded that many white workers are drifting away from the Democratic Party, and there is only so much Democrats can do about it; their best strategy is to avoid going out of their way to offend traditional values, which some Democratic elites unfortunately are inclined to do. Here again, the DLC has called for a more moderate approach as the best way to secure victory in the general election campaign.

In sum, according to the DLC analysis, the challenge Democrats faced is that powerful segments in the party favor positions that are not winners. (Republicans obviously have a similar problem of their own.) The leadership of Old Labor still pushes for economic populism and for restrictions on trade. Educated professionals in the party thrill at the rhetoric of economic populism (for many it is like eating vicariously of the forbidden fruit), and they are especially keen on various forms of cultural and social liberalism. DLC Democrats nevertheless believed that, notwithstanding these first preferences, enough Democrats could be brought to see the wisdom of choosing a candidate somewhat more moderate than themselves in order to win the election. This, they argued, was Bill Clinton's formula. It had proven the best way—the only way—to capture the presidency.

This position was at odds with the views of Richard Gephardt, who continued to argue for the positions of Old Labor, including opposition to the free trade policies of the Clinton administration, which Clinton had considered one of his great achievements. A more thoroughgoing critique of the DLC position came from Howard Dean, in his plea to restore the "Democratic wing of the Democratic Party." Even before the Iraq War emerged as so important an issue, Dean argued against a moderate line. He never appealed to the constituency of Old Labor, but far more to the young, the highly educated, and the more ideologically motivated upper-class segments of the party. The way to make the Democratic Party into a majority was to energize its base and turn out real Democrats in much larger numbers. As Dean put it, "We're not going to beat George Bush by being Bush Lite. The way to beat George Bush is to give the 50 percent of Americans who quit voting because they can't tell the difference between the Democratic Party and the Republican Party—give them a reason to vote again."[26]

This position was more than campaign rhetoric. It represented a view, shared by a number of experts, that enlarging and energizing the base, rather than appealing to the swing voter in the middle, was the best way to win elections. Dean and his advocates rejected the Clinton formula, which in any case had given Democrats only the presidency, while costing them the House and Senate. The new line was that it was energy and conviction, not soft-sell moderation, which was the key. According to Joe Trippi, "There's something very appealing about taking a party back, and that crosses party lines. . . . The middle tends to go to the most energized party." These arguments had implications for the nomination race as well. They were meant to convince potential Dean supporters that what they were feeling in their hearts could be confirmed in their heads: Howard Dean was electable. Dean's opponents took the opposite position, arguing that it was only by appealing to the swing voter in the middle on moderate grounds that the Democrats had any hope of winning. Democrats had to pick up the votes of some voters in a few states, such as West Virginia or Ohio or Arkansas. As a strategist for Wesley Clark, Matt Bennett demanded to know, "Tell me the states that Gore lost in 2000 that Dean thinks he wins with new voters."[27]

What began to shift the equation in this argument in the Democratic Party was the reemergence of the national security issue following September 11. A number of persons on the Left, especially among the highly educated and professional class, began almost immediately to express concern about the administration's response to the terrorist attack, believing that its definition of the issue as a "war" on terrorism was misguided. Among a large part of the academic Left, support for the war in Afghanistan was lukewarm, and the objections collapsed only because the operation ended so quickly. Opposition mounted, however, as President Bush adopted a more assertive and nationalist line and began to use his more "absolutist" rhetoric of the "axis of evil." Parts of what had been the internationalist contingent of the Democratic Party and which had backed President Clinton in the war in Kosovo now began to desert President Bush for his "unilateralist" tendencies. Finally, the launching of the Iraq War activated a full-scale antiwar movement that altered the balance of forces in the Democratic Party. An increasingly large number of the educated and the professionals in the party viewed opposition to Bush's foreign policy and to the Iraq War as the litmus test for the nomination. An increasing share of the educated Democrats would not listen to DLC arguments about "moderation," above all its argument for "moderation" in foreign affairs. The DLC—at least the part of it that supported vigorously the war on terror and the Iraq invasion—found itself overwhelmed by events. Its constituency grew smaller as the war in Iraq proved more difficult and costly than its supporters imagined. By the beginning of 2004, two-thirds of Democrats counted themselves as opponents of the war, with this figure much higher among upper-class Democrats.

## The Field

The determination of the field of candidates is a function of the decisions made by individuals to run or not to run. This sounds almost like a tautology, but it serves to focus attention on the political context in which these individual decisions are made. The class of Democratic contenders in 2004 was large and rich, containing five candidates (soon to be six if you count Howard Dean) who entered with some reasonable expectation—as judged by the commentators—of winning the nomination for president (or vice president): John Kerry, Joe Lieberman, Richard Gephardt, Robert Graham (who withdrew), Wesley Clark, John Edwards, and then Howard Dean. In addition, there were three unlikely fringe candidates whose intentions probably had more to do with advancing their own political careers or giving voice to an ideological view on the national stage. This group consisted of Ambassador Carol Mosley Braun, the first African American female senator, Congressman Dennis Kucinich, and the Reverend Al Sharpton. Sharpton, who supplied some of the liveliest commentary during the campaign, was engaged in an election of his own, seeking to end the reign of Jesse Jackson as the unofficial spokesman or "king" of civil rights activism and take the fallen crown for himself.

A fieldologist might describe the 2004 group as constituting something close to a "full field," meaning that it contained most all of those who had a reasonable shot. This was the first such group for the Democrats since 1988. (Republicans had fairly large, if not full, fields in three of the last four races—2000, 1996, and 1988—and even in 1992 President Bush faced some competition in Patrick Buchanan). In 2000, only Bill Bradley challenged Al Gore, whom many in the party treated almost as an incumbent; in 1996, President Clinton ran unopposed for reelection; and in 1992, a number of first-tier Democratic candidates, judging that President George Bush would be unbeatable, decided to tend to their local constituents (an error none would repeat this time). By 2004 there was accordingly a backlog of Democrats with presidential ambitions. For some of the seasoned Washington politicians in the group, it was clearly now or never.

There were nevertheless a few politicians of stature who were mentioned and who considered running, but in the end decided not to. The list consisted of Tom Daschle, Joe Biden, Hillary Clinton, and Al Gore. In the first two cases, both men gave the race considerable thought, but determined in the end that it was not reasonable. Daschle, as Senate majority leader after 2001, was hurt by the Democrats' loss of the Senate in 2002, and he had his own Senate seat to defend in 2004 (which in the end he lost). Joe Biden debated entering late, during the summer of 2003, but finally judged that there was no reasonable prospect of victory. In a Washington rarity, his public statement corresponded to his private judgment: "At this date, everything would have to fall perfectly into place and I would have to put on hold what influence I have in the U.S. Senate in pursuit of what is now too much of a long shot."[28] Hillary Clinton's case was a bit different. At this stage in her career, when she needed time to establish a record in her own right independent of her position as First Lady, it would have taken an extraordinarily favorable set of circumstances to have induced her to run. But when a decision needed to be made, George Bush was still highly popular. There was also the small matter of her promise to New Yorkers to serve a full term, a repudiation of which would have required the most artful parsing of what "full term" meant. Better, as former Bill Clinton adviser (and current professional Hillary nemesis) Dick Morris pointed out, to plan for a Democratic defeat in 2004 in order to prepare a clear path to the nomination in 2008.

Al Gore's case was the most intriguing, as he still had the greatest name recognition among Democrats and a sizable following. But there were also many, including a good number in his own entourage in 2000, who thought that another race against George Bush would be a disaster for the party. Other candidates had made it clear that they were not going to step aside for Al Gore or await his decision; they were ready to go. The exception was Joe Lieberman, who from either an excess of gratitude or a rational calculation that a display of disloyalty would sink him, declared that he would not run if Al Gore did.

Americans watched the continuing drama of Al Gore's evolutions with much fascination, beginning with his widely acclaimed concession speech and dignified departure from the political scene in January 2001 to his yearlong phase of introversion, during which he played and looked the part of a professor from the 1960s, down even to the growth of the obligatory scraggly beard. But Gore reemerged refreshed and clean-shaven in the summer of 2002, appearing as a fire-breathing populist, his southern or mountain accent growing noticeably stronger by the day. He became a fierce critic of the administration, opposing the Iraq War resolution and attacking Bush on his education program. In the fall of 2002, following the midterm election, Gore embarked on a comeback tour, and all signs pointed toward another run. But then, with the crowds less than enthusiastic, Gore pulled the plug and announced on December 15 that he would not be a candidate "this time around."

Gore remained active during the nomination phase, and his attacks on the Bush administration grew harsher. His final act came in a dramatic endorsement of Howard Dean in December 2003, shortly before the Iowa caucus. The surprise here was not that Gore did not back his former running mate, Joe Lieberman, but that he failed in the courtesy of informing him in advance, leaving Lieberman standing in the lurch, his excess of loyalty completely unrequited. (Gore's aides spoke of equipment malfunction in reaching Lieberman.) Given Al Gore's political position, the choice of Howard Dean was fully consistent. Of all the major Democrats, Gore had already moved furthest from Bill Clinton's moderate stances of 1996. Gore was closest to Howard Dean, not just in his positions and in his populism, but also in the intensity of his expressions of anger at George Bush. He even began to resemble Dean in his physical appearance, albeit a hulkier version, and he commended Dean for continuing his own plan, launched in 2000, "to remake the Democratic Party . . . to take it back on behalf of the people of this country."[29] To a disappointed Joe Lieberman, Al Gore was no longer the kind of Democrat that he had remembered: "Al is supporting a candidate who is so fundamentally opposed to the basic transformation that Bill Clinton brought to this party in 1992, moving it to a more middle-of-the-road stance on economic policy and other areas."[30]

Of the ten candidates who entered the race, the top four finishers in order (and the only candidates to have won at least one primary) were John Kerry, John Edwards, Howard Dean, and Wesley Clark. A word should be said about each, beginning from the bottom of the list.

The very existence of a campaign by Wesley Clark was one of the great surprises of the 2004 contest. Hardly anyone could even have imagined such a candidacy before the midterm elections of 2002, and from all accounts

Clark himself never thought of himself as a candidate (or a Democrat) until around this time. At first, mention of Wesley Clark in the Democratic mix occurred mostly in the context of his serving as an informal adviser to Howard Dean. There was much talk, at least in the Dean camp, of Clark becoming Dean's vice-presidential choice. Not only would Clark balance the ticket geographically, leavening the radical image of Vermont with a touch of Arkansas heartland, but he would also help inoculate a Dean candidacy from the kind of charges Republicans were sure to level: softness, pacifism, and a lack of credibility within the military. How better to counter such arguments than to run a general who had earned a medal in Vietnam and who had headed allied forces as NATO's chief commander during the Kosovo War? Dean's stratagem made sense for the fall election, but it was even more astute for his nomination bid. Clark's name being bandied about as a potential vice-presidential nominee could help Dean win support from Democrats who admired him, but worried that he might be unelectable.

Having Wesley Clark on the Democratic ticket with Howard Dean struck many as such a brilliant stroke that a few began to conclude that it might be better if Clark himself, not Howard Dean, were at the head. Wesley Clark, a man known in the military as one who always preferred to give rather than to take orders, quickly embraced this view. By the late summer of 2003, the Clark option was also being backed by a shadowy contingent in the Democratic Party establishment that included many advisers of former President Bill Clinton (if not Bill Clinton himself). This group saw Clark as the only candidate who could stop Howard Dean. The ABD contingent (Anybody But Dean) had come to the conclusion that Democrats could not nominate a candidate who favored the war—that much was now conceded to Howard Dean—but that it was important to field a more credible antiwar candidate who was friendlier to the party establishment and more moderate on domestic policy questions.

There was never any possibility that Howard Dean would step aside to accommodate Wesley Clark. Clark was seen in the Dean camp as an interloper or a Johnny-come-lately, and his candidacy was viewed very much in the way that those in Eugene McCarthy's camp had seen Bobby Kennedy in 1968. Inevitably, the personal relations between Dean and Clark grew acrimonious, as they were now battling for part of the same constituency. To the Dean people, Wesley Clark was not a real Democrat—indeed, they questioned whether Clark was a Democrat at all. Clark was reported to have backed President Bush and to have spoken not so long ago on his behalf. For his part, Clark intimated that Howard Dean was soft and unpresidential: "I just don't believe that, at this time in American history, the Democratic Party can field candidates who can only represent the education, health, job, and compassionate sides of the party. . . . We have to deal with the challenges facing America at home and the challenges facing America abroad."[31]

Clark presented himself, like Howard Dean, as an outsider, only as an outsider who was both expert and experienced in the one area where Americans wanted insider credentials: the conduct of national security policy. In Clark's own words:

> If you want a lawyer to lead this country, pick a lawyer. If you're looking for a doctor, get a doctor. But if you want a leader, somebody who's actually been there, who's helped negotiate agreements, who's led alliance in war, then get a leader. And I'm the only person on that stage of candidates who's ever laid awake at night and prayed the bombs that I ordered to drop would hit the proper target and not innocent people. And I think you need in this country someone who's done it both at home and abroad, and that's why I'm running. I'm the only person who's been there and actually done it.[32]

Clark's bid for the presidency began with great promise. He was the last candidate to join the race, not entering until September 2003. The late entrance had many causes, the chief one being that no one much entertained a Clark candidacy until Howard Dean demonstrated the strength of an antiwar campaign. There were evident problems with a late start—most of the critical "invisible primary" stage was already over—but it also had some advantages. Clark could profit from the sentiment that the existing candidates, like suitors who had pressed their case too assiduously, were a bit shopworn. In addition, Clark hoped to present his candidacy as a kind of modern-day draft, driven by a groundswell of popular support as evidenced by the Internet activity of two separate Draft Clark groups. Although Clark was not exactly a national hero in the mold of Colin Powell in 1996, his backers believed that he had sufficient prowess for Americans to regard him as a man on a horse. This image evidently had a certain appeal for Madonna, who became a Clark supporter: "Our greatest risk is not terrorism . . . but a lack of leadership."

In the post-September 11 world, "leadership," especially (although one might not say it) manly leadership, was a subtext to the whole 2004 election campaign. Democrats knew it was important. Manliness was a key to Kerry's campaign, from his leather Harley outfits to his own military prowess to his invitation to "bring it on," and Dean's own feistiness and aggressiveness served to dispel any implications of a softer side. For the moment, Clark was the beneficiary of this mood. He immediately rose to the top of the field of Democrats in a few national polls, a position he might have continued to occupy if only he had been able to avoid campaigning.[33] In the polls in September and October, Clark ran stronger than

Dean among men, southerners, and Democrats of lower income. Dean led only in his solid base, the wealthiest and most educated of Democrats. Clark also enjoyed great early success in raising money, as the wallets of many of the rich and famous opened up to him.

The Clark candidacy serves as yet another reminder of how difficult it is to run for the presidency of the United States. Clark by all accounts is a person of great intelligence, and he has enormous experience running complex organizations. Yet his campaign was plagued from the first moment with problems. It was inevitable, of course, that when Clark changed positions from being a man on a horse to a candidate on the stump, some of the luster of his appeal would begin to wear off. In the studio and on the podium, he would begin to look more like the other candidates. Beyond this fact, however, Clark made a series of embarrassing gaffes, which began almost from the first day. The whole logic of the Clark campaign had been that he was to be a tough antiwar candidate, yet in an early appearance he allowed himself to say that he "probably would have voted for the Iraq War resolution." He recanted the next day. Clark also seemed unprepared to deal with the charges, backed by some recent statements supportive of George W. Bush, that he was in fact a Republican. Misstatements abounded. Clark boasted that, if president, he could assure that there would be no terrorist attacks, another statement he had to retract.[34] Finally, though his statement was taken out of context (when is this not the case in presidential races?), Clark at a critical moment seemed to be trying to pull rank on John Kerry: "He's a lieutenant and I'm a general." This might work in the military, but is not a prescription for winning favor in civilian life. As Senator Ernest Hollings of South Carolina said, "We're going to teach that fellow in South Carolina that there are more lieutenants than there are generals."

For all the problems, Clark's campaign nevertheless had a powerful rationale, but it was a rationale that was based almost entirely on a circumstance in which he was the sole plausible rival to Howard Dean. The strategy was predicated on Dean wiping out much of the opposition in Iowa—Clark chose not to compete there—after which Clark would engage Dean *mano a mano* in New Hampshire and then in the South. Clark's candidacy made less sense against John Kerry. By the time Kerry had won Iowa, Kerry had become mostly an antiwar candidate. Kerry was also a military man and as much a hero as Wesley Clark. Finally, Clark was hardly in a position to attack John Kerry from the right, when he was trying if anything to run to his left on national security issues. (Surprisingly, given initial indications, Clark also campaigned to the left on many social issues, including abortion, where he took a position well to the left of *Roe v. Wade*.)

There was little left to the campaign at this point, and after suffering a series of defeats against John Kerry, he withdrew in early February.

Howard Dean, the scrappy governor of Vermont, began his campaign before the Iraq War was launched, and there was always more to the campaign than this single issue. As one observer noted, "It was less his opposition to the war than his opposition to Bush that attracted so many frustrated Democrats."[35] His early stump speech sang a continual refrain that began: "What I want to know is why so many Democrats in Washington aren't standing up against Bush's"—and then you fill in the blank—"give-away tax plan," "unilateral war in Iraq."[36] Howard Dean played the outsider, not just to George Bush, but to the establishment in his own party. John Edwards and Wesley Clark also played on the outsider theme, but never with the edge or attitude of Howard Dean. Dean took on not only his rival candidates, but also the Democratic National Committee, the Democratic Leadership Council, and even, indirectly, former President Clinton.

Psychologically, Dean seemed most comfortable in the outsider role. Dean had learned the technique from Jimmy Carter in the 1976 campaign, where he had first cut his teeth as a political organizer. But the model on which he relied, even if unconsciously, came from Mr. Outsider himself, Ross Perot, who made his mark by promising to "clean up the mess" in Washington. Similarly, Dean insisted that "we need a change in Washington, and we're not going to get it by electing someone from Washington." Some of his rivals "want to say they are against the establishment, but they are the establishment."[37] Dean took his outsiderism to such an extreme that at one point he reportedly likened Washington insiders to "cockroaches," a comment he clarified by saying that he had only declared that, if elected, he would send them "scurrying like cockroaches." As the campaign geared up, it appeared to be a good time to be an outsider. The Democratic losses in the 2002 midterm election discredited the party's congressional contingent, leaving an opening for a governor. Much the same thing happened on the Republican side after the GOP's 1998 losses, when Republicans began looking outside of Washington, helping Governor George W. Bush to move quickly to the front of the pack.

Dean's campaign was run largely to the Left, but this image was leavened by his strong emphasis on balancing the budget. As governor in Vermont, he had earned something of a reputation as a fiscal conservative and a moderate on certain issues, including gun control. This image helped his campaign, even with many on the Left, as it was proof that Dean was, in the tradition of the true outsider, a straight shooter who defied simple categories. The cyber movement he came to lead put an enormous emphasis on procedural matters, a democratic style, and honesty and directness in one's views. In the dichotomy that Dean cultivated, outsiderism meant sincerity, insiderism duplicity. As he put it, "The definition of a gaffe in Washington is somebody who tells the truth but shouldn't have."[38]

Yet it was perhaps just this candor and sincerity that proved his undoing. Cultivating outsiderism is like performing a high tightrope act. Eventually the very qualities that put a candidate there risk getting him into trouble. Dean's blunt talk, his willingness to be frank, his cultivation of a different kind of style, the creative, loosely run organization worked on the way up, but at a certain point, when people start thinking of the candidate as the nominee, they can become liabilities. Over the fall and winter, admittedly under the kind of scrutiny that no other candidate received, Dean's frankness led him from one troubling or impolitic statement to the next, from an unfortunate invitation to court southerners with Confederate flags (insulting both to many southerners and to African Americans), to his statement about Saddam, to his impolite treatment of a Bush supporter at an Iowa town meeting. An outside candidate cannot remain Peter Pan, but at some point must make a smooth transition to adulthood. According to a critical assessment of Howard Dean written afterward by his pollster, Paul Maslin, "Dean's erratic judgment, loose tongue, and overall stubbornness in refusing to be scripted, to be disciplined, or to discipline himself wore our spirits down."[39] Harsh words, but even the most Deaniacal of the Deaniacs in the end would acknowledge a grain of truth to this description.

John Edwards began the race as a dark horse, but eventually emerged from the pack of the candidates to be the last rival standing to John Kerry. It was rumored that Edwards had decided to run for the presidency chiefly because he feared another race for his Senate seat in North Carolina. (He gave up that seat, which went to the Republican, Richard Burr.) It was also rumored that Edwards had his eye on the vice-presidential nomination and on burnishing his credentials for the future. John Edwards was only in his first term as a senator, which made a race for the presidency look premature. But his connections with the trial lawyers assured him all along of a steady supply of funding, which helped keep the campaign afloat even during the single-digit months.

By necessity—and perhaps also by choice—his limited experience in Washington enabled him to run as something of an outsider. He was not yet quite part of the establishment—half in, half out. Edwards crafted a unique message to fit that niche, and it was this message that proved to be his greatest asset. Edwards became the cheerful and upbeat populist. When encountering the word "populist," the first thought is likely to be of a candidate who exhibits a touch of anger. But Edwards was different. He preached a Gore-like message of "two Americas," but his voice was mellifluous, not harsh, and he delivered his speech far more with sadness than anger: "Today, under George W. Bush, there are two Americas, not one. . . . One America that does the work, another America that reaps the reward. . . . One favored, the other forgotten. . . . One privileged, the other burdened." The upshot, too, was the possibility of reconciliation, to make the two Americas one. With his southern drawl, it was like listening to music. Edwards honed this message in the last month before the Iowa caucus at the same time he renounced any kind of negative campaigning. Sensing that Iowans and Democrats had heard enough attacks from one Democrat on another, he cast himself as the beneficent candidate. To burnish his populist message and give it some verisimilitude—something that Al Gore had never really been able to achieve—he played heavily, like Richard Gephardt, on his humble, working-class origins. It was only in America, as he often said, that the "son of a mill worker can go toe-to-toe with the son of a president."

Edwards offered his own version of electability to Democrats, arguing that he could appeal not only to the swing voter in the North (which Kerry and Gephardt and Lieberman all claimed to be able to entice) but also the swing voter in the South. Edwards alone could do what Bill Clinton and Jimmy Carter had done: win a sufficient number of southern whites to bring some southern states into the blue column. As Edwards frequently told his listeners, "I can beat [Bush] in all regions of the country, including the South."[40] (This was the same argument that had been advanced by Robert Graham of Florida while he was in the race, and Clark, who was from Arkansas, echoed it.) No one who observed John Edwards's campaign could fail to notice, even if they did not mention, his good looks and youthful appearance (it was difficult to believe he was already fifty years old.) These qualities are usually treated generally as assets that make a candidate "attractive," but the truth is that they can also serve as liabilities. One of the first to suffer from this cruel paradox was Dan Quayle, who, the moment he was selected for the vice-presidential nomination in 1992, came under suspicion of lacking the intelligence and gravitas to be president. And these judgments had something to do with his looks. John Edwards never quite fell to the level of Dan Quayle, but there was some truth nonetheless to Andrew Ferguson's observation that "in person, as on television, Edwards can't escape the sense of weightlessness that his good looks impart."

Finally, there was the nominee, John Kerry. Surveying the biographies of presidential candidates, a rough distinction can be drawn between "candidates by design"—those who from a very young age have their sights on the presidency—and "candidates by accident"—those who for one reason or another come much later in life to entertain presidential ambitions. John Kerry is most definitely a candidate of the first type, while George W. Bush is more likely of the second. John Kerry began to experience presidential longings from the moment John F. Kennedy came on the scene. Camelot, in fact, cast its mystical charm on two young men of that generation who became Democratic nominees: Bill Clinton and John Kerry. All accounts of Bill Clinton's life report the story of how a young Bill Clinton, traveling as a high school student from Arkansas to Washington, D.C., as a Boy's Nation delegate, maneuvered himself to the front of the group in order to shake hands with JFK on the White House Lawn. The photo shows an awkward young man stretching out his hand in order to get what might be his one brush with fame. From that moment, Clinton's plans to become a saxophone player began to take second place to his dreams of becoming president of the United States. In the same year, 1962, John Kerry also met JFK, only under vastly different circumstances. And therein, as the saying goes, lies a tale. Kerry, then a student at Yale, moved in the higher circles of American society. His girlfriend at the time was from a family that was friends with the president. A photo, taken on the family yacht during a spin off the coast of Rhode Island, shows a confident youngster (John Kerry) seated just a few feet from the president. Both men, equally lean and fit, are clad in casual boating attire that the elite alone know instinctively where to find. No stretching or groping for the president's hand here.

As his biographers recount, John Kerry modeled himself on John Kennedy. The image of JFK as a naval military hero, commanding the legendary PT109, was enough to induce John Kerry to enlist in the same service. Like JFK, Kerry became a hero in his own right, although in a way that some of his critics charged was partly tainted by a calculating self-consciousness that sought to use his record as a springboard for his political career. And use it he did. When John Kerry famously made his military service the cornerstone of his Democratic Convention acceptance speech—"I'm John Kerry and I'm reporting for duty"—it was not, as some a few weeks later tried to suggest, a departure from usual practice; his service record was front and center in the campaign from its inception. John Kerry officially kicked off his campaign from Norfolk, with a warship as a backdrop, and the autobiography he published for the campaign draws the reader back continually to his Vietnam service. The same goes for the widely cited official biography by Douglas Brinkley, prepared with Kerry's cooperation, which was entitled *Tour of Duty: John Kerry and the Vietnam War*. This point is confirmed by Thomas Oliphant, the *Boston Globe* columnist (and friend of John Kerry), who summed up Kerry's first year on the campaign trail as follows: "The initial year of his presidential campaign was almost fatal because of two rookie mistakes influenced by hubris: Kerry bought into front-runnerism via fund-raising yardsticks, and, worse, he bought into a presentation based mostly on himself, his war record, and his résumé."[41] Oliphant's suggestion is that Kerry toned down this appeal as the Democratic race went on, which may have been the case for a while. But Kerry revived it—or it was revived mightily for him—in what was the single most important moment for John Kerry in reigniting his nomination campaign. In Iowa, just two days before the vote, Jim Rassmann, the man whom John Kerry saved from the waters of the Mekong River in Vietnam, and to whom Kerry had not spoken since 1969, contacted the campaign and then flew to Iowa to offer a moving testimonial of John Kerry's courage and heroism. The effect was electric. The theme of heroism now had a specific face to it. From then on, too, Kerry took frequently to campaigning with the "band of brothers" from Vietnam.

The other aspect of the image to emerge from the photo with JFK is that of John Kerry as a member of America's elite. John Kerry was not originally from a family of great wealth, but it was a family of pedigree and refinement, and Kerry's education at St. Paul and Yale reflected this. It was evident even more in his demeanor. Kerry had been called a man without the common touch, and this image was always something that his campaign worried about and sought to dispel. Howard Dean, a short man who had the image of a scrappy fighter, was known to despise Kerry for his sense of entitlement, even though Dean had also come from a wealthy family. Still, he never had the elitist image or demeanor of John Kerry.

## Positioning

In addition to the candidates' appeals on the basis of their unique personal characteristics and qualifications, they also run on their stands on the major issues and (sometimes) on a theme or style of leadership—whether they are "outsiders" (or "populists") or "insiders." The Democrats vying for the nomination can be compared on these matters by plotting their positions on a diagram (table 3.2).

The major issues in the 2004 nomination campaign fall along two basic dimensions. The first (on the horizontal axis) is their position on the Iraq War, which became the single most important item of controversy. The candidates can be placed into one of three spaces: those who were against the war (Howard Dean and Wesley Clark); those who were in favor of it, however much they might have criticized its conduct (Joe Lieberman and

Table 3.2.   **Rosetta Stone of the 2004 Democratic Primary Contest**

|            | *Antiwar* | *Middle* | *Prowar* |
|------------|-----------|----------|----------|
| *Populist* | **Dean**  |          | Gephardt |
| *Middle*   | **Clark** | **Edwards**<br>Kerry |  |
| *Moderate* | Graham    |          | Lieberman |

Richard Gephardt); and those who moved between these two positions (John Kerry and John Edwards), albeit ending much more on the antiwar side. The second issue dimension, which is presented on the vertical axis, represents an amalgam of their positions on domestic economic and welfare issues, including trade protection. Some of the specific items here include views on Bush's tax cuts, Bush's education policy, the form of health care proposed, and the view on NAFTA. With a bit of liberty taken, the positions here are grouped into the three categories of more radical or populist, middle, and moderate. The more radical position came to be identified with opposition to NAFTA and free trade, support of universal single-payer health care, and full opposition to the Bush tax cuts and education program. Howard Dean and Richard Gephardt were more to the radical side here, with John Edwards edging in their direction; John Kerry is properly placed in the middle; and Joe Lieberman, who defended NAFTA and parts of the Bush tax cuts, is located on the moderate side. From all signs, Wesley Clark—if he ever had to get around to it—was intending to position himself somewhere near the middle. Finally, on the question of style or theme of leadership, the candidates are distinguished either as outsiders (in bold) or insiders (regular type). Included among the outsiders are, most notably, Howard Dean, who was the constant scold of the "Washington politics-as-usual club," as well as Wesley Clark and John Edwards, who sang a milder and sweeter anti-establishment theme. The insiders were those who could not, and did not try, to slip the label of being experienced hands from Washington: John Kerry, Richard Gephardt, and Joe Lieberman. All three of them sought to depict this position to their advantage, contrasting their maturity and knowledge to the inexperience of the outsiders. Typical, for example, was Gephardt's observation, directed against Dean, that "in a time of terrorism," voters would be sure to vote for President Bush "if they have doubts about the experience and the ability, the steady hands, of the alternative."[42]

It is notable over the course of the campaign that the two main candidates in the middle on the issues, John Kerry and John Edwards, both tacked to the Left, moving in the direction of Howard Dean on the war and Richard Gephardt on trade policy. Dean and Gephardt served as the magnets, drawing others toward them on these major issues. Still, both Kerry and Edwards at certain times sought to profit from their more moderate position in comparison to Howard Dean. In the last phase of the campaign, the race—if it really still was one—was between Kerry and Edwards, the two major candidates who were most closely situated to each other. Edwards, a mild kind of outsider, tried to run a bit on the populist side on the trade issue, although Kerry denied that there was any real difference between them. There was precious little over which to argue, which may explain why it ended so quickly.

As a senator, John Kerry had a strong record as a Democrat on the Left. But in this race, he was the candidate most conspicuously in the center, in part because of the nature of his opponents and the issues of the campaign; Kerry might carry the burden of being another "Massachusetts liberal," but Dean gave him the opportunity to appear centrist by comparison. Although being in the center is not always an advantage—and while John Kerry's victory certainly cannot be explained purely on the basis that he was in the middle—that position did allow him at times to counterpunch, and it placed him in an excellent position to pick up the votes of those on one side against those on the other. In Iowa, near the end, he was able to gain from Dean on his left and from Gephardt on his right. He was always the consensus pick, the person who was most electable. In this respect, he bore a stunning resemblance to Bob Dole, the Senate insider and war hero who captured the Republican nomination in 1996 not by generating much personal enthusiasm but by being the one candidate almost everyone could agree on, the one who could be counted on neither to split nor to embarrass his party.

## The Race

The abbreviated nomination contest in 2004 unfolded in three phases: the contest in Iowa, a three-week shake-out period in which three of the four remaining major national candidates (Lieberman, Clark, and Dean) dropped out, and the brief, anticlimactic showdown between John Kerry and John Edwards.

In past races, the Iowa caucus has been important not for deciding who would win the nomination but for beginning to decide who would not. It started the process of winnowing the field. This time, matters were different. Iowa was practically the national primary. When the caucus meetings ended in the early evening of January 19, almost everything was over but the shouting, which Howard Dean added a few hours later. Some may complain that the 120,000 Iowans who turned out had too much say in the race. Iowans acted in some instances on the basis of incidents that were particular to the Iowa campaign, but it quickly became clear that their verdict was entirely in line with the sentiment of Democrats nationwide.

Two general lines of explanation, not entirely incompatible, have emerged about what happened in Iowa. One is that a real and strong shift took place in the final weeks of the campaign against the two perceived front-runners, Richard Gephardt and especially Howard Dean. In this view, Howard Dean had a "real" lead in December and January and lost it. In the other explanation, this lead never really existed. The polls had measured a mirage. People had not begun to focus closely on the event until near the end, and when they took their first serious look, it did not take them long to conclude that Howard Dean was not the man. Elections focus the mind. Faced with a choice, Democrats decided they were not going to nominate Howard Dean. No one can ever resolve this matter definitively, but it is hard not to believe that some very real damage occurred to the image of Howard Dean in December and January. Doubts must have been growing among Iowans. Even for those who were joining in late and talking with others, Dean's stature must have been less than it had been. It is true also that John Kerry and John Edwards gained, but if it is possible to "sequence" a decision, it seems most likely that the positive view of John Kerry and his superior electability followed a negative decision reached about Howard Dean. Dean's nonelectability was the precondition of Kerry's and Edward's advance. A strategic factor also came into play. Up to the end, Iowans thought the real race in their state was between the putative front-runners, Dean and Gephardt. Because of their opposing views on the Iraq War, the votes of their initial supporters were not transferable between them. The decision against Dean or Gephardt meant a vote for Kerry or Edwards.

What were some of the reasons for the change in Howard Dean's standing that began to erode his image beneath the surface of his poll numbers? Besides his comment on the capture of Saddam Hussein, the following points are noteworthy.

First was the cumulative effect coming from all the scrutiny of being the front-runner. Dean had been the front-runner for months, and he was the constant target of the other candidates and of the media. After a debate in Iowa a week before the campaign, during which Dean faced the usual gang attack from most of his rivals, he announced that he had had his fill and was "tired of being a pincushion here."[43] (George Bush no doubt had the same sentiments in 2000, when he was virtually the sole target of all of his rivals in the early debates.) It was not just the rivals, however, who targeted Dean, but also the media. Perhaps the critical focus on Dean was no more than the usual attention journalists give to the front-runner, in this case to a front-runner who seemed to invite controversy and who provided a steady supply of grist for the journalistic mills. But William Greider, a respected political observer, argued that the opposition to Dean went much further: "In forty years of observing presidential contests, I cannot remember another major candidate brutalized so intensely by the media, with the possible exception of George Wallace. . . . For the record, reporters and editors deny that this occurred. Privately, they chortle over their accomplishment."[44] If Greider is correct, and mainstream journalists were less than impartial, the question becomes why they took this tack. Greider attributes it to the journalists' opposition to reform, but an equally plausible account might have been their belief that Howard Dean was unelectable. Hostility to President Bush, more than opposition to Howard Dean, may have been the explanation. To this extent, Republicans may have too freely telegraphed their hope that Dean would be nominated. The conservative journal *National Review* published a cover picture of Dean with the headline "Please Nominate This Man," and Karl Rove himself was reported to have let slip his wish, "Yeah, that's the one we want."

It is likely that some of the candidates, if they appreciated Dean's declining status, would have tried to help him. Although all of the candidates had an ultimate interest in knocking Dean out of the race, each also wanted to see Dean knock all the others out first, in order to turn the contest into a two-man race with Dean. The candidates who were not engaged in Iowa (Clark and Lieberman) or who were not in a do-or-die situation there (Edwards) would have helped their chances by a Dean victory in Iowa, preferably a narrow one. It was probably only because everyone thought him to be so strong and so likely to win in that race that they continued to attack him.

Second, some have mentioned the endorsements Dean received, which allegedly tarnished his image as an outsider. Gore, Bradley, and Harkin all kissed Dean's ring, and Dean went running off at the last moment to Plains to receive the near-blessing of Jimmy Carter. For some reason, or so many argue, this display dampened enthusiasm for him. Iowa voters might well not have liked being bossed by big shots. It is more likely, however, that the endorsements meant what they usually mean: next to nothing. What they did reveal was something of the condition of the party establishment, which seemed unwilling at the time to fight for one of their own, such as John Kerry.

Third, the intensity of the race in Iowa between Gephardt and Dean led each side to launch blistering attacks on the other, including a series of strong television ads. Contrast ads can help to drive the other side down in a two-person race, but in this case what both candidates lost sight of was the fact that there were two other candidates—Edwards and Kerry—standing on the sidelines and appearing as choir boys. The ad war between Gephardt and Dean, which followed from their assessment that it was a two-man race, was rightly dubbed a "murder suicide."

Fourth, Dean was the only candidate at this point who was running a national strategy. All of the other candidates, including Kerry, saw Iowa as a last-ditch fight to the finish. While he spent much time in Iowa at the end, he was also the only candidate in Iowa who looked past Iowa and was concerned about Clark in New Hampshire and contests in other states down the road. Some of Dean's energy was diffused, while the energy of his opponents was focused completely on the Hawkeye state.

Finally, and likely of much greater consequence, there were two incidents dealing with Iowans that placed Dean in an unfavorable light. One was a comment Dean had made in a Canadian public affairs program about the Iowa caucus in 2000, which "mysteriously" surfaced on January 9, ten days before the caucus. Dean demeaned the process, claiming that caucuses "are dominated by special interests . . . that tend to represent the extremes." The analysis may have been good political science (from a decade ago), but awful politics. For residents of the other forty-eight states, it is perhaps hard to imagine the pride and self-importance that the voters in Iowa and New Hampshire have developed about their privileged role in the presidential selection process and how those sentiments can lead them to react with unusual sensitivity. Gephardt understood and immediately called Dean's statement "unbelievable. . . . It would lead one to believe that he is cynically participating in these caucuses." Cynically? The other incident, two days later, involved a testy exchange between Dean and an elderly Bush supporter who tried to argue for being "a good neighbor." With characteristic anger, Dean replied, seemingly thwarting the injunction to love thy neighbor as thyself, "George Bush is not my neighbor." He then went on to cut off his interlocutor to make his point: "You've had your say and now I'm going to have mine."[45] If all politics is local, Dean had committed two cardinal sins: thinking that what you say in Canada will never count and being rude to an ordinary citizen. Tracking polls showed that this moment was a crucial turning point in the battle for Iowa.

Kerry's victory in Iowa left no logic in the race to any other candidacy except Edwards's. Iowa had shown, in its rejection of Richard Gephardt, that the prowar constituency in the party was too small to nominate a candidate. This also meant—as everyone had already concluded—that there was no place for Joe Lieberman (who represented a tiny constituency of a few prowar Democrats and some intellectuals at *The New Republic*). It also meant that enough of the antiwar constituency was satisfied now with Kerry (or Edwards) on his position and that there was no need to resort to a risky outsider. There was thus no logic left to the Clark campaign. The only choice left was between Kerry and Edwards. Edwards tried to sell his brand of economic populism with a slightly greater cultural conservatism and a more down-to-earth appeal, which might carry over to independents. In his final gambit, he tried to draw a line on trade. "Senator Kerry supported NAFTA and other trade agreements," Edwards told CNN. "I was against NAFTA and some of the trade agreements that he was for, and I think they've cost us millions of jobs. And I think voters need to see the difference in our views on what needs to be done about trade and how trade can work for America and American workers."[46] Kerry answered by saying that his position on the issue was indistinguishable from Edwards's. This exchange availed Edwards nothing, not least because he would not take the rhetorical gloves off in the way that might have been his only hope. Some suggested that he was mindful of his status as a potential Kerry running mate, had concluded the main prize was already beyond his grasp, and was determined to say nothing that would spoil his relationship with Kerry. In any event, what Edwards offered in appeal, Kerry more than made up for in gravitas and in his manliness as a hero.

On March 2, the last flickering flame of Edwards's campaign went out. On March 3, the general election began.

## Notes

1. Robert Novak, "Comeback Tour Was as Faulty as Campaign," *Chicago Sun-Times*, December 16, 2002.

2. Thomas B. Edsall and Sarah Cohen, "Kerry Leads Democratic Hopefuls in Funds Raised," *Washington Post*, p. A7.

3. Howard Dean in an address on foreign policy, delivered in Los Angeles on December 16, 2003, available at www.davidlimbaugh.com/121603.htm (accessed January 5, 2005).

4. "Dean First to Single out Democratic Presidential Rivals for Criticism," March 28, 2003, CNN.com, available at www.CNN.com/2003/ALLPOLITICS/03/28/sprj.irq .democrats.ap/ (accessed January 5, 2005).

5. The exit polls from the one genuinely contested race among the Democratic candidates—Iowa—show this point. More voters listed economic problems and health

care issues as being more important than the Iraq War and national security, but there was much greater differentiation on the Iraq War. Voters approving of the war avoided Howard Dean, while voters who strongly disapproved gave him his strongest support (although still slightly less than John Kerry). Extrapolating to the race as a whole, the candidates were neither helping nor hurting themselves, relative to the other candidates, by their stands on economic and health issues. But the war mobilized voters for different candidates.

6. Howard Dean on Larry King Live, August 4, 2003, available at transcripts.CNN .com/TRANSCRIPTS/0308/04/lkl.00.html (accessed January 5, 2005).

7. Jill Lawrence, "Saddam's Capture Forces Dean to Reshape Message," December 16, 2003, *USA Today,* available at www.usatoday.com/news/politicselections/ nation/2003-12-16-dems-cover-usat_x.htm (accessed January 5, 2005).

8. John Kerry, speech at Drake University, December 15, 2003. James G. Lakey, "Democratic Hopefuls Hit Dean on His Stance against War in Iraq," *Washington Times,* December 16, 2003, available at www.washtimes.com/national/2003 1216-114006-6931r.htm (accessed January 5, 2005).

9. "Beyond the Mainstream," *Washington Post,* December 18, 2003, p. 34.

10. "Democrats Play Catch Up with GOP," *Wall Street Journal,* February 14, 2002, p. A21.

11. Eric M. Appleman, "Democrats Set Ground Rules," Democracy in Action website, November 10, 2001, available at www.gwu.edu/~action/dncrb111001.html (accessed January 5, 2005).

12. William Mayer, "Forecasting Presidential Nominations," in *In Pursuit of the White House: How We Select Our Presidential Nominees*, ed. William G. Mayer (Chatham, N.J.: Chatham House, 1996), p. 57.

13. David S. Broder, "No Way to Choose a President," *Washington Post*, December 31, 2003, p. A19.

14. " The Fast-Forward Primary," *New York Times*, January 6, 2002, p. A25.

15. Eric M. Appleman, "Democrats Set Ground Rules," Democracy in Action website, November 10, 2001, available at www.gwu.edu/~action/dncrb111001.html (accessed January 5, 2005).

16. As one reporter described the situation at the beginning of January, "Insurgent candidates have won the nomination before, of course . . . but no insurgent has become a prohibitive favorite before a vote has been cast." *The Economist,* January 3, 2004, p. 17.

17. Dan Balz and Thomas B. Edsall, "Mr. Dean and Campaign Money," *Washington Post*, August 19, 2003, p. A18.

18. Guy Taylor, "Dean Campaign Says No to Public Funding," *Washington Times*, November 9, 2003, available at www.washtimes.com/national/20031109-123650-1901r .htm.

19. Taylor, "Dean Campaign Says No to Public Funding."

20. "Dean Asks Supporters to Decide His Position on Public Financing," *USA Today*, November 11, 2003, available at www.usatoday.com/news/politicselections/nation/2003- 11-05-dean-money_x.htm.

21. Taylor, "Dean Campaign Says No to Public Funding."

22. Thomas B. Edsall and Dan Balz, "Kerry Says He Will Forgo Public Funding," *Washington Post*, November 15, 2003, p. A1.

23. Edsall and Balz, "Kerry Says He Will Forgo Public Funding."

24. Joe Trippi, "The Grassroots Can Save Democrats," *Wall Street Journal*, November 30, 2004, p. A16.

25. "Waiting for Al," CBS News.com, July 29, 2002, available at www.cbsnews.com/stories/2002/07/29/politics/main516633.shtml (accessed January 5, 2005).

26. Susan Page, "Dean Urges a Different Direction from Clinton," *USA Today*, January 15, 2004, p. 1A.

27. John F. Harris, "Democrats Wrestle with 'Electability,'" *Washington Post*, January 16, 2004, p. A1.

28. Erin Kelly, "Biden Announces He Won't Join Presidential Race," *USA Today*, August 12, 2003, p. A7.

29. Available at www.iowapresidentialwatch.com/dailyArchive/Dec2003/12-10-03.htm.

30. Available at www.iowapresidentialwatch.com/dailyArchive/Dec2003/12-09-03.htm.

31. Jim VandeHei, "Clark Rules Out Joining Dean Ticket," *Washington Post*, January 5, 2004, p. A6.

32. Available at www.iowapresidentialwatch.com/dailyArchive/Dec2003/12-09-03.htm.

33. David W. Moore, "Clark Leads Democratic Candidates," Gallup Organization, October 10, 2003, available on the Gallup Organization website.

34. Paul Schwartzman, "Clark Tries to Shake Earlier Comments," *Washington Post*, January 15, 2004, p. A5.

35. John Margolis, "From Out of Nowhere," in *Howard Dean: A Citizen's Guide to the Man Who Would Be President*, ed. Dirk Van Susteren (South Royalton, Vt.: Steerforth Press, 2003) p.11.

36. John Margolis, "From Out of Nowhere," p. 11.

37. John F. Harris and Dan Balz, "Dean Goes on Offensive in Iowa," *Washington Post*, January 13, 2004, p. A1.

38. From *Newsweek* cover story, "Doubts about Dean," January 12, 2004. Citation noted at www.forrelease.com/D20040104/nysu018.P2.01042004132221.23190.html (accessed January 5, 2005).

39. Paul Maslin, "The Front-runner's Fall," *Atlantic Monthly*, May 2004, p. 103.

40. Harris, "Democrats Wrestle with 'Electability.'"

41. Thomas Oliphant, "The Kerry I Know," *The American Prospect*, August 2004, p. 20.

42. David Halbfinger and Diane Cardwell, "Dean Lays Out a Domestic Plan to Wake Up His Party," *New York Times*, December 19, 2003, p. 36.

43. Harris and Balz, "Dean Goes on Offensive in Iowa."

44. William Greider, "Dean's Rough Ride," *The Nation*, March 8, 2004.

45. Dan Balz and John F. Harris, "In Iowa, Dean Is Again Target," *Washington Post*, January 12, 2004, p. A1.

46. Available at www.CNN.com/2004/ALLPOLITICS/02/18/elec04.prez.main/index.html.

*Chapter Four*

# The General Election Campaign

The calendar of presidential election campaigns in America has been changing. A couple of decades ago the final choice of the nominees did not occur until late spring. By custom and by deference to the conventions, which are the official bodies charged with the nominations, both candidates waited until after the conventions met in late summer before starting the campaign. The real campaign was generally launched with the traditional Labor Day "kickoff" in early September. A new schedule began to develop in the 1990s. The front-loaded nomination system produced much earlier decisions—as early as March, and a de facto presidential campaign, still slightly hidden beneath the table and pursued with delicacy, began soon after. This jump start on the official campaign became known as the interregnum period. Bill Clinton in 1996 was the first to master its dynamics, pouncing on Bob Dole in the spring with a set of campaign ads that defined Dole before he could define himself. By 2000, both sides, in order to avoid falling victim to Dole's fate, launched their respective campaigns earlier.

Gone, then, are the days when the candidates did not mention their opponent publicly until the convention. Under the new calendar, the face-off between the candidates begins when the identity of each party's nominee is established. In 2004, this development reached its full logical conclusion. As soon as it was clear that John Kerry would be the Democratic nominee on March 2, George Bush called to congratulate him. Both sides then quickly went into full campaign mode, attacking and defending with the kind of intensity previously reserved for October. The relentless fundraising and the airing of attack ads by the campaigns and outside groups only increased as the interregnum went on. Indeed, while the concept of an "interregnum" as a distinct, transitional phase was necessary to understand the elections of 1996 and 2000, it has by now lost much of its utility, except perhaps to help distinguish a period when the general public is still not fully focused on the political battle. It is only a slight exaggeration to say that the general election campaign began on March 3, 2004.

March to November now marks the period of the campaign, but what exactly is meant by "the campaign"? When the campaign begins, much—perhaps most—of what will decide the election is already in place: the candidates are known; the basic situation in the nation is set; and the record of the incumbent or incumbent party over the preceding three years and two months has been defined. "The campaign" itself refers conceptually to two starkly different frames. One is the campaign as simply a period in time, a more-or-less passive recipient of inputs in the form of external events that, when they are important enough, can alter the character and perceptions of the basic situation. Time does not stop when the campaign begins, and the longer the campaign goes on, the greater the chance things may occur that can affect people's judgment of the record of the incumbent or incumbent party. Events in this period are accordingly seen a bit differently, being interpreted through an intensely "political" lens. The other campaign is the active creation of candidates, parties, consultants, contributors, and volunteers. Strategies, decisions, speeches, and advertisements are its currency. Here, the campaigns try to shape and manage the perception and judgments of the existing record as well as the perception and judgments of the new events that are occurring during the campaign period itself. This campaign has a calendar that has four "scheduled" moments of opportunity when the strategists have a chance to harness events and to shape or reshape the contest: (1) The final choice of the parties' nominees, when the two campaigns make their first efforts to define themselves and especially the opposition; (2) the selection of a vice-presidential running mate; (3) the conventions; and (4) the debates.

These moments unfolded in 2004 in a basic strategic situation that remained quite stable over the course of the campaign. At the beginning of the Bush-Kerry contest, there were two great themes in play: the hardy perennials of national security and economic performance, or, as it used to be said, "peace and prosperity." Polls showed that President Bush was most trusted by the electorate to wage the general war on terror, although doubts were growing about the situation in Iraq. The trust for Bush as the leader in the war on terror was the single greatest obstacle to Kerry's election. During the campaign Bush would strive, despite a series of unfortunate events, to maintain that advantage, while Kerry would seek to mitigate or overcome it, mostly by stressing the difficulties in Iraq and ultimately the error of the entire venture. By contrast, polls showed John

Kerry leading on the question of who would best strengthen the economy. Bush hoped to close that gap with a continued economic recovery and an attack on Kerry's economic prescriptions, while Kerry would press his advantage by emphasizing the slow pace of job recovery. Both candidates incorporated additional issues during the campaign, but their fundamental challenges never changed through Election Day.

## Moment of Opportunity: Early Definition

Despite John Kerry's success in the Democratic primaries—or perhaps because that success came so quickly—the American public in early March still had little feel for the man and who he really was. Kerry had been a nationally known antiwar leader long ago in the 1970s, and he had served in the Senate since 1985, but he was not a nationally recognized senator on par with a John McCain or a Ted Kennedy. His political identity was to many still largely a blank slate.

Once Kerry was assured of the nomination, the task for both campaigns immediately shifted to trying to fill in that slate. The Bush campaign, which was flush with a campaign war chest of over $100 million that had been built up over the past year, wasted no time launching an ad campaign to try to define Kerry for himself. The theme was twofold: Kerry was a liberal addicted to higher taxes, and he was inconsistent on national security (a "flip-flopper"), willing to change his positions to suit the political moment. He had voted for the congressional authorization giving Bush the power to use force against Iraq, but against the $87 billion funding measure. He famously proclaimed that he had voted for it before voting against it. These themes, especially the second one, would remain a staple throughout the campaign. Up until his final speech on election eve in Dallas, President Bush was placing John Kerry into the "flip-flop hall of fame"—regrettably, Bush did not list the other inductees. CNN's William Schneider, one of the nation's most astute political analysts, attributed much of Bush's ultimate victory to the Republican plan "to define John Kerry in a way [they] wanted and to stick with that definition for the entire campaign."[1]

Initially, Kerry's campaign was financially ill-equipped to compete, having less than $10 million on hand.[2] Looking for ways to blunt Bush's attack, Kerry proposed monthly debates with Bush (a nonstarter for Bush) and took up a highly combative posture. His oft-repeated taunt of "Bring it on" was meant to convey that he would not sit back and take it, like Michael Dukakis was alleged to have done in 1988. (Clearly, any political analyst who could know what "it" is would possess the decisive insight into American politics.) In a couple of instances, Kerry's combatitiveness might have gotten the better of him. At a Florida fund-raiser on March 7, he declared, "I've met with foreign leaders who can't go out and say this publicly, but, boy, they look at you and say 'You've got to win this. You've got to beat this guy [President Bush]. We need a new policy.' Things like that."[3] Kerry drew criticism when he refused to name names. A few days later, in a supposedly private comment, he called the Republicans "the most crooked, you know, lying group I've ever seen."[4] Asked to apologize, he refused.

Democrats also challenged Bush's credentials as commander in chief. Michael Moore called Bush a "deserter," and Democratic National Committee chairman Terry McAuliffe accused him of being "AWOL." Kerry himself had earlier delicately encouraged discussion of Bush's military service when he commented, "Just because you get an honorable discharge does not in fact answer" whether Bush had fulfilled his National Guard commitment.[5] The circumstances surrounding Bush's National Guard service in Alabama were raised anew by the old media in a series of inquiries and stories, and Bush, who might have thought that this chapter of his record was closed in 2000, was compelled to release more records of his military service.

Kerry launched a new fund-raising drive to close the money gap, and liberal "527" groups, which were able to receive unlimited contributions, stepped up their efforts. Democratic groups such as MoveOn.org and Americans Coming Together (ACT) raised millions of dollars and launched anti-Bush ads, often coordinating their activates among each other (although not directly with the Kerry campaign itself, which is prohibited by the law). Democrats also swung into action and tried to emulate the financial success of Bush's fund-raising operation, whose "Pioneers" and "Rangers" had been acknowledged for encouraging friends, employees, and colleagues to donate the maximum $2,000 hard-money contribution to the campaign.[6] If imitation is the purest form of flattery, the Democrats complimented the Republicans by creating a similar system and inventing titles equally as imaginative as the Republicans', like "Minutemen Corps," "Paul Revere's Night Riders," and "D.N.C. Patriots."[7] As with the "Pioneers" and "Rangers," these labels gave new meaning to the notion of soldiers of fortune, and the valiant in the Democratic Party, like those in the Republican Party, were rewarded with access to the party and to the candidate commensurate with their sacrifices.

It was one of the remarkable feats of the Democratic campaign that, despite its late start and the disadvantage of a contested nomination race, it was able to catch up and—when the efforts of all the supporting groups are taken into account—raise almost as much money ($1.08 billion) as the Republicans ($1.14 billion).[8] But there were two problems with Democratic operation. The Kerry campaign itself, meaning the official organization operating under the direction of the candidate, did not always have the cash when it needed it, and much of the money raised was not directly under its control. Money that was given to the Democratic 527 groups was theirs, not the official campaign's. In a postelection analysis, Kerry's media adviser, Ted Devine, observed that the 527s often "didn't do what we wanted done. . . . We would have run ads about Kerry; we would have had answers to the attacks in kind, saying they were false, disproved by newspapers."[9]

The rapid-fire intensity from the start of the interregnum period went well beyond that seen in 2000, although many in the nation were probably unaware. The ad wars were concentrated in the eighteen swing states, many of them in the industrial Midwest. The consensus today is that, overall, Bush made better use of this first moment of opportunity than Kerry and laid a firmer foundation for the fall campaign. As one Democratic strategist conceded, "They were ahead of us; they had a strategy set by the beginning that they were going to live and die by, and we didn't."[10] It would be highly surprising if it had been otherwise. President Bush did not have to wage a nomination battle, and the campaign organization had nearly two years to organize the campaign and raise funds. Bush's task was also easier, as there was more room for shaping voters' views of the lesser-known Kerry.

## Bush's Spring of Discontent

Just as it seemed that Bush had Kerry on the defensive through more skillful campaigning, the other element of the campaign—the effect of external events—took a decided turn for the worse for the president. In the economic realm, the issue of "outsourcing" of jobs, which Richard Gephardt and John Edwards had emphasized during the primary contest, gained significant traction. Many manufacturing jobs, including those in the swing states of the industrial Midwest, had been moved overseas. Bush was on the defensive and seemed ill-prepared to deal with the fallout from this issue, which nearly drowned out the positive news on the economic front: a massive 308,000 new jobs had been created in March.[11]

It was events in Iraq, however, that proved the greater drag on the president's fortunes. The political boost President Bush received from the capture of Saddam Hussein in December 2003 had long since faded, and he was now buffeted by a series of occurrences that would have weakened any incumbent president. The first was broader than Iraq itself and went to the heart of President Bush's strong suit as leader in the war on terror. Richard Clarke, a former terrorism expert whose government career had spanned the presidencies since Reagan, leveled several accusations at the Bush administration, beginning with the claim that the administration lent insufficient urgency to the terrorist threat prior to the September 11 attacks. In his book *Against All Enemies*, in numerous media interviews, and in his widely viewed testimony to the 9/11 Commission on March 24, Clarke also asserted that the Iraq War was a diversion from the war on terror—a key charge of John Kerry's—and that in the days following the September 11 attacks, Bush seemed overly eager to pin at least some of the blame on Saddam Hussein in Iraq. Richard Clarke was not an individual distinguished by his humility—he took it upon himself in his commission testimony to apologize to the victims on behalf of the U.S. government—and some of his public charges were contradicted by earlier statements he had made. But his intelligence and record of service were more than enough to earn him a hearing, especially when there were so many who were eager to listen. His charges did damage to the president, and some on the 9/11 Commission, which now began to show partisan rifts, used the occasion to raise further questions about Bush's handling of intelligence information in the month before the attack.

The events on the ground in Iraq in March and April took a rapid turn for the worse. U.S. forces faced a two-front battle that made matters appear as if the whole country was in chaos. In Fallujah, long a bastion of Sunni Baathist insurgents, four American contractors were killed and mutilated. Marines began a large-scale military operation to root out the enemy, but scenes of civilian casualties and urban ruins led to a decision to cease action, which insurgents celebrated as a major victory. Simultaneously, armed radical Shiite followers of the firebrand cleric Moqtada al-Sadr revolted when a warrant was issued for al-Sadr's arrest and seized the city of Najaf, site of one of the holiest shrines in Shiite Islam. American casualties surged.

The most damaging event, however, came on April 28, when several photos were aired on *60 Minutes II* that showed Iraqis being mistreated by U.S. soldiers at the Abu Ghraib prison in Baghdad, which had been notorious under the Hussein regime as a chamber of torture. The "irony" was devastating, and it made an immediate impact throughout the world. One photo showed American prison guards relishing the formation of a pyramid out of naked prisoners. Another showed a cloaked and hooded man standing on a box with wires attached to his hands. The Red Cross disclosed that it had previously noted abuse at U.S.-run Iraqi prisons, and a classified report by

Major General Antonio Taguba had detailed "sadistic, blatant, and wanton criminal abuses against prisoners." President Bush decried the actions of what he characterized as a few rogue prison guards, and on May 5 he did interviews on two Arab satellite news channels, declaring the abuse "abhorrent" and assuring the Arab viewers that it "does not represent the America that I know." On May 7, Donald Rumsfeld testified for six hours before a congressional committee. He apologized while warning that other photos existed even more graphic than those already in circulation. Many called for Rumsfeld's resignation, and questions were also raised about the treatment of the "unlawful combatants" in Guantanamo Bay, Cuba. Of all the difficulties Bush encountered during this period, the prison scandal probably caused the most harm. It sapped confidence in the rightness of the mission and lent support to the general sentiment that the situation was a mess. It seemed to be disgrace, not difficulty, that Americans could not accept. It was in May, while Abu Ghraib dominated the headlines, that Bush dipped below 50 percent approval and lost his lead to Kerry.

Even with Bush facing a mountain of bad news, Kerry confronted the difficulties of trying to "define" himself. The same bad news that was hurting Bush kept John Kerry out of the public eye. Many Democrats were fretting that Kerry had failed to put his own stamp on his candidacy and that the Republicans would continue filling in the blanks of his political identity. The Kerry campaign rolled out a series of ads that made a concerted effort to present him as a centrist and an "entrepreneurial Democrat" in the mold of Clinton and the Democratic Leadership Council. His effort for the moment was to combat the "liberal" label and try to give more balance to his record.

## Bush Regains His Footing

If the events of April and May worked against President Bush, those of June and July helped him, though not as much. As the incumbent, Bush was vulnerable to bad news, but as the head of state he was able to benefit from ceremonial occasions promoting a sense of national unity. In early June, the D-day memorial dedication in France and the death and funeral of Ronald Reagan put President Bush in the spotlight with major speeches and allowed him to look back on former presidents and wars. Bush used these occasions to connect World War II with the war on terror, and the public was reminded of Bush's close associations with Reagan, whose popularity was evidenced by the outpouring of public grief during the solemn memorial services.

At the end of June, the transfer of power in Iraq took place from the Coalition Provisional Authority led by Paul Bremer to an Iraqi interim government. The turnover aided Bush somewhat by raising hopes that an Iraqi government might be put in place that eventually would be able to stand on its own. Still, the violence continued unabated, and John Kerry was unable to fully capitalize. His problem remained the same, as he seemed to waver between putting the emphasis on condemning the war or on running to the "right" of Bush by offering a stronger and better plan to prosecute it. He chose a bit of both, proposing now to add 40,000 soldiers to the forces in Iraq. The United States, he argued, was mismanaging the war. The effort in Iraq needed more international contributions and more troops. This would require a new president, given the good will George Bush had squandered within the international community.

Another development in the area of national security was the release of the 9/11 Commission's findings on the terrorist attacks. The report came as something of a relief to the White House, as there were worries that it might focus too much blame on the administration for not preventing the September 11 attacks. But in a balanced way the report apportioned responsibility among preceding administrations and placed the chief "blame" on an entire mind-set and organizational structure that was in place in Washington. One point in the report that did bear on the administration's judgment was the finding of a lack of a "collaborative relationship" between Saddam Hussein and Al Qaeda. Democrats leaped on this point, claiming that it further undermined the administration's stated justification for the war in Iraq, while Republicans, led by Cheney, countered that the "collaborative relationship" conclusion was focused on September 11 specifically, not the broader Iraq-Al Qaeda relationship, for which there remained substantial evidence. In what became a common pattern, much of the old media emphasized the former argument, while much of the new media stressed the latter.

In early July, the Kerry campaign sought to seize control of the general theme of moral values. Recognizing his potential vulnerability, Kerry, like Clinton before him, was determined to define the moral issue on his own terms.[12] Instead of the Republican Party's emphasis on what Kerry called the "little political, hot-button, cultural, wedge-driven, poll-driven values"—a reference no doubt to the issue of single-sex marriage—Kerry sought to reframe the values questions as one of honesty in policy making: "The value of truth is one of the most central values in America, and this administration has violated it. . . . Their values system is distorted and not based on truth."[13] The moral issue in this sense had been raised a few days earlier in a more controversial manner at a star-studded Kerry fund-raiser featuring Whoopi Goldberg and John Mellencamp, where Bush was pilloried for being a liar, a thug, and a killer, while Goldberg made vulgar plays on the president's name. Kerry had praised the performers for representing the "heart and soul" of America, and asserted that his ticket had "a better sense of right and wrong."[14] Bush saw an opportunity to insert a wedge, taking exception to Kerry's claim that Hollywood was the "heart and soul" of America. And he derided Kerry's contention, made earlier, that he (Kerry) represented "conservative values."

## Moment of Opportunity: Vice-Presidential Selection

The second moment of opportunity in the campaign belonged to John Kerry, with his decision on a vice-presidential running mate. In early July, he named John Edwards, who was the first campaign rival to be selected since Ronald Reagan chose George H. W. Bush in 1980. In this case, though, there was no melding of different currents in the party. Kerry and Edwards had run on almost identical programs during the primary, and there were few, if any, differences between them that needed explaining. But the two men were clearly different in personality and background. Edwards brought a connectedness to voters that the more aloof John Kerry lacked, and Kerry admitted to feeding off of the younger man's energy as the two campaigned together. Plus Edwards, the son of a mill worker, could talk in a populist way that the blue-blooded Kerry could not. Despite his multimillionaire status, Edwards had a Clintonesque capacity to speak to working-class audiences and "feel the pain" of the disadvantaged. Style points aside, Kerry hoped that Edwards would put North Carolina and some other southern states in play for the Democrats.

Two possible drawbacks to Edwards's selection were his lack of governing experience and his career as a lawyer. Edwards had spent only five years in national politics, and as a trial lawyer who brought large suits he was a member of a profession that at the moment was not widely celebrated in American society. The choice was widely acclaimed, especially in much of the old media, but the selection did not give Kerry the kind of boost that Al Gore's selection of Joseph Lieberman gave him in 2000. As time went on, the weaknesses of the choice became more apparent, although it is only speculation who, if anyone, might have helped Kerry more. Edwards added nothing to Kerry's stature, brought with him no identifiable constituency, and could not carry North Carolina for the ticket, let alone any other southern state. Kerry's second moment of opportunity—a moment not afforded to Bush, who already had a vice president—was, in the last analysis, not put to fruitful use.

## Moment of Opportunity: The Democratic National Convention

The Democrats entered their convention week buoyant at their prospects for the election in November. Party strategists were eager to tell any and all members of the media—including "bloggers," who for the fist time ever had space reserved for them on press row—that the party was more united than ever behind a presidential candidate. The race, Kerry's advisers offered, was coming to resemble that of 1980, with President Bush in the role of Jimmy Carter and John Kerry playing "The Gipper." In 1980, polls consistently showed Carter with low job approval and high wrong track numbers. According to the mythology of the 1980 campaign, voters had decided to fire Carter, and all Reagan needed to do was present himself as a credible alternative. The Kerry's strategists argued that the 2004 polls displayed a similar desire to fire Bush.

The primary goal of the convention accordingly became to convince voters of Senator Kerry's fitness to become Commander in Chief Kerry. Once that threshold was crossed, Kerry could then turn to domestic issues where he held an advantage in the polls over Bush. But how to cross it? Here Kerry faced several difficulties, some of his own making, others reflecting divisions within his political base. Kerry's last twenty years had been spent as a legislator, not an executive, and within the Senate he had not held a major leadership post or been directly responsible for any pieces of landmark legislation. He had built one of the more dovish records on foreign policy and defense in the Senate from his election in 1984 until 1997, when he began to echo President Clinton's tough rhetoric against Saddam Hussein. His record of votes on domestic issues was also highly liberal. There was much, in short, to gloss over. Kerry also had to deal with trying to unify Democrats on national security issues. A majority of Democrats were antiwar, but a significant minority supported the Iraq War while being critical of Bush's plan of execution. The same was true of many swing voters. Kerry sought to handle these dilemmas by a political balancing that emphasized his Vietnam service. He would resume the cloak of the reluctant warrior who fought for his country when called, but who could also offer a levelheaded assessment of the prospects for success in a difficult situation. Both elements—pro and antiwar Democrats—could find reason to support Kerry.

Conventions were once seething cauldrons of political infighting and intrigue over party platforms and nominees, but the modern convention is a scripted and organized show designed to sell the party and its candidate to the American public. In a display of disdain for what many journalists called party infomercials, the major networks reduced their coverage of the conventions to only three prime-time hours of the four-day event, forcing both parties to schedule their most prominent speakers to appear at those times. Viewers were treated, among others, to former President Carter, who lamented Bush's policy failures with regard to the Middle East, Iran, and North Korea; former President Clinton, who mused about a return to the better days of the Clinton economy; Senator Ted Kennedy, who tried to stir the echoes of his family's past; and Howard Dean, who issued a (for him) mild declamation on the future of the party. All of them, including ex-Senator Max Cleland, who introduced Kerry, played up Kerry's service in Vietnam. The result was a convention that seemed to focus more on the past than on the future. The most positive and prospective message of the convention was the keynote address delivered by an Illinois state senator, Barack Obama, who was all but assured of election to the U.S. Senate. Unfortunately for Democrats, Obama's speech was delivered on the night on which the network coverage went dark.

On the final night of the convention John Kerry strode through the crowd to the podium, smartly saluted the audience, and announced, "I'm John Kerry, and I'm reporting for duty." The speech that followed brimmed with homespun history. Kerry offered loving details of his childhood and suggested that his time served in Vietnam would put him in good stead to act as commander in chief. He spent a scant ninety seconds explaining his twenty years in the Senate, before mentioning his plans for the future, which could be found in more detail at JohnFKerry.com. Minimizing both record and issues, Kerry staked his claim for the presidency on biography to a greater extent than any presidential candidate since Dwight D. Eisenhower in 1952, except that Eisenhower never had to call attention to his own biography. It was a well-delivered oration, but longer on style than content.

One remarkable aspect of the convention was the degree to which the social and cultural liberalism of the delegates was kept under wraps. At previous Democratic conventions full-throated affirmations of a woman's "right to choose" and calls for gun control were de rigueur rhetoric from the podium, but not at the 2004 convention. With the exception of a single speech by Representative Barney Frank, which was not delivered during prime time, no pronouncements were made in favor of same-sex marriage. The only social policy that the Democrats dared to support was increased funding for embryonic stem cell research. Beyond this one paean to liberal social policy, however, the silence suggested a tacit recognition that the

Democratic Party was not eager to play up the cultural divide. Outright denunciations of the war in Iraq were likewise strictly limited, although Michael Moore was granted a privileged and highly visible seat in the presidential box next to Jimmy Carter.

As the convention closed, most analysts applauded the Democratic Party for having run such a successful convention. The party had kept anti-Bush vitriol to a minimum, rekindled fond memories of Democrat presidents past, and established its nominee as a man of character who, in his own words, could "make America stronger at home and respected in the world." All that was left was to see how large a margin Kerry had opened over his rival in the postconvention polls. Those polls suggested that Kerry had indeed improved his standing with voters: he was seen as more likable and as a stronger leader. But he received little if any of the anticipated "bump" or "bounce" in the head-to-head polls against Bush. (By past standards, most candidates can expect a six-point bump, with the nominee of the out-party receiving closer to nine points.) Most postconvention polls showed Kerry and Edwards ticking up two or three points, but others — including a Gallup survey — actually showed Kerry losing ground to Bush.[15] These perplexing poll results puzzled pundits, forcing many to reevaluate the success of the convention. Many now wondered whether the convention had underplayed a discussion of issues in favor of personal biography. But there was another and more hopeful view for Democrats. It was that the American public was now so firmly divided that there were fewer swing voters or persuadables in the electorate. If Kerry had received no postconvention bump, the silver lining was that Bush would be unable to receive one either. The electorate was "unbumpable." As long as Kerry could maintain his lead through August, he would be in the driver's seat heading into the debates and the final weeks of the campaign.

## Kerry's August Decline

Instead, throughout the month of August, Bush whittled away at John Kerry's five- or six-point lead. Bush may have profited a bit from the national glow surrounding American success in the Olympics and from the participation of athletes, including women athletes, from Iraq and Afghanistan. The Bush campaign also scored a coup when it badgered Kerry into conceding on August 9 that, knowing everything that he then knew, he would still have voted to authorize the Iraq War (though Kerry went on to explain that he would have exercised the authority differently).[16] This admission, often repeated without the qualification, not only deflated many of Kerry's supporters, but it also contributed to a growing impression that Kerry's position on Iraq was more than nuanced; it was opaque. Bush's efforts to claim that Kerry now agreed with him almost certainly prompted Kerry's turn, a month later, to a clear antiwar stance. But this matter, important as it was, was put on hold when the ad of an anti-Kerry organization threw the entire race into a spin, effectively eliminating a key prop of Kerry's campaign strategy.

On August 5, Kerry's campaign-by-biography came under challenge from the Swift Boat Veterans for Truth, a new 527 organization consisting of men who had served in John Kerry's swift boat unit in Vietnam. This group came out with its first attack ad questioning Kerry's heroism in Vietnam and by extension his fitness to serve as commander in chief. The ad featured fellow swift boat vets addressing the camera and stating that Kerry did not deserve the medals he received. Accompanying the criticism were pictures of the men as young soldiers standing near Kerry in Vietnam. Although the group's initial ad buy was small—about $500,000 and limited to three states—it created a firestorm of enormous proportions. Much of the interest was generated by the new media, where the allegations were aired and analyzed. The attention quickly led to a spike in online donations for the group that paid for a second attack ad that contained another, and potentially more damning, set of charges against Kerry. It featured snippets of John Kerry's testimony before a U.S. Senate committee in 1971, speaking in opposition to the Vietnam War. Interspersed were clips of former prisoners of war commenting on how Kerry's statements adversely affected their treatment at the hands of their North Vietnamese captors. In his Senate testimony Kerry cited reports accusing soldiers of having raped and pillaged the countryside in a fashion reminiscent of Genghis Khan. One former POW stated that "John Kerry gave the enemy for free what we endured torture not to admit." These two ads, although miniscule in what they cost, turned out to be far more influential than all of the other ads of the campaign, on which millions were spent. At the end of August, the Kerry campaign finally broke down and bought advertising time in the markets where the swift boat vet ads had aired, but by then the Internet and media coverage had enhanced the reach of the ads to the extent that almost 80 percent of the population was familiar with their content.

The ads and the subsequent release of a book, *Unfit for Command*, written by one of the founders of the 527 group, John O'Neill, and making specific allegations about Kerry's combat and postwar actions, sparked a debate within the Kerry campaign about how best to respond. The initial decision was to ignore the message and to attack the messenger as being a pawn of the GOP.[17] The seed money for the group had come from a deep-pocketed Republican from Texas who had previous associations with Karl

Rove, and two individuals ultimately had to quit the Bush campaign because of their association with the swift boat ads.[18] Kerry called on President Bush to denounce the swift boat veterans directly. Bush responded by
calling on Kerry to join him in condemning all 527 groups in their efforts
to influence the election. The back-and-forth over the arcane legal provisions governing the actions of 527 groups continued for a couple of weeks,
while the charges made by the swift boat vets were allowed to fester nearly
unchallenged.

As it became clearer that Kerry could not eliminate the swift boat vets'
challenge through indirect means, his campaign team (aided by the mainstream media) adopted a new tactic: discredit the most attenuated charges.
The *Boston Globe*, the *New York Times*, and the *Chicago Tribune*—among
others—ran accounts calling into question some of the swift boat veterans
claims that challenged Kerry's heroism in Vietnam. Few papers, however,
tackled Kerry's persistent and problematic claims to have ventured into
Cambodia during his four-month stint as a swift boat captain.[19] Nor did
many wish to examine the POWs' charges that Kerry's congressional testimony had caused them distress.

Besides creating disarray in the Kerry campaign over how to respond,
the initial swift boat ad effectively took away Kerry's Vietnam security
blanket. Kerry could no longer freely invoke Vietnam without the risk of
having to personally engage the questions about his war record and his
postwar activities. Many Democrats, including former President Clinton,
now advised him to drop the subject, and the campaign began to downplay the issue, with some going even so far as to deny that Kerry had ever
made very much of his service in the first place.[20] One way or another,
the question of military service in Vietnam faded from the campaign as
an issue. Bush certainly did not want to talk about it, and now Kerry
dared not to. In fact, Kerry by and large ceased taking questions of any
kind from the press. With his biography now a matter of contention, a
pivotal part of Kerry's candidacy was diminished. By the end of the
month of August, when the Republicans began their convention, John
Kerry had lost his lead and the two candidates were in a statistical dead
heat in the polls.

## Moment of Opportunity: The Republican Convention

The Republicans had chosen a risky place to hold their convention—New
York City, where Democrats held a huge edge and where thousands might
be expected to demonstrate against the president. This decision had been

made in days when Republicans were more confident of their standing and could still hope for a grand celebration for the president. The situation had changed, and as Republicans began to arrive in New York, there were enormous fears of massive demonstrations that would put the Republicans in a bad light. In fact, the choice of the setting in New York, just blocks away from Ground Zero, turned out to be one of the great symbolic coups of the campaign, especially when contrasted with the Democrats' choice of the safe venue of Boston, John Kerry's hometown.

The setting in New York City offered the GOP the perfect backdrop against which to defend George Bush's record in the war on terror and—in what became the central subtext of the convention—to connect the war on terror (where Bush was highly regarded) with the decision to liberate Iraq. Speaker after speaker took up this theme, praising Bush's steadfastness and resolution and contrasting it to John Kerry's "nuanced" irresolution. On the opening night Senator John McCain offered the old warriors' case for the war, and former New York City Mayor Rudy Giuliani gave the rally 'round the victims speech. The next night, Governor Arnold Schwarzenegger gave the immigrants' speech of appreciation for American opportunity and of respect for Republican foreign policy toughness. Although the Democrats had the rest of Hollywood, the Republicans had the Terminator, and it was no match. For those who preferred some red meat, Democratic Senator Zell Miller, who delivered the keynote address, served it up raw. In a withering criticism of his party's nominee, Miller went through Kerry's Senate record on national security, ticking off all of the weapons' systems he had opposed—"against the Patriot Missile that shot down Saddam Hussein's scud missiles over Israel; against the Aegis air-defense cruiser; against the Strategic Defense Initiative; against the Trident missile, against, against, against." Miller then asked, "This is the man who wants to be the commander in chief of our U.S. Armed Forces? U.S. forces armed with what? Spitballs?" By comparison, Dick Cheney's speech later the same evening seemed like the model of sobriety.

Enough had been said on the issue of national security so that when President Bush appeared on the final night, he could turn to domestic affairs and announce the broad outline of his domestic policy agenda before offering a general defense of his foreign policy and its goals. Bush's policies in a second term would further the growth of what he called an "ownership society." Government policies would be revised to help citizens accumulate wealth. Education reforms would continue so that individuals would have the skills to take high-paying jobs, the tax system would be reformed to encourage savings and to reduce compliance costs, the tort system would be changed to minimize frivolous lawsuits, and the health-care system would be altered to encourage greater patient engagement in the process, thus reducing extraneous costs. Most importantly, the Social Security system would be revamped to allow workers to accumulate private investments. The individual pieces of Bush's agenda all conformed—or could be made to conform—to conservative themes, although to themes that no longer put limited government first. Most importantly, Bush's proposals could be bundled into a thematic package, at least rhetorically, which marked an advantage over Kerry's programs—corporate and middle-class tax cuts combined with tax increases on high-income earners, plus a new health-care plan—which lacked thematic consistency. Bush's emphasis on a program resulted, at least temporarily, in an inversion of roles between the challenger and the incumbent, in which the incumbent seemed to offer a bolder policy vision than the challenger.

One of the most noteworthy facts about the two conventions was how markedly different they were in tone from what the parties had presented four years earlier. In 2000 the GOP blunted its rough edges and tried to appeal to the center by presenting a racial rainbow of speakers to the television audience, keeping strident social conservative rhetoric to a minimum. The Democrats, on the other hand, talked up abortion rights and gun control and environmentalism with great fervor. In 2004 the image was reversed. The Democrats paraded military men to the podium and invoked God and made only the most oblique references to liberal positions on social policies such as abortion and same-sex marriage. The Republicans, for their part, offered mostly country music entertainment, bragged about cutting taxes and banning partial-birth abortion, and called for a constitutional amendment prescribing marriage as being the union of a man and a woman. Republicans felt more confident in the ascendancy of their ideas, at least among the voters to whom they were appealing, than the Democrats.

The stalwart defense of Bush's strategy in prosecuting the war on terror and the enunciation of a thematically unified policy agenda helped Bush to achieve a rarity in presidential campaigns: the incumbent received a larger convention bump than the challenger. Postconvention polls showed Bush surging ahead by four to six points—one *Newsweek* poll improbably said eleven points—although this lead began to open as the convention started. The success of the GOP convention in framing the issues in Bush's favor led many analysts to downgrade the Democratic convention even further. Democrats began to grow restless. Although the general election campaign by the old clock had just started, in reality it had been ticking for six months. Kerry had exhausted all but one of the moments of opportunity available to change the course of the campaign.

## The Postconvention Campaigns: Events

The postconvention campaign contained the same elements as the preconvention campaign—events and strategies—but in a different proportion. Events dominated the period before the conventions, and there was much speculation about what might happen as the electoral clock counted down. A dramatic capture of Osama bin Laden might tip the race decisively to Bush; a major terrorist attack in the United States might also shake up the race, though in uncertain ways. In the end, the fall campaign was filled with the intervention of a series of external events—they seemed to come one after another like a cascade—but none had a decisive effect that altered the course of the race. Perhaps, too, the events came so fast and were so divergent in their implications that they offset themselves. The paradoxical verdict is that events played a relatively smaller role in the fall campaign than during the spring.

The most horrifying of these events was a terrorist incident in Russia that came hard on the heels of the Republican convention. Chechen Islamic terrorists occupied an elementary school in the town of Beslan on September 1, taking more than a thousand hostages. The standoff ended when the terrorists set off bombs inside the school, killing more than three hundred persons, most of them children. The episode dramatically reinforced the central theme of the GOP convention—the war on terror must go on—and probably contributed to the rise of the "security moms" as a segment of women voters acutely attuned to concerns of national security. At just this time as well, Bill Clinton entered a New York hospital for heart surgery, a medical fluke that sidelined the Democrats' best fund-raiser and most skilled politician for most of the fall campaign.

These events were soon overshadowed by an episode that dramatized the gap between the old and the new media. On September 8, Dan Rather, first on his CBS evening news show and then on a segment for *Sixty Minutes II*, reported that President Bush had received preferential treatment to get into the Texas Air National Guard and once there had failed to fulfill his duties. A key piece of evidence in this new indictment was a series of private memos said to have been written by Bush's superior officer, Lt. Col. Jerry Killian, who had died in 1981, which showed Killian's exasperation with the antics of Lt. Bush. Here, finally, was the new, "hard" evidence that news sources had for years been seeking. A copy of one of the memos was posted on the CBS News website. Vietnam and military service were once again improbably front and center in the campaign.

Almost immediately, however, the story came under attack, mostly by forces on the Internet, which raised questions about the memos' authenticity.

Powerline.com, a blog run by three respected lawyers, picked up the thread, and ran a report demonstrating that the memos, supposedly produced on a typewriter in the 1970s, used a modern font and could be perfectly reproduced, spacing and all, using the Microsoft Word word-processing program. Other "holes" were spotted in the story as well. By the weekend, mainstream media outlets such as ABC News and the *Washington Post* were examining CBS's claims more critically, even as Dan Rather continued to insist that the information used in formulating his report came from an "unimpeachable" source. Rather was putting his own and his network's prestige—as well as the prestige of much of the old media—on the line. The next week Rather made a final stab at defending the memos by airing an interview with Killian's former secretary, who indicated that while she did not think the memos were authentic, they probably reflected Killian's views at the time. This "fake but accurate" defense of the memos, which did not exactly meet the highest journalistic standards, was greeted with widespread derision. Within a few days, Bill Burkett, an ex-guardsman with a political ax to grind against Bush, was revealed as the source of the phony memos. Dan Rather apologized.

The effect of "Memogate" on the race was hard to discern, as the candidates' poll numbers did not change. But with Bush ahead, anything that froze the campaign worked in his favor. Precious time had been lost for Kerry, and the controversy kept almost all other news from making a dent in the public's consciousness. The story also worked against the sentiment circulating in the aftermath of the swift boat ads that John Kerry was the only victim of unfair attacks. Bush was now every bit as much of a victim, if not more so. The old media in general, and Dan Rather in particular, proved to be energizing symbols for Republicans, who could now be just as entitled to righteous indignation as the Democrats.

Nature played a part, as well. In August and September, Florida was battered by four hurricanes, throwing the state into turmoil. The series of disasters gave President Bush an opportunity to shore up his position in the Sunshine State. Learning another lesson from the travails of his father, who was judged by many Floridians to have botched relief efforts after Hurricane Andrew in 1992, George W. Bush responded vigorously, if not profligately. One survey noted that 70 percent of Floridians gave Bush an excellent or good rating on his performance, compared to a 50 percent poor or fair rating for his father. Bush's investment in disaster relief paid off handsomely, with some 16 percent of voters saying that they would be "more likely" to vote for him.[21] The course of world history has been known to turn on smaller things.

Other unforeseen occurrences followed. In early October, health care became a more salient issue when a severe flu vaccine shortage developed. A

Kerry ad blamed it on a Bush administration foul-up: "Seniors and children wait. Not enough vaccines for pregnant women. A George Bush mess."[22] Oil prices accelerated their recent climb, reaching a record high of around $55 a barrel and driving prices at the pump to $2.50 a gallon or more in some locales. And job creation figures continued to oscillate, reaching a respectable 150,000 in early September but falling to less than 100,000 in October.[23] Stocks tumbled sharply in October. These news items were not helpful to the Bush campaign. The trends of underlying economic improvement were temporarily obscured or offset by immediate events, and it was more often John Kerry than George Bush who profited from the issue of the economy in the final stages of the campaign.

These unfavorable events were partly compensated for, however, by two vicarious victories for President Bush in the international arena. On October 9, the Afghan election was held, the first democratic election in that country's history, and Hamid Karzai, the strong American ally, would eventually be chosen. Here was a key test of the administration's policy of democratization, and the election was a rough success. It is an indication of the political lens through which news is viewed in the final stages of a political campaign, however, that an event that would normally be celebrated as a major achievement of the nation as a whole tends to be treated largely in terms of the political credit it can bestow. The Afghan election generally received far less attention in the press than its significance warranted. The other event was the Australian election, also on October 9, in which voters returned John Howard and his party to power against an anti–Iraq War challenger. Many Republicans had feared another rejection of a leader who had allied himself closely with the Bush administration, similar to what had occurred in Spain in March, when José María Aznar's party went down to a stunning defeat. Howard's victory avoided this reversal.

In the final week, the *New York Times* reported what was widely touted as the great October surprise. The International Atomic Energy Agency had concluded that up to 400 tons of Saddam's high explosives were missing from a base in Iraq, presumably due to U.S. incompetence. The initial story—which CBS had developed jointly with the *Times* and meant to hold until two days before the election—conjured up the impression of another spectacular failure, on the scale of Abu Ghraib. But after a couple of news cycles the event turned out to be less significant and more ambiguous than it originally seemed. It was possible that the missing explosives—which were, in any event, a small proportion of the total in Iraq—were either removed by U.S. forces or were already gone when those forces arrived on the scene. But this report was played up by Kerry as the smoking gun proving

Bush's malfeasance, and he devoted most of the last week of the campaign to pounding on it.

These events posed a bigger threat to Bush than they might have because the pages and broadcasts of the old media almost uniformly stressed the interpretation most harmful to Bush. When no negative interpretation was possible—the Afghan and Australian elections—the news was rather systematically downplayed, whereas when a story was harmful to the president—or helpful to John Kerry—it received extensive attention. According to Robert Lichter of the Center for Media Affairs, which conducted an analysis of presidential campaign press coverage by major newspapers and the networks, John Kerry "received better press than anyone since 1980, receiving a record breaking 77 percent positive evaluations" compared to just 34 percent for President Bush.[24] In the past, Republicans might have railed against these tendencies in vain. In 2004, two things worked to mitigate the damage. First, the old media was extraordinarily incautious in dropping its veneer of impartiality. Not only had it overplayed its hand in Memogate, but in October ABC news director Mark Halperin circulated a memo to his reporters urging them not to hold Bush and Kerry equally accountable, as Bush's "distortions" were worse than Kerry's. His reporters had a duty to the public to go after Bush harder. The reporting in October, as the election drew nearer, recalled a stunning claim that had been made in mid-July by *Newsweek* assistant managing editor, Evan Thomas, who claimed that the establishment media "wants Kerry to win and they're going to portray Kerry and Edwards as being young and dynamic and optimistic and there's going to be this glow about them, collective glow, the two of them, that's going to be worth maybe 15 points." The weekend before the election, looking at the polls, Thomas revised his exaggerated estimate downward, speaking now of a figure more in the range of five points for Kerry. But his point was clear.[25]

The hubris of the old media interacted with a second factor to shield Bush from the wave of negative reporting. The new media was coming into its own as a counterweight to the old, as could be seen from the bloggers' role in discrediting CBS's story on Bush's military service. In the swift boat veterans' story and the CBS memo scandal, the promise and the peril of the new media were fully revealed. As CBS discovered, the fact-checking ability of the Internet is near infinite and immediate. In the absence of the Internet, the Bush campaign would have had to suffer through a multitude of negative stories about Bush's service record or use its own resources and time to debunk the story. Of course, the Internet could also act to the detriment of a campaign. The Kerry campaign learned the Internet does not need to follow the normal news cycle. In years past, the swift boat veterans' story might have been quickly buried by the old media. In the new media, however, bloggers and talk show hosts can stay on a story for as long as they like. Back-and-forth musings about whether or not Kerry really went into Cambodia and links to each new ad by Swift Boat Veterans for Truth provided millions of readers and listeners with access to information and arguments that they would previously never have received. As a result the swift boat vets turned limited advertising buys into a larger phenomenon and created enough interest to warrant continued coverage of the swift boat veterans' efforts in the old media. The Bush campaign, for its part, found itself on the wrong end of an Internet rumor about a secret plan to reinstitute the draft after the election, which may have stimulated youth voting in 2004. Although it adds another layer of accountability to the old media and the political campaigns, the new media has problems of its own. The new media's own standards of accountability are shaky, and, outside of conspiracy theories, the Internet (and blogging in particular) has thus far proven a more reactive than creative medium.

The final event with a bearing on the race was a videotape by Osama bin Laden, which surfaced the Friday before the election. In the tape, bin Laden quoted Michael Moore approvingly and appeared to threaten retribution against states that voted for Bush. Commentators wondered: Could this be the *real* last-minute surprise that will break the race open one way or the other? Worse, was it the prelude to an actual preelection attack? The answer was no and no. According to Kerry pollsters, their man's numbers saw a "slight wobble" overnight, but had recovered by Sunday.[26] Exit polls indicated that a bit more than half (56 percent) of voters saw the tape as important, and these voters split 50-50 between Bush and Kerry.[27] Events may have set the stage for the final denouement, but the campaign of speeches and strategy would have to decide.

## Moment of Opportunity: The Debates

With the Republican convention coming later than usual, and Election Day coming earlier, the clock was ticking on the 2004 campaign. Only one scheduled moment of opportunity now remained for John Kerry to reverse the lead that Bush had opened up: the debates. But before the debates, Kerry took a calculated risk and tried to force a change on the campaign by moving more clearly into an antiwar position on Iraq. On September 20 he delivered a major speech in New York in which, adopting Howard

Dean's language, he unambiguously labeled the conflict in Iraq "the wrong war, in the wrong place, at the wrong time." The war was predicated on bad information, which the president should have been able to recognize at the time, and the timing of the war should have been delayed to allow UN inspectors more time to do their job. Worst of all, the war in Iraq was a diversion from the war on terror. Preparation for the war had removed resources from Afghanistan that could have been used to capture Osama bin Laden and other Al Qaeda terrorists. Despite a deteriorating situation in Iraq, the administration still was trying to paint a picture of the war through rose-colored glasses. Kerry would implement a better plan than Bush to get a democracy installed and U.S. troops returned home. Kerry seemed to be energized by this turn to a clearer antiwar position, as were many Democrats, and his stump speeches gained a new pep. But adopting a new position risked accusations of another flip (or flop). Furthermore, whatever his critique of the past, Kerry's proposed policy was not very different from Bush's. As he moved left on Iraq, Kerry was more likely to tap into dissatisfaction with the war, but he also ran the risk of becoming too closely associated in the public mind with activists who seemed like they would rather lose the war than lose the election. Judging by the polls, Kerry's speech did not fundamentally change the trajectory of public support for the candidates.

This meant that all the hopes of the Kerry campaign had to ride on the debates, the last regularly scheduled chance to change the direction of the race. In order for Kerry to make up ground in the debates, however, the debates first had to occur, which meant negotiating with Bush's team over how many debates would occur and under what circumstances. Many thought that the Bush campaign would seek to limit the number of debates to two, as Clinton had done in 1996. Instead, Bush agreed to three debates (plus a vice-presidential debate), but insisted that the foreign policy debate occur first rather than last. The strategy, it seems, was to use the first and most widely watched debate to show Bush in his strong suit. A strong performance by the president would solidify his lead and effectively "decide" the race. It was not to be.

On the day of the first debate President Bush visited with victims of the most recent of the four hurricanes that hit Florida, while Senator Kerry rested and prepared further. The difference seemed to show even in appearance. Bush looked tired, while Kerry looked confident and vibrant. Instead of the knockout blow that GOP partisans had been looking for, it was Kerry who sent Bush reeling. In addition to scoring debater's points on President Bush's turf of foreign policy, Kerry also narrowed the likeability gap as Bush was seen scowling and sighing softly in reaction to Kerry's attacks, reactions that were soon compared with Al Gore's in the first 2000 debate. Kerry appeared in command, while Bush seemed more unsure of himself and often appeared to be repeating his talking points. At the end of the debate Kerry partisans were rushing to microphones to tout their candidate and reiterate the theme, confirmed in the nomination contest in the spring, that Kerry was a great campaign "closer." Bush supporters struggled to argue that the event was really a draw.

Most instant polls showed that Kerry had won the debate, and as is often the case, it was the postdebate interpretation by journalists and pundits that hardened the public verdict against Bush. The first debate and its immediate aftermath was the high-water mark for the Kerry campaign in the fall. More than sixty million people had tuned in to watch. Kerry's self-assured demeanor and crisp answers helped to dispel much of his image as a weak-kneed flip-flopper that the Bush campaign had tried to cultivate over the previous six months. Polls showed a race that had moved from a roughly six-point lead for Bush into a statistical dead heat. Better yet for Kerry were indications from poll questions that asked voters to say which candidate would handle certain issues better, where Kerry had narrowed Bush's advantage on security issues by almost half. The senator finally seemed to be closing the credibility gap on terrorism and national security with the result that he could turn his attention to domestic issues where his electoral advantage truly lay and on which the next two debates would focus.

In the hoopla surrounding Kerry's first debate victory, there was nevertheless a rhetorical opening that Kerry had given to Bush. In an answer to a question about the United States's use of preemptive attacks, Kerry defended the idea but went on to suggest that any U.S. action should pass a "global test." The Bush campaign pounced on the phrase, using Kerry's words in the subsequent debates and in advertising to argue that he would subjugate U.S. interests to the whims of French and German policy makers as well as the UN. Democrats accused Republicans of twisting Kerry's meaning, arguing that he only intended to say that the United States should always be able to rationally defend its position to the world at large. Nevertheless, the interpretation Republicans put on Kerry's comment was consistent with the view many Americans had already formed of Kerry's foreign policy approach.

Debates are not singular events, but represent an iterative process. Candidates must provide a coherent message across four and a half hours of interaction, trying to present their policies in a credible way and to "wear" well with the electorate. Bush began to make headway on these dimensions as the debates continued. He recovered in no small part with his answers to a series of questions during the last two debates that called for responses that touched on policies that related to "moral values." One of the questions came in the second debate, in which citizens formulated questions for the candidates to answer in a "town hall" style of debate. The question asked why government funds should be available to pay for abortions. Kerry talked about his Catholic upbringing, his service as an altar boy, and how his faith sustained him in Vietnam before alluding to the proposition that abortion was a constitutional right and that failure to provide funding for low-income women would be tantamount to denying them their rights. Kerry's meandering response set up Bush's best line of the night when he stood to answer and volunteered that he was still trying to decipher Kerry's answer. He then went on to state his opposition to federal funding and partial-birth abortion and his support for parental notification and the Un-born Victims of Violence Act (which allowed for prosecution on behalf of the baby if it suffered harm or death in the womb as a result of a crime)—all issues on which Kerry held the opposite opinion.

Overall in the second debate, both men gave reasoned answers, but the exchanges marked the beginning of what would become a familiar pattern in the final debate. Kerry was eloquent but aloof, while Bush offered answers that had a more human touch and that were also better calibrated to reach out to Catholic swing voters and values voters in the Midwestern battleground states. After the second debate the Kerry team was quick to declare victory, but this time they were met by equally enthusiastic Bush supporters. Many in the media declared the debate a draw or gave a slight edge to Kerry on points. The ABC instant poll showed a 44-41 percent Kerry "win," for all practical purposes a draw.

At the start of the third debate, members of the Kerry team talked about "sweeping" the debates, and Democratic supporters had their brooms in hand ready to make the point. From the standpoint of a pure debate, Kerry once more put in a strong performance, attacking Bush on the state of the economy, on the shortage of flu vaccine available, on health care and tax cuts. This time, however, President Bush gave almost as good as he got in nearly every exchange. And yet, if Kerry had not had difficulty with three "softball" questions that moderator Bob Schieffer tossed out near the end to allow the candidates to provide insights into their personal qualities, he might have had reason to celebrate his triumph. One question queried the candidates about the role of religious faith in their lives, a second asked whether homosexuality was an expression of choice or genetics, and a final "question" essentially gave a chance for the candidates to praise their wives. On all three Bush's answers came easily, while Kerry's seemed more labored.

It was on the delicate question about the nature of homosexuality, however, that Kerry got into trouble. Bush had the first response, and he began by saying that he did not know whether homosexuality came from nature or by choice, but that regardless of sexual orientation every person should be treated with dignity. He then took the occasion to note that he objected to judges imposing radical redefinitions of the institution of marriage on the rest of America. When Bush finished, Kerry supported his contention that homosexuality was genetic by invoking the name of a homosexual who would, Kerry argued, agree with him that she was just being who God made her to be. Instead of citing a well-known celebrity such as Ellen DeGeneres, Rosie O'Donnell, or Martina Navratilova as his example, he mentioned the daughter of Dick and Lynne Cheney. The allusion to Mary Cheney's sexual orientation came from out of nowhere. Whereas John Edwards had mentioned Mary Cheney in the debate with Vice President Cheney in the context of praising her parents' love for her, Kerry made no such effort to wrap his statement in the same feigned flattery. What made matters worse was that Kerry's comment was widely seen as calculated to score a political point—either to suggest hypocrisy on the part of the Cheneys for supporting President Bush (who advocated a constitutional amendment opposing gay marriage) or to make an appeal to social conservatives by reminding them that Cheney had a gay daughter. Whatever Kerry's intent, thousands of mothers objected to the use of an opponent's child as a political weapon against her parents. The error was compounded by the words of Mary Beth Cahill, his campaign manager, and John Edwards' wife, Elizabeth, in the aftermath of the debate. Cahill declared that Mary Cheney was "fair game" for political attacks, and Edwards hinted that the Cheneys' outrage at Kerry's comment was a sign that they were ashamed of her. ABC snap polls showed the final debate to be another draw. But if the votes of a vast swath of married women were in play before the final debate, Kerry's performance may have helped to move some of them into Bush's camp.

Altogether, the 2004 debates reinforced an old lesson that many nevertheless seem to need to relearn from scratch in every election. "Winning" debates on debating points is not the same as winning them politically. There is only one real test: To what extent did the debates help a candidate, relative to his opponent, achieve his strategic objectives? By this standard, both candidates could lay claim to some success. Kerry successfully used the first debate to revive his campaign psychologically, reduce his vulnerability on national security issues, and close the gap with Bush in the polls. He demonstrated that he was not the caricature the Bush team had painted him to be, but was instead articulate and thoughtful. But while Kerry's individual performances were uniformly praised, the sum effect was less than the parts. Over time, it was Bush who displayed a more human touch, and it was Kerry, not Bush, who contributed sound bites that became ammunition for the other side—the "global test" comment and the Mary Cheney statement. Kerry made the better impression, but Bush used the debates to appeal to key swing groups—married women and Catholics. Bush took more away from the debates. Kerry's problem answers, some of which slid right past the instant analysis, became the subject of extended discussion afterward in the new media. Above all, strategic success in the debates for Kerry meant overtaking Bush; for Bush, it meant holding his lead. In this biggest test of all, Bush ended the debate season still holding a modest lead over Kerry in most polls.

## Endgame

Both campaigns outwardly suggested satisfaction with the state of the race entering the homestretch. And both sides were sincere. The Kerry team focused on the idea that the president's approval rating hovered at 50 percent and clung to the conventional wisdom that late deciders always go decisively for the challenger. All Kerry had to do, according to this wisdom, was stay within striking distance and he would win. For Kerry, one key to making this theory a reality was to accentuate the negative. The net job loss under Bush's term, the rise in anti-Americanism around the world, the increase in the number of persons living in poverty and without health insurance, and, of course, events in Iraq were staples of the campaign. He also jumped on any new piece of disappointing news, such as the shortage in flu vaccine, to make the point about things in America deteriorating under the Bush administration. By this reckoning the higher the wrong track number went, the better Kerry's chances for victory. Yet Bill Clinton had won handsomely in 1996 despite bad "wrong track" numbers. There were always a variety of possible reasons voters might be dissatisfied, not all of which they would lay at the president's feet. The fact that Kerry never sustained a poll rating higher than 50 percent throughout the fall in spite of wrong track numbers that occasionally neared 60 percent should have been a warning sign.

The Bush campaign based its optimism on its reading of the electoral map. By mid-October many of the states that Kerry had hoped would be in play were not. By contrast, many of the states that Bush had targeted were. While the Kerry team made feints for Colorado and Nevada as the

Bush team did with Oregon, New Jersey, and Hawaii, of the nine states legitimately "in play" during the final weeks of the campaign only three were red states: Ohio, Florida, and New Hampshire. The remainder, Pennsylvania, Michigan, Wisconsin, Minnesota, New Mexico, and Iowa, were blue states that contained many of the values voters that Bush had been cultivating throughout his presidency and through the debates. There was perhaps an element of wishful thinking in the Bush camp as well. Throughout the year they repeated the mantra that the economy was as strong in 2004 as it had been when Clinton was reelected in 1996. Statistically the claim bore some truth, but most of Clinton's 1996 economic statistics marked a significant improvement from when he began his first term in 1993, while many of Bush's showed a decline. Polls showed that the issue of the economy was working in favor of John Kerry more than George Bush.

For both sides the path to electoral victory was simple. Kerry needed to flip either Ohio or Florida. Bush needed simply to hold serve or to flip a couple of smaller blue states to make up for the loss of Florida or Ohio. To accomplish their goals both sides consulted the last election to see what they could do to change the outcome. The Kerry campaign sought to discover how to edge out Bush in Florida or Ohio. The Bush campaign, with four years to prepare, had decided to put an enormous effort in the Get Out the Vote (GOTV) operation, where Karl Rove believed Democrats had bested them in 2000. To win outright in 2004 would require more than simply tactical superiority during the campaign season. It would demand a long-term strategy to insure that more voters showed up to vote Republican on Election Day. Immediately after the 2000 election Rove set out to discern which voters who had an affinity for Bush and the GOP on policy matters failed to show up at the polls on Election Day. Rove concluded that a large chunk of Bush's missing electorate were values voters such as evangelical Christians and faithful Catholics as well as ex-urban and rural residents who looked askance at some of the cultural norms of metropolitan areas. Having identified part of the problem, Rove then set out to find ways to motivate these "missing" voters to go to the polls and pull the lever for Republicans and President Bush.

Under Rove's guidance the GOP began a massive voter registration drive in districts where Republican candidates underperformed against the demographic profile of the district. The effort went as far as to try to pinpoint likely voters based on their shopping habits and magazine subscriptions. Ideally, the Republicans would know which people would vote Republican before they fully realized it themselves. The Republicans also used the Internet to build networks of individuals across the country who would not just canvass their neighborhoods for votes, but would canvass their friends in other states as well. The test run for this new GOP GOTV machine in the 2002 midterm elections proved highly successful. Rove also realized that it helps if one's likely supporters are motivated to head to the polls by something more than their interest in the candidates. Popular initiatives can be of great help, and local Republicans put issues on the ballot in Arizona (immigration) and Florida (parental notification when a minor seeks an abortion). No doubt GOP leaders would have supported some sort of tax reform initiatives in other battleground states as a means of motivating the base, if manna from heaven had not fallen into their laps in the form of the same-sex marriage debate. In response to the Massachusetts court decision, eleven states, including swing states like Ohio, Michigan, and Oregon, placed ballot questions before their voters asking them to pass laws and state constitutional amendments declaring that marriage was limited to one man and one woman.

In contrast with Bush's and Rove's long-term strategic vision, Kerry and his team sought to gain a tactical advantage against Bush at every opportunity, perhaps in the belief that victory in every skirmish would guarantee that they would win the greater campaign. In striving to win each news cycle, the campaign sometimes caught itself working against Kerry's strategic interests. Kerry decided to spend the last week of the campaign focusing on domestic issues and began his offensive by ridiculing Bush and Cheney for talking only about security. Just then, the *New York Times* ran the story alleging missing explosives in Iraq. Kerry immediately jumped on the story as a sign of the Bush administration's incompetent handling of Iraq and continued to hammer at the story for several days. Kerry's thrust may have hurt the president a bit, but it may have appeared that his campaign was merely reacting rather than shaping the discussion.[28] Kerry's response to the Osama bin Laden tape—attempting to make political points by pointing out that Bush had failed to capture or kill bin Laden—struck some as equally opportunistic.

Bush did manage, however, to take advantage of opportunities as they arose in the homestretch. The most important of these was presented by Kerry in a lengthy interview that ran in the *New York Times Magazine* on October 10, in which he admitted that he was "not much changed" by the terrorist attacks of September 11, and he hoped to reduce terrorism to a "nuisance." His greatest hope was that America could go back to the way it was before September 11. Republicans and the new media wasted no time jumping on the comments. Bush responded by saying, "Now just this weekend, Senator Kerry talked of reducing terrorism to quote—nuisance—end-quote, and compared it to prostitution and illegal gambling. I couldn't disagree more. Our goal is not to reduce terror to some acceptable level of nuisance. Our goal is to defeat terror by staying on the offensive, destroying terrorist networks, and spreading freedom and liberty around the world."[29] Cheney attacked Kerry's "pre-9/11 mind-set."

By Election Day, Bush had a slight lead in most national polls, although everyone understood that all would depend on turnout. Hidden deeper in the polls were a couple of Bush advantages that offered another clue to the outcome. First, Bush had much better favorability ratings than Kerry. In an election eve average of six major polls, Bush was rated favorably by 51 percent, unfavorably by only 44 percent. Kerry's favorable-unfavorable split was 47-46.[30] Second, in a related vein, it was clear that Bush's voters were voting for him, while about half of Kerry's voters were only voting against Bush, not for Kerry. Both of these observations indicated more enthusiasm for Bush in the electorate. Kerry had run all year on the hope that it would be enough to not be George W. Bush. His hope was about to be put to the test.[31]

According to a Pew Research survey, 86 percent of voters said they had learned enough about the candidates to make an informed choice, and more than two-thirds expressed satisfaction with the choice of candidates.[32] The only question left was which one they would choose.

## The Results

George Bush was selected in a close race in which more people, 118 million, voted than in any previous election. The president won a total of 51 percent of the vote to John Kerry's 48 percent. Compared to the 2000 election, Bush improved his share of the total vote in forty-eight out of fifty states, with some of his biggest gains coming in the blue states. For the aficionados of the now famous red-blue maps, the nation as a whole appeared redder after 2004, with New Mexico and Iowa added to the Republican column and New Hampshire alone switching to the Democrats. The county version of the red-blue map showed expanding swaths of red, with blue areas receding and being largely confined to urban zones and university-town enclaves. Probing just beneath the surface of geography to sociology, it is clear that Democratic support in 2004 relied in large measure on knowledge-based communities, support from minority groups, and support from large parts of the urban public employee and social services sector.

During the campaign, some analysts drew a sharp distinction between a strategy aimed at energizing the base (and making more extreme appeals) and a strategy aimed at going after the swing voter (and being kinder and gentler). A base strategy, in most of these accounts, was dangerous and foolish, a swing strategy virtuous and wise. This view was summed up by one of the nation's leading analysts, Morris Fiorina, who in the case of the Republicans expressed concern (or perhaps joyful anticipation) that they had trapped themselves into a losing base strategy. Republicans, Fiorina reported, were "attempting to win in 2004 by getting out the votes of a few million Republican-leaning evangelicals who did not vote in 2000, rather than by attracting some modest proportion of 95 million other nonvoting Americans, most of them moderates, not to mention moderate Democratic voters who could have been persuaded to back a genuinely compassionate conservative."[33]

Fiorina's assessment of the merits of the two strategies may make sense, but his account of the plans of Republican practitioners was far too one-dimensional. The Bush campaign never supposed that a base strategy alone could assure victory. The challenge all along was to find the proper combination of the two strategies, with the critical decision being a judgment about the proportion of effort to be invested in each one. These proportions had to be calculated not in a generic sense, but with respect to each area or venue in which the campaign operates. It may be advisable (and efficient), for example, to have the candidate pursue mostly a swing strategy in his comments and speeches, while it might make sense (and be more efficient) for parts of the organizational component to concentrate more on a base strategy.

Bush's strategists clearly gave greater weight to a base strategy than has been the case in many past campaigns. This approach rested on the assessment, which Democrats shared, that the base component of the vote today is more significant. The election results appear to confirm these conclusions. The election of 2004 was one of the "basest" of recent elections. There was a greater proportion of partisans than in any election since 1980—74 percent identified as either Republican or Democrat—and more of these partisans combined to vote for "their" candidates. Partisan "yield" as a share of the total vote is at its high point in modern times. John Kerry certainly earns plaudits for his ability to hold on to Democratic voters—he suffered only an 11 percent defection rate to Bush, which was the equal of Al Gore's percentage in 2000. The only problem for Democrats is that George Bush lost only 6 percent of Republicans to Kerry. Bush had one of the lowest partisan defection rates, if not the lowest, since presidential polling began. It was clear that affection for Bush in the Republican base carried him far. To no small degree, Bush's win was, as Michael Barone noted, a triumph of love over hate.

An analysis of partisanship, however, takes one only so far. People do not vote Republican or Democratic just because they are Republicans or

Democrats; they must be motivated to do so. Campaigns aim to reinforce the ideas, beliefs, interests, and prejudices that make people vote one way or another. There were many indications of the importance of these motivating base appeals in the elections results. One sign was the degree of ideological appeals. Self-described conservatives gave Bush 84 percent of the vote, while Kerry took 85 percent of the liberal vote. These figures are all up from past years.

Another factor motivating voters in 2004 was moral values. In 2004, as in 2000, frequency of attendance at religious services was an important correlate of presidential choice, with those who attended religious services once per week or more voting overwhelmingly for Bush. It is not primarily because these voters attend religious services, however, that they are inclined to vote Republican; rather this factor serves as a proxy that identifies a constituency that shares many ways of looking at things. The differences between the religious and nonreligious vote would be even greater, but for the countervailing pull of many highly religious Hispanics and blacks who continue to vote Democratic at higher than the average rates. White Christians identifying themselves as evangelical or born again supported Bush over Kerry by a 78-21-percent margin. The appeal of Republicans among the religious part of the electorate is also illustrated in the support that Bush had among voters who thought the most important qualities in a candidate were religious faith (he won 91 percent of these voters) and in the constituency that listed "moral values" as the most important issue of the campaign (of whom he won 80 percent). (See table 4.1.)

Analyzing coalitions is important not only for the sake of identifying the different elements of voting strength behavior but also for providing clues about direction and policies. Important members of a coalition naturally expect that their views will be taken into account. The 2004 election in this respect sent a signal that the Republican Party is committing to halting a slide toward government imposition of secularism. The Democratic Party, which has generally aligned itself with secular forces in the judiciary and elsewhere, will have to decide how much to fight against or accommodate itself to this new reality.

Yet as important as base mobilization was in 2004, it was clearly not the only or even the most important part of the overall strategy of the parties. Both campaigns implemented had a swing vote strategy deigned to appeal to the same segment of voters. But the dimension on which voters were swinging in 2004 was not in the first instance traditional elements of domestic politics (where compassionate conservatism made the difference) but rather questions relating to national security and the war on terror. As former Democratic candidate for the presidency Michael Dukakis observed, "I don't

**Table 4.1.   Influences on the 2004 Vote**

| | % of Electorate | Bush | Kerry | Bush minus Kerry |
|---|---|---|---|---|
| **Some Significant Sociological Elements** | | | | |
| *Religious affiliation* | | | | |
| Protestant | 54 | 59 | 40 | 19 |
| Catholic | 27 | 52 | 47 | 5 |
| Jewish | 3 | 25 | 74 | −49 |
| *Religious observance* | | | | |
| Weekly | 41 | 61 | 39 | 22 |
| Occasionally | 40 | 47 | 53 | −6 |
| Never | 14 | 36 | 62 | −26 |
| *Married* | | | | |
| Yes | 63 | 57 | 42 | 15 |
| No | 37 | 40 | 58 | −18 |
| *Married with children* | | | | |
| Yes | 28 | 59 | 40 | 19 |
| No | 72 | 48 | 51 | −3 |
| *Ethnicity* | | | | |
| White | 77 | 58 | 41 | 17 |
| African American | 11 | 11 | 88 | −77 |
| Latino | 8 | 44 | 53 | −9 |
| *Size of Community* | | | | |
| Urban | 30 | 45 | 54 | −9 |
| Suburban | 49 | 52 | 47 | 5 |
| Rural | 25 | 57 | 42 | 15 |
| *Gender* | | | | |
| Male | 46 | 55 | 44 | 11 |
| Female | 54 | 48 | 51 | −3 |
| **Most Important Issue** | | | | |
| Moral Values | 22 | 80 | 18 | 62 |
| Economy/jobs | 20 | 18 | 80 | −62 |
| Terrorism | 19 | 86 | 14 | 72 |
| Iraq | 15 | 26 | 73 | −47 |
| Health care | 8 | 23 | 77 | −54 |
| Taxes | 5 | 57 | 43 | 14 |
| Education | 4 | 26 | 73 | −47 |
| **Most Important Personal Quality** | | | | |
| Will bring change | 24 | 5 | 95 | −90 |
| Strong leader | 17 | 87 | 12 | 75 |
| Clear stand on issues | 17 | 79 | 20 | 59 |
| Honest/trustworthy | 11 | 70 | 29 | 41 |
| Cares about people | 9 | 24 | 75 | −51 |
| Religious faith | 8 | 91 | 8 | 83 |
| Intelligent | 7 | 9 | 91 | −82 |

*Source:* CNN.com Election Poll.

think that George Bush won this election because of gay marriage or evangelical Christianity or any of this stuff. He won it, in my judgment, on the national security issue." This dimension could be seen not only in the issues rated as most important, but also in evaluations of candidates' qualities. Leadership and willingness to take a clear stand outweighed the personal qualities of intelligence and empathy by 34-16 percent. Kerry was unable to make headway in the two areas where he needed most to do so—convincing Americans that he was a steady leader who would wage the war on terror vigorously. The terror issue was also partly responsible for the single largest identifiable contingent of general swing voters in 2004: a segment of women voters. A huge shift to Bush took place from 2000 in the voting behavior of women, where he gained a full 5 percent. While George Bush still lost the woman's vote in 2004, he did so narrowly—51 to 48 percent. There were many reasons for this shift, but evidence from within the campaigns suggest that much of it was the result of security considerations: Bush was seen as the candidate better suited for protecting Americans from terror.

The other general element of the swing vote shift focused on domestic issues, and perhaps less with any single issue than with general views relating to families. One of the largest gaps between the parties now is associated with marriage and the traditional family. The Republicans had an enormous advantage among voters who were married, especially married with children, where the gap between Bush supporters and Kerry supporters was 19 percentage points, 59 to 40. Singles strongly favored the Democrats, marrieds the Republicans. If the Republican Party, as some like to characterize it, is a God-centered party, it is also a traditional family-centered party, and there appears to be a clear link, at least for Republicans, between "moral values" and what were once referred to as "family values." The themes of Bush that appealed to this constituency were not just some of the progovernment policies linked to compassionate conservatism, like "no child left behind," but also the tax policy that reduced the marriage penalty and increased the deduction for children. How Republicans will be able to broaden and solidify their hold over the marriage constituency remains one of the major challenges of the second Bush administration.

There was, however, another facet of the parties' pursuit of swing voters. It concentrated on making inroads into groups that possess a strong degree of collective identity in their voting behavior. A variety of approaches can be employed, including enacting specific policies that appeal to the group as a group, demonstrating that group members can advance in society, and appealing to general issues that invite members within these groups to split along the same lines as the rest of the population. Republicans in 2004 went on the offensive to pursue each of these strategies in regard to three traditionally Democratic groups: Jews, African Americans, and Latinos. Jews, who were invited to notice that Bush was one of the most pro-Israel presidents since Truman, gave him an increase of 6 percentage points since 2000 (from 19 to 25). African American voters—by far the sturdiest members of the Democratic base—responded by providing Bush 2 percent more nationally, or 11 percent of their total. Yet Bush did much better among blacks in a number of key states, like California (18 percent), Ohio (16 percent), Pennsylvania (16 percent), and Florida (13 percent). Finally, among Latinos, whom Bush had taken great pains to cultivate, his vote share increased from 35 percent in 2000 to 44 percent in 2004. More significantly, the Latino vote is beginning to divide along the same lines as the rest of the electorate. The most religious and entrepreneurial Latinos may be trending Republican.

A word, finally, needs to be said about the "Catholic vote." It was widely recognized on both sides that Catholics, once reliably Democratic, represented a key swing group in 2004, as they have since at least 1980. By some estimates, Catholicism was the dominant religion in two-thirds of the battleground states. John Kerry was only the third Catholic candidate to run for the presidency, but his Catholicism was hardly an issue, one way or the other. It was to some his secularism, or rather the secularism of a part of the Democratic Party, that was his most important "religious" quality. Bush won among Catholic voters by a 52-47-percent margin, and by a much larger margin among white Catholics (and observant Catholics). It is now abundantly clear that there is no longer a "Catholic vote," in the sense of Catholics forming a cohesive bloc of voters; the elimination of the Catholic vote for Democrats has by implication been a huge gain for Republicans. Bush's success with this group is by itself a refutation of the notion that Republicans ran a purely "base" campaign.

## Notes

1. William Schneider, comments from an "Election Watch" panel of November 4, 2004, available at www.aei.org/events/seriesID.11/series_detail.asp.

2. Howard Kurtz, "Ad Attacks Kerry Vote on Iraq Funds," *Washington Post*, March 17, 2004, p. A7.

3. Paul Farhi, " Kerry Challenged on Claim of Foreign Support: Powell Says Democrat Should Identify Officials with Whom He Spoke," *Washington Post*, March 15, 2004, p. A10.

4. Dan Balz, "Kerry Decries GOP as 'Crooked' and 'Lying,'" *Washington Post*, March 11, 2004, p. A6.

5. "Kerry Questions Bush Guard Service," February 9, 2004, www.foxnews.com/story/0,2933,110803,00.html.

6. The fund-raisers were ranked according to how much they took in, using a tracking system with their own code to monitor their progress. "Pioneers" could claim to have helped raise $100,000, "Rangers" $200,000.

7. Paul Farhi, "Democratic Spending Is Team Effort: Groups' Ads Level Field for Kerry," *Washington Post*, March 24, 2004.

8. This is an estimate of the total amount available to each side, taking into account the official campaign organizations, the party organizations, and the funds spent by groups known to be allied with either campaign. The estimates that appear are discussed in Thomas Edsall and James Grimaldi, "On Nov. 2, GOP Got More Bang for Its Billion" *Washington Post*, p. A1.

9. Edsall and Grimaldi, "On Nov. 2, GOP Got More Bang for Its Billion."

10. Edsall and Grimaldi, "On Nov. 2, GOP Got More Bang for Its Billion." The strategist is unnamed.

11. Amy Goldstein and Jonathan Weisman, "Bush Hails Job Gains Figures from March: Tax Cuts and Policies Effective, He Says," *Washington Post*, April 3, 2004, p. A6.

12. Kerry rarely spoke about his religious faith. He did proclaim to Larry King that it "guides you. It's your rock. It's the bedrock of your sense of place, of where it all fits."

13. Dan Balz and Jim VanderHei, "Kerry Vows to Restore 'Truth' to Presidency: Democratic Ticket Assails Values as 'Distorted,'" *Washington Post*, July 11, 2004, p. A1.

14. Jim VanderHei, "Values Become Key Campaign Issue: Kerry, Bush Show Their Differences," *Washington Post*, July 9, 2004, A6.

15. David Moore, "Presidential Race Remains Close; No Convention Bounce," August 1, 2004. Available at Gallup website: www.gallup.com/poll/content/login.aspx?ci=12565 (accessed January 5, 2005).

16. Kerry reportedly answered the question as follows: "I'm ready for any challenge, and I'll answer it directly. Yes, I would have voted for the authority. I believe it is the right authority for a president to have, but I would have used that authority, as I have said throughout this campaign, effectively. I would have done this very differently from the way President Bush has."

17. Because the Democratic convention ended a full month earlier than the Republican one, Kerry would have to make his public funding ($75 million) last that much longer than Bush. To ensure that they would be on a level playing field with the Bush campaign during the last two months of the race, the Kerry team decided to drop its campaign-directed advertising and to rely on pro-Kerry 527 organizations and the Democratic National Committee to keep it in the game through August. At the end of August, the Kerry campaign finally broke down and bought advertising time in the markets where the swift boat vet ads had aired, but by then the Internet and media coverage had enhanced the reach of the ads to the extent that almost 80 percent of the population was familiar with their content.

18. Kenneth Cordier, a Vietnam vet who was featured in one of the ads, was dismissed on August 21 as an adviser to the Bush campaign. Benjamin Ginsberg, a lawyer for the Bush campaign, resigned on August 25 after having acknowledged that he had given legal advice to the swift boat group.

19. One of the exceptions was a lengthy article in the *Washington Post* by Michael Dobbs, "Swift Boat Accounts Incomplete Critics Fail to Disprove Kerry's Version of Vietnam War Episode," August 22, 2004, p. A1.

20. According to *Newsweek*'s account of the campaign, President Clinton told Kerry in early September to "spend less time talking about Vietnam and more time engaging on Iraq." See Evan Thomas and *Newsweek*'s Special Project Team, "The Inside Story: How Bush Did It," *Newsweek*, November 15, 2004, p. 102.

21. A Mason-Dixon survey reported that 16 percent were more likely to support Bush, 5 percent less likely. Grant Boxleitner, "Response to Hurricanes Could Help Bush . . . a Little," Gannett News Service, October 11, 2004, www.usatoday.com/news/politicselections/nation/president/2004-10-11-bush-florida_x.htm (accessed January 5, 2005).

22. Howard Kurtz, "Kerry Ad Says Flu Vaccine Shortage Is Typical of Bush's Policy Blunders," *Washington Post*, October 17, 2004, p. A6.

23. As it turned out, the October figures were revised significantly upward, but not until three days after the election, too late to help Bush.

24. Jennifer Harper, "Study Finds Press Pro-Kerry," *Washington Times*, November 1, 2004, available at www.washingtontimes.com/functions/print.php?StoryID=20041101-122452-4025r (accessed January 12, 2005).

25. *Media Bias Journal*, October 19, 2004, online at www.fairpress.org/pblog/archives/cat_newsweek.htm (accessed January 5, 2005).

26. "Down to the Wire," *Newsweek*, special election issue, November 15, 2004, p. 124.

27. Available at www.CNN.com/ELECTION/2004/pages/results/states/US/P/00/epolls.0.html (accessed November 2004). Curiously, Fox News reporter Geraldo Rivera reported that John Kerry had indicated to him after the election that he believed that the bin Laden tape had cost him the election. The comments came when the two men shared a holding room while waiting for the opening of the Clinton Library in Little Rock, Arkansas. "Exclusive: Kerry Says UBL Tape Cost Him Election," November 19, available at www.foxnews.com/printer_friendly_story/0,3566,139060,00.html, 2004 (accessed January 5, 2005).

28. Bush's advisers later held that he had been hurt by the story, but only a little, and they were actually pleased that Kerry spent so much time talking about it. See Richard Lowry, "Bush's Well-Mapped Road to Victory," *National Review*, November 29, 2004, p. 45.

29. George Bush, campaign speeches, October 11, 2004, available at www.presidential rhetoric.com/campaign/speeches/bush_oct11.html (accessed January 5, 2005).

30. www.realclearpolitics.com/bush_kerry_favorability.html (accessed December 2004).

31. Available at www.CNN.com/ELECTION/2004/pages/results/states/us/p100/epolls.o.html.

32. The Pew Research Center, "Voters Liked Campaign 2004, But Too Much 'Mud-Slinging," November 11, 2004, people-press.org/reports/display.php3?ReportID=233.

33. Morris Fiorina, "The Polarization Myth," October 20, 2004, available at cnnstudent news.CNN.com/2004/US/10/19/polarization.myth (accessed January 5, 2005).

## Chapter Five

# Congressional and State Elections

The contests for House and Senate made 2004 a comprehensive victory for the national Republican Party. If George W. Bush's personal victory was narrow, his party's was broad. In recent decades, many presidential candidates have won landslides without helping their party, but Bush confounded history by achieving the reverse: a modest margin against his rival that translated into a big win for congressional Republicans. Few doubted, moreover, that this party victory should be credited to Bush's personal party leadership. Ten years after the dramatic Republican sweep of 1994, in which the party surged to majorities in the House, Senate, and governorships and moved toward parity in state legislatures, Republicans have maintained control of these institutions and narrowed the margin in the state legislatures. But this has been no easy task.

After the heady days of 1995, when conservatives began vigorously promoting their policies, congressional Republicans crashed against the rocks of political reality. Much of their revolutionary agenda was vetoed or lost in the labyrinth of the consensual Senate. They were unable to outmaneuver the politically astute Bill Clinton, and the public blamed them for the two government shutdowns of late 1995 and early 1996. When they tried to impeach President Clinton in 1998–1999, they suffered more politically than he did.

In the electoral arena, Republicans lost a handful of House seats in 1996 and suffered similar incremental losses in 1998 and 2000; in the Senate, the GOP made no gains in the midterm year of 1998 and then proceeded to lose four seats in 2000. Adding insult to injury, George W. Bush did little in 2000 to lengthen his coattails, running a campaign that was often critical of the GOP Congress on policy and legislative technique, implicitly (and sometimes explicitly) juxtaposing his civility and moderation with Congress's partisanship and hard-line policy approach. By January 2001, Republican majorities, which were never large, hung by a thread. A switch of five seats in the House would tip it to the Democrats, and a 50-50 split in the Senate remained Republican-controlled only due to the tie-breaking vote of Vice President Dick Cheney. Four months later, Vermont Senator James Jeffords's defection handed organizational control to Tom Daschle and the Democrats. In 2002, Republicans, defying historical precedent, reversed their downward slide. They gained six seats in the House and two in the Senate, enough to win back their Senate majority and double their margin in the House. For Republicans, 2002 provided a salutary combination of a president with powerful personal appeal (especially to Republican voters), a focused and well-honed message on national security, and a strong grassroots organization.

Although Republicans could do little to control the larger electoral environment in 2004, it tended to favor them. Bush's popularity among the party faithful persisted, although his relations with most Democrats and some independents were more strained than in 2002, primarily due to the controversial Iraq War. At the congressional and state levels, Republicans sought to replicate and refine the strategy, tactics, and message that had proved so successful in 2002. Democrats, on the other hand, were unable to agree on the lessons of 2002 or stake out a clear position on the Iraq War. Hence, there was a lack of consensus on the party's message. Democrats

Table 5.1.   Change in Party Strength 1990–2004
(Republicans-Democrats-Independent)

| Year | Senate | House | Governors | State Legislatures |
|------|--------|-------|-----------|--------------------|
| 1990 | 44 R–56 D | 167 R–267 D–1 I | 19 R–29 D–2 I | 25 R–69 D (4 Ties) |
| 1992 | 43 R–57 D | 176 R–258 D–1 I | 18 R–30 D–2 I | 31 R–64 D (3 Ties) |
| 1994 | 52 R–48 D | 230 R–204 D–1 I | 30 R–19 D–1 I | 50 R–47 D (1 Tie) |
| 1996 | 55 R–45 D | 228 R–206 D–1 I | 32 R–17 D–1 | 46 R–50 D (2 Ties) |
| 1998 | 55 R–45 D | 223 R–211 D–1 I | 31 R–17 D–2 I | 47 R–50 D (1 Tie) |
| 2000 | 50 R–50 D | 221 R–212 D–2 I | 27 R–21 D–2 I | 49 R–46 D (3 Ties) |
| 2002 | 51 R–48 D–1 I | 229 R–204 D–1 I (one vacant) | 26 R–24 D | 52 R–43 D (3 Ties) |
| **2004** | **55 R–44 D–1 I** | **232 R–201 D–1 I (one vacant)** | **28 R–22 D** | **49 R–47 D (2 Ties)** |

*Source:* U.S. Census Bureau, *Statistical Abstract of the United States.*

could, at least, agree that they needed to redouble their voter mobilization efforts to combat GOP efforts in this area.

The last decade of slim Republican majorities in Congress has been characterized by increased partisanship, as measured by party loyalty and discipline exhibited in floor votes. This development may be considered another sign of the new "system" that has accompanied the current realignment. The Republican victory in 2002 only increased this trend. In 2003, Congress set a new record when 365 roll call votes saw unanimous House or Senate Republicans voting against a unanimous bloc of Democrats. Although partisan voting declined slightly in 2004, it was still the fourth highest on record. Overall, in 2004, Republicans voted to support the official party position 90 percent of the time in the Senate and 88 percent of the time in the House; Democrats voted to support their party position 83 percent of the time in the Senate and 86 percent of the time in the House.[1]

In partisan combat, Republican congressional leaders have learned how to govern. As one analyst remarked, "The leadership is very, very comfortable and mature in managing the day-to-day legislative agenda of the House. They have a very keen sense of where the votes are—what is possible and what is not possible. That wasn't there a few years ago."[2] Throughout his first term, Bush used his close relationship with Republicans in Congress to pursue a focused agenda. In his first four years in office, Bush enjoyed an overall congressional support score of 81 percent for those measures that actually reached a floor vote, the highest of any president since Lyndon Johnson. Even in his reelection year, he achieved support scores in excess of 70 percent in both houses.[3] At the beginning of 2004, some observers detected signs that congressional Republicans were beginning to distance themselves from the president, but there was little question that both saw their political futures as intertwined.

## The Context of the 2004 Elections

Political scientists define "structural" factors in an election as how many seats each party must defend and where, the layout of House districts, and the campaign finance laws that affect party fund-raising.

In the 2004 congressional elections, Republicans, especially in the Senate, held the advantage. Democrats held nineteen of the thirty-four Senate seats in play, and many of these Democrats hailed from states that had voted for Bush in 2000. Ten of the nineteen Democratic seats were in states Bush won in 2000, while Al Gore won only three of the states with GOP seats up for election. By early 2004, it was clear Democrats would be facing an even greater uphill climb than they had anticipated. One after another, southern Democratic senators announced their retirements: Ernest Hollings in South Carolina, Bob Graham in Florida, John Edwards in North Carolina, Zell Miller in Georgia, and John Breaux in Louisiana. The recent Republican surge in the South made these five Democratic open seats competitive, with perhaps a slight advantage to the Republicans. Bush had won all of these states in 2000, and in twelve of eighteen open-seat senatorial elections held in the previous two presidential elections, the party that won the state's presidential electoral votes also won the Senate seat.[4]

While the environment did not bode well for Democrats, Republicans faced obstacles to electoral success. They were losing a few Senate incumbents, too, in Oklahoma (Don Nickles), Illinois (Peter Fitzgerald), and Colorado (Ben Nighthorse Campbell). Illinois seemed the Democrats' best opportunity to pick up a seat. A handful of Republican incumbents were also facing tough challenges. Lisa Murkowski of Alaska, who had been appointed by her father when he vacated his Senate seat to become governor in 2003, was deemed vulnerable by Democrats due to the circumstances of her ascendancy, though Alaska was one of the most Republican states in the union. At various points in the campaign season, Democrats thought that GOP incumbents in Pennsylvania (Arlen Specter), Kentucky (Jim Bunning), and Missouri (Kit Bond) were potentially vulnerable.

No incumbent's defeat, however, attained higher priority than the Republicans' effort to unseat Senate minority leader Tom Daschle, whose ability to stymie Bush had attracted considerable attention. Daschle first won his seat in 1986 by 9,500 votes and had held it by emphasizing constituency service and campaigning on a moderate line in South Dakota, one of the reddest of the red states. Daschle faced a tough opponent in John Thune. Thune, like Daschle, had represented all of South Dakota as its congressman-at-large from 1997 to 2003. In 2002, he was recruited by the Bush White House to run against South Dakota's other Democratic senator, Tim Johnson; he lost by 524 votes. The Daschle-Thune contest was destined from the beginning to be the most closely watched Senate race. In the view of George Allen, chairman of the National Republican Senatorial Committee (NRSC), Daschle's defeat would be "like picking up three seats in itself."[5]

If the Senate electoral environment was discouraging for Democrats, on the House side it was downright depressing. Most in the party had high hopes in 2002, but those had been dashed. Two recent pickups in vacancy elections were offset by an equal number of defections to the Republican side. Now Democrats needed a net gain of thirteen seats to attain an outright majority, and few analysts believed that such a gain was realistic in the absence of a major and unforeseen national surge for Democrats. At the heart of the Democrats' problem was the fact that, due to a combination of gerrymandering and incumbency advantage, only a small number of House elections were at all competitive. Most incumbents started as prohibitive favorites, and of the thirty-three open seats, fewer than half were in play. Thirty-five Republicans would be running without any Democratic opponent at all, while only twenty-nine Democrats would not face a Republican. In April, *Congressional Quarterly Weekly Report* estimated that only twenty-nine seats were truly competitive, and most of those leaned toward the Republicans.[6] Only fourteen of those competitive races were for seats held by Republicans. If Democrats held every one of their own competitive seats, they needed to win thirteen of the fourteen GOP seats to reach the number required to attain a majority. Democratic strategists argued that typically high incumbency reelection rates would not hold in a political climate characterized by the undiluted partisan responsibility of unified party government, but most observers were skeptical.

Adding to their difficulties was a redistricting scheme that made a number of Texas Democratic incumbents vulnerable. At the behest of House Majority Leader Tom DeLay, himself a Texan, the Texas legislature redrew U.S. House districts after 2002. A partisan division between the Texas legislature and the governor had made agreement impossible after the 2000 census; consequently, the courts devised a redistricting plan that strongly favored Democrats. Receiving only 44 percent of the combined House vote in 2002, Democrats won seventeen of thirty-two House seats. In the same election, Republicans gained complete control of the state legislature, and a scramble to redraw the district lines ensued. Some Democratic state senators stayed away from Austin to prevent a quorum, actually fleeing to Oklahoma to avoid arrest by the state police. When enough Democrats agreed to conduct business, the legislature approved a new districting plan that deliberately endangered seven Democratic incumbents. One (Ralph Hall) promptly changed parties to avoid an electoral challenge; another announced his retirement, leaving a GOP-leaning open seat. Federal courts refused to intervene, and Democrats braced themselves for disaster in the Lone Star State. They faced the possibility of having to win five or six seats outside of Texas just to break even. (Colorado legislators tried a similar maneuver, passing a new redistricting plan that would have solidified two shaky Republican districts, but the courts struck down the maneuver.)

The Texas redistricting imbroglio served to highlight a broader trend in U.S. House districts. Nationally, district lines were drawn in ways that made more efficient use of Republican votes than of Democratic votes. To put it another way, Democratic voters were crammed into fewer districts, while Republican voters were spread more thinly across a greater number of districts. This phenomenon was partly due to Republican electoral successes at the state level in recent years, which resulted in a postcensus redistricting process tilted toward the GOP. In addition the Voting Rights Act Amendments of 1982 required that mapmakers strive to maximize the possibility of racial minority winners, which forced the creation of "minority-majority" districts, and further increased the concentration of Democratic voters. Finally, the Republican advantage simply reflected the natural distribution of voters across America. As one could see from national red-blue maps—or better yet, county-level purple maps showing gradations of voter concentration—Democrats were highly concentrated in the major urban centers and in a sprinkling of college towns; Republicans were spread more evenly across the rest of the country. According to congressional scholar Gary C. Jacobson, this amounted to "a huge structural advantage" for Republicans.[7]

As the election year began, a few additional factors foreshadowed a battle for Congress fought at the margins, with the Republicans enjoying an edge. Congress as an institution enjoyed good approval ratings, approaching 50 percent—not impressive in absolute terms, but historically high when compared with years in which large anti-incumbent trends developed.[8] The public also favored the Republican Party in general polls seeking to determine which party voters supported for the U.S. House. Not surprisingly, the GOP retained an advantage in early fund-raising. In 2003, the National Republican Senatorial Committee raised significantly more money than their Democratic opponents, and had more than three times as much cash on hand at the end of the calendar year ($8.6 million to $2.5 million).

The Bipartisan Campaign Reform Act (BCRA) ended large "soft money" contributions to the parties, with uncertain partisan consequences. Parties possess the greatest interest in challenging entrenched incumbents of the other party, and some believed that the loss of soft money would mean that fewer challengers would be able to mount strong campaigns, all other things being equal. Naturally, this scenario implies an advantage for the party in power. To the extent that soft money was replaced by independent expenditures from advocacy groups known as 527s, and 527 dollars were funneled overwhelmingly into the presidential race, this left relatively little for the congressional contests. Voter mobilization efforts by 527s, however, could have increased turnout further down the ballot. Finally, the relatively modest shifts in party strength in elections after 1994 hinted that neither party was in serious danger.

Two other factors influenced the outcome of the congressional elections. First, the Republican edge in the blue-red division of the states meant that, all other things being equal, they had something of a built-in advantage in Congress. Each state, regardless of population, is guaranteed two senators and one representative. If roughly thirty states continued leaning Republican—in an era of declining split-ticket voting and increasing partisanship—it would present Democrats with a serious long-term obstacle, especially in the Senate.

Second, Republican control of Congress and close cooperation between the White House and Republican congressional leaders bolstered the already significant advantages of unified party government, making the legislative process unusually well-directed to the political advantage of the majority. For example, on the verge of the election year, the Bush administration pushed Congress to act on a prescription drug entitlement, having reportedly been told by consultants that the president's reelection would be endangered by failure to deliver on this promise. (Lest anyone doubt the electoral connection, when the Department of Health and Human Services spent $22 million for television and newspaper ads beginning in February 2004, Democrats filed a complaint, claiming the department was engaged in electioneering at public expense.) The tight relationship between congressional Republicans and the White House produced a legislative environment that furthered Republicans' reelection bids by forcing Democrats to reckon politically with the GOP agenda.

Republicans used their control of Congress to weaken Democrats' standing with the public. The Senate continued its high-profile political wrangling over Bush's judicial nominations. After the 2002 elections gave Republicans their slim Senate majority, Democrats retreated a bit, releasing a few controversial nominees for a floor vote (and ultimate confirmation). The renewed political maneuvering surrounding judicial nominations meant that Republicans could charge Democrats with obstructionism in both the presidential election and Senate elections of 2004. Congressional Republicans also forced Democrats to put themselves on record concerning the question of same-sex marriage. In July, a 48-50 procedural vote thwarted Republican hopes to bring a constitutional amendment banning same-sex marriage before the Senate. The House waited until September 30 to bring the amendment to the floor; it attained a 227-186 majority, but fell short of the constitutionally required two-thirds vote. While the amendment failed, it had political consequences for both its supporters and opponents in Congress. In addition, the congressional votes likely mobilized more social conservatives to take action at the state level. If Congress would not act, the states would—a sentiment that boosted Republican turnout in the states. Likewise, when some liberal groups sought to attract young voters by claiming the Bush administration had a secret plan to revive the military draft, House Republicans brought to a surprise vote a bill (sponsored by Charles Rangel, D-NY) reviving the draft—just so it could be defeated. Not even Rangel voted for the measure, which lost 402-2. Although the vote did not completely put to rest the draft rumors, it may have mitigated their effect.

Republicans consistently employed legislative tactics to try to reduce the "gender gap"—the tendency of women voters since the 1980s to support Republican candidates less often than men. A medical tort reform bill aimed at limiting malpractice lawsuits was focused on obstetricians and gynecologists and named the Healthy Mothers and Healthy Babies Access to Care Act. Other legislation with a more general import—such as the Medicare prescription drug benefit or the draft measure—could also be framed as a "women's issue." On average, women live longer than men and are more likely to care for an elderly parent. And what mother wants her son to be drafted?[9] At the same time, several Democratic measures that would have presented political difficulty for Republicans—like an increase in the minimum wage—were blocked from floor consideration, courtesy of House rules that increasingly limited amendments and conference committees that fashioned bills to comport with the majority's political strategy.

Nor did the Republican strategy work only in one direction. Not only were floor votes used to affect the election, but the election was also used to leverage votes. For example, a five-year, $146 billion extension of several tax cuts—which would normally have aroused significant opposition from Democrats—was brought to a vote in late September. Daschle, already under fierce attack in South Dakota as an "obstructionist," allowed the vote to go forward. The tax cut extension encountered few obstacles in the Senate, passing handily by a 92-3 margin. Citing the damage done to them in 2002, Democrats also mounted little opposition to Bush's late summer nomination of former Representative Porter Goss to head the Central Intelligence Agency.[10]

## House Contests

Republicans and Democrats chose opposing strategies for the 2004 congressional races. Democrats sought to campaign on national issues and banked on a national surge to regain control of the House. As Democratic Congressional Campaign Committee (DCCC) chairman Representative Robert Matsui observed in June, "If it is a status quo election . . . we might pick up a few seats, but not enough to take the House. But I'd always been assuming that there were going to be winds of change in this election cycle."[11] Republicans eschewed the kind of national campaigns they ran in 1980 and 1994, instead encouraging each candidate to tailor his message to the peculiarities of his district. Representative Thomas M. Reynolds, chairman of the National Republican Congressional Committee (NRCC), explained, "We build these races from the ground up so that they can withstand the influence of upper-ballot races."[12] In the eyes of GOP strategists, this approach made it easier to defend seats held by moderate Republicans in blue states like Connecticut and New York. Nevertheless, most generic polls linked the fate of Republicans everywhere to Bush's fate. For the year prior to the election, polls gauging party preferences in House races almost uniformly showed Republicans' standing moving up or down in tandem with the president's.[13] As the presidential race entered the homestretch, it became clear that neither Bush nor Kerry would break the race open and achieve a landslide victory. To maintain control, Republicans did not need a Bush landslide. Democrats, on the other hand, needed a big Kerry victory. By early September, Democratic Representative Steny Hoyer admitted, "It would be less than candid to say there was a great wind out there at this point in time. There is not." NRCC chief Tom Reynolds was even more blunt: Democrats "need[ed] a monsoon," not just a breeze, and they were unlikely to get it.[14]

Ultimately, Democrats focused on about twenty open-seat races and a handful of Republican incumbents, four in Pennsylvania, two in Connecticut, and a smattering of others.[15] Republicans focused on defending their incumbents, promoting about fifteen challengers, and pursuing a handful of open seats. Overall, U.S. House candidates spent $620 million in the 2004 election cycle, with Republican candidates outspending Democrats $348 million to $270 million. The average GOP House candidate spent $572,288, the average Democrat $487,797. Three of the ten most expensive races were in Texas, where the radically altered district map was in effect for the first time. Of the national party committees, the NRCC raised nearly twice as much money as the DCCC: $175 million to $92 million.[16]

Several other indicators suggested that the end result would be what most analysts had predicted in the spring. A number of polls showed no swelling demand for change in Congress. In a mid-October *New York Times* poll, 51 percent of registered voters said their representative in Congress "deserves reelection," while only 27 percent said "it's time to give a new person a chance." At the same time, a CNN/*USA Today*/Gallup poll found that likely voters thought their U.S. Representatives deserved reelection by a 69-19-percent margin, and thought the same of "most members of the U.S. House of Representatives" by a 53-32-percent margin.[17]

In the absence of a Kerry landslide or a throw-out-the-bums groundswell, House Democrats were left with little on which to pin their hopes. By the fall, analysts designated between thirty-five and forty-two seats as somewhat competitive, with only seven to twelve of those representing true "toss-ups."[18] By *Congressional Quarterly*'s count, it was the smallest number of competitive seats at that stage of a race in at least two decades. When Tom DeLay was reprimanded twice by the House Ethics Committee for fund-raising practices and arm-twisting tactics, Democrats thought DeLay-as-boogeyman could be "an effective new weapon" in their campaign to re-take the House.[19] But few voters knew of either DeLay or his problems, and fewer yet were willing to draw a connection between him and their local Republican candidates. DeLay was no Newt Gingrich, the well-known and controversial Republican face that launched a thousand Democratic attack ads in 1996.

## Senate Contests

In the Senate, neither party ran a unified national campaign, in the sense of coordinated advertisements with a common slogan. For both parties, taxes and national security were the dominant themes. Unlike the House, there was little doubt among analysts that presidential politics would deeply influence the outcome of the Senate races.

In Senate primaries, the Bush White House intervened, sometimes openly and sometimes more subtly, in an effort to secure electable Republican nominees. As he did in several races in 2002, Bush openly recruited and backed Mel Martinez (FL), John Thune (SD), and Jim DeMint (SC), supported incumbent Pennsylvania Senator Arlen Specter in his tough but successful renomination battle against conservative Representative Pat Toomey, and reportedly nudged Peter Coors into the Colorado Republican Senate primary. Some of Bush's targeted recruits, such as Representative Jennifer Dunn of Washington and former Governor Jim Edgar of Illinois, declined his entreaties.

Republicans faced a complete meltdown in Illinois, which the White House was powerless to affect. Democrats had nominated the charismatic black state senator Barack Obama, Republicans investment banker and teacher Jack Ryan. Ryan, already the underdog, was forced in June to leave the race after embarrassing revelations leaked out of his divorce records. Illinois Republicans scrambled madly to find a replacement, even asking former football great and Chicago Bears coach Mike Ditka to run. In the end, black conservative Alan Keyes, former Reagan administration official and candidate for president and Senate (in Maryland), agreed, despite a demonstrable lack of connection to Illinois.[20]

In the South and other red states, Republican Senate candidates sought to align themselves with President Bush, while Democratic candidates sought to distance themselves from Kerry. In October, the *Los Angeles Times* noted that if Democrats had a fighting chance to regain the Senate, "it's because some of their candidates are sounding like Republicans."[21] Democratic senatorial candidates contending for the five open seats in the South found rough sledding. As University of Georgia political scientist Charles Bullock predicted, "[T]hey are going to have to do like Democrats running from the South did in the 1960s, 1970s, and 1980s, and that is try to disassociate themselves from the national party . . . and encourage voters not to think of them as running on the same ticket with John Kerry."[22] Some made clear their opposition to abortion, gun control, and gay marriage. For their part, Republicans in those races tied themselves closely to Bush. Republican John Vitter, running in Louisiana, said simply, "I'm supporting President Bush. They support John Kerry."[23] It was the same story in red states outside of the South. In Alaska, Democrat Tony Knowles went "to great lengths to distance himself from Mr. Kerry."[24] In South Dakota, Tom Daschle felt compelled to run advertisements showing himself hugging George W. Bush shortly after the terrorist attacks (NRSC head George Allen complained that the ad was "probably the most duplicitous ad that I've seen in this entire election year"[25]).

The South Dakota race became the most heated and costliest Senate race in the country because it was a contest between a strong incumbent and a strong challenger. In a state with a population of 750,000, Daschle raised $19 million, Thune $16 million. Daschle emphasized his legislative work on behalf of South Dakota and the benefits of his seniority. To illustrate the latter point, Daschle would describe the advantages, for South Dakotans, of his big office and desk location in the Senate chamber: "[S]ome would have our South Dakotans believe there is nothing wrong with trading that office and that desk in the front row in the center aisle for another desk in the far corner in the back. But I think there is a big difference." Former Representative Thune attacked Daschle as the "chief obstructionist," and emphasized issues like abortion, gay marriage, and national security, arguing that Daschle had abandoned his South Dakota roots in favor of Washington Beltway liberalism. Thune insisted on bringing the discussion back to national issues: "If [Daschle] is just a conduit for federal money, any senator can do that. But a senator is about more than that; it is about representing the values and beliefs of the people you represent."[26]

Daschle called Thune a "follower" for being too closely allied with Bush. Senate Majority Leader Bill Frist (R-TN) traveled to South Dakota to campaign personally for Thune, breaking a taboo against Senate leaders' campaigning against each other. Throughout the campaign, the new media played a role in bolstering Thune. In particular, a number of "bloggers" tracked coverage of the race in the state's dominant newspaper, the Sioux Falls *Argus Leader*, indicating what they considered instances of the *Argus Leader*'s pro-Daschle bias. The paper found itself under increasing pressure to revise its coverage. To one observer, "The blogs and other alternative media outlets became the tail wagging the media dog."[27]

Other races became prominent from time to time, flitting across the national radar screen. In Illinois, Alan Keyes provoked a fuss when he argued that homosexuals, including Vice President Dick Cheney's daughter Mary, were "narcissistic." In Kentucky, incumbent Jim Bunning lost most of his significant lead when he began acting strangely, missing a debate and making a series of bizarre comments that led some to question his physical or mental health. In Alaska, Lisa Murkowski artfully tied her challenger, former Governor Tony Knowles, to the national Democratic Party's opposition to Alaskan oil drilling, though Knowles himself supported it. Tom Coburn, the Republican doctor (and former representative) running for an open Senate seat in Oklahoma, was attacked for alleged Medicaid fraud and for involuntarily sterilizing a female patient in the 1970s; moderate Democrat Brad Carson drew closer in the polls, until he accused Coburn of being "an abortionist," a charge that backfired badly.

Unlike the House, Democrats raised more money than Republicans for Senate races. The DSCC raised $87 million to the NRSC's $75 million, and individual Democratic Senate candidates outspent Republicans by an average of $3.1 million to $2.5 million. In nine key races, the Democratic candidate raised more money in five (Alaska, Colorado, North Carolina, Oklahoma, and South Dakota), and the Republicans raised more money in four (Florida, Kentucky, Louisiana, and South Carolina).[28] Party strategists generally agreed that the top-tier candidates on both sides did not lack the resources they needed.

Every race had its own particular features, but as Election Day approached, analysts concluded that Democrats would have to win every one of the six closest Senate races to regain a majority in the Senate—or win some surprise upsets elsewhere.[29] As in the House, despite a moment of hopefulness in the summer, it seemed unlikely that Democrats would regain control of the Senate. Jon Corzine, who had claimed in June that

Democrats would have fifty-two Senate seats if the election were held then, conceded in late October that he "wouldn't be too surprised if we stayed where we were or moved to 50-50."[30]

## The Results

In the end, Republicans expanded their majorities in both houses of Congress, netting three seats in the House and four in the Senate, bringing their totals to 232 in the lower chamber and fifty-five in the upper.[31] They made their gains in the Senate by sweeping all five of the southern open seats. Three of the five—Isakson in Georgia, DeMint in South Carolina, and Burr in North Carolina—won by significant margins. In Louisiana's unique system, John Vitter won outright, avoiding a December 4 runoff by garnering 51 percent of the vote against two Democrats. He became the first Republican senator since Reconstuction elected in Louisiana. Only Florida was close, as Mel Martinez beat Betty Castor by one percentage point. The Senate elections dramatically confirmed a trend that began in the 1980s and gathered strength in the 1990s and early part of this decade: The South has realigned and is now a Republican stronghold. As a result of the 2004 elections, Republicans held twenty-two of the twenty-six Senate seats from the South. Democrats retained only one senator in Florida, one in Louisiana, and two in Arkansas.

In the biggest Senate race of the year, John Thune deposed Tom Daschle in South Dakota. Journalists declared Daschle's defeat a "devastating blow to Senate Democrats."[32] He was the first Senate floor leader to be defeated for reelection since Ernest McFarland lost to Barry Goldwater in 1952. As Stephen Moore of the Club for Growth, a conservative advocacy group, put it, "What we've essentially done is defeat the other side's general."[33] Compared to Thune's 2002 loss to incumbent Senator Tim Johnson, his 2004 winning margin was a blowout—a whopping 4,508 votes. Despite his vast campaign resources, his proven ability to bring federal dollars to his state, and a fair amount of goodwill stored over twenty-six years in Congress, Daschle was unable to overcome Thune's attacks. As political scientist Ross Baker remarked, the minority leader "still had to contend with the fact that the party he represented, and was the voice and face for, was very much out of favor with South Dakotans."[34]

For Democrats there were only two bright spots. In Illinois, Barack Obama handily defeated Alan Keyes. Obama, who would be the third black senator in U.S. history, set an Illinois record with his 70-percent vote share. Within six weeks, Obama's face graced the cover of *Newsweek* as a

Democratic "rising star." In Colorado, moderate State Attorney General Ken Salazer defeated brewing magnate Peter Coors by a 51-47 margin. Salazer and Martinez became the first Hispanic senators since Joseph M. Montoya of New Mexico, who left the Senate in 1977. Elsewhere, Democrats missed opportunities. In Oklahoma, Republican Tom Coburn easily held on to the GOP open seat. Similarly, Alaska's Lisa Murkowski won despite Democratic attempts to cast her as a beneficiary of nepotism. And Kentucky Republican incumbent Jim Bunning survived, barely. Altogether, Republicans won eight of the nine truly competitive Senate races. Not one Republican incumbent was defeated for reelection. At forty-four seats, Democrats controlled a smaller part of the Senate than at any time since before the 1930 election.

Exit polls showed that Republicans built their nine key Senate wins—the eight close races plus Georgia—on fundamentally the same ground as Bush and their copartisans in the House: muting, if not overcoming, the gender gap; making substantial inroads among Hispanics and Catholics while retaining huge majorities of white evangelicals; and winning income groups starting at the $50,000 bracket (or, in some cases, as low as $30,000). Seven of the nine Republicans won the Catholic vote outright. While the gender gap persisted, Republicans mitigated its effect in a variety of ways. Alaska's Murkowski won the men's vote by a wide margin and held her losses among women down to a small margin; in three states, Republicans won big among men and essentially broke even among women; in two more states, Republicans won both men and women, though men by more. The classic "mirror image" gender gap—men and women on opposite sides, by roughly the same margins—appeared in only three of the nine states. These, perhaps not coincidentally, happened to be the three closest races—South Dakota, Kentucky, and Florida. In the three states where Hispanics formed a large enough sample to be meaningful—Oklahoma, Georgia, and Florida—Republicans won them outright. Though Senate Republican winners followed a national template in many ways, they were creative in assembling regional coalitions. While the core national Republican coalition combines majorities in suburbs and rural areas, only three of the nine winners (Murkowski, DeMint, and Bunning) followed that route. Burr won solely on his overwhelming strength in the suburbs. Thune and Coburn put together urban-suburban majorities, losing rural areas narrowly; Vitter and Isakson put all three together; Martinez in Florida lost the suburbs, but forged a coalition of urban and rural.[35]

In the House, net Republican gains were traceable to Texas. Republicans won five of the six new districts that were in play in Texas (losing, ironically, only the district encompassing George W. Bush's ranch in Craw-

ford). Four Democratic incumbents were defeated, including Charles Sten-
holm and Martin Frost, who had fifty-two years of House experience between them. With twenty-one GOP representatives, Texas surpassed California as the state delegation with the largest number of Republicans. In
the rest of the country, Democrats broke even, losing one seat each in Indiana and Kentucky and gaining one seat each in Georgia, Illinois, New
York, and Colorado. Republicans and Democrats traded one seat for another in Louisiana. Thus, in order to win the thirteen seats they needed for
control of the House, Democrats actually had to gain eighteen outside of
Texas, but they only won two. The aim of a House Democratic majority,
which receded a bit in 2002, receded farther in 2004. Recycling Democrats' favorite meteorologic metaphor, DCCC chief Robert Matsui acknowledged, "[W]e did not get the wind, the uplift, that we had expected
in this campaign."[36]

As one commentator argued, "The overriding theme of the House campaign, in fact, was not change, but stability."[37] As was widely predicted,
few House races provided any real suspense on Election Night. In only ten
contests of 435 did the winner prevail by fewer than 5 percentage points.
In 2000, that figure was 18; in 2002, 24. Outside of Texas, 99.2 percent of
House incumbents who sought reelection won it, the highest incumbent reelection rate in at least half a century; only six seats changed party hands.
Even including the anomalous Lone Star State, the incumbent reelection
figure was 98.2 percent. As usual, House incumbents outraised challengers
by an average of more than 5 to 1.[38] A total of sixty-eight women were
elected to the House, an increase of five. The 109th Congress would also
see a total of forty blacks (an increase of three), twenty-three Hispanics (an
increase of one), three Asians (no change), one American Indian (down
from two), and one Asian Indian (there had been none).[39]

House Republicans maintained the absolute majority of the national
vote they achieved in 2002. Exit polls showed the House vote closely
tracked the presidential vote. House Republicans lost among women, but
won bigger among men—and held down the gender gap by winning
among married women; gained the same 44 percent share of the Hispanic
vote that Bush boasted; won income groups starting at $50,000; held their
own among independents; gained a small plurality among Catholics, majorities of both Catholics and Protestants who attend church regularly, and
an overwhelming majority (74 percent) of white evangelicals. Republicans won big among voters who cited terrorism, moral values, and tax cuts
as their most important issues, and obtained the support of 88 percent of
voters who were supporting Bush. Not surprisingly, the South was the Republicans' best region, where they won 56 percent of the House vote; they

held small pluralities in the West (50-48 percent) and the Midwest (50-49 percent). As in the presidential race, the Northeast was the Democrats' best region, where they won 57 percent of the total House vote. Democrats won the big cities, but lost the suburbs by a bit and rural areas decisively. In all, there was little change from the last presidential election year, except for increased support for Republicans from Hispanics. And there was not much variation between the 2004 presidential vote and the House vote; Bush did modestly better than House Republicans among women, Jews, Catholics, and antiabortion voters, but there was otherwise remarkable consistency between the two. Democrats who hoped for a national "wind" were not completely misguided: those voters who made their House voting decision in the last month of the campaign preferred Democrats, but not by a large enough margin to make the difference. It was too little, too late.[40]

Altogether, there could be little question that 2004 was a party victory for Republicans or that the victory was built on the base of Bush's narrow but solid win. Not since 1964 did an incumbent president winning reelection bring in a net gain for his party in both the House and the Senate. Clinton had lost seats in the Senate in 1996, as had Reagan in 1984 and Nixon in 1972. Senate Republican gains were clearly owed to Bush's strength at the top of the ticket. In all of the key races—South Dakota, Alaska, Oklahoma, Kentucky, and the Southern Big Five—Bush did better at the polls than the GOP's Senate candidate, winning by an average of 18 percentage points to their 6. Isolating the Southern Big Five, the Republican senatorial candidate trailed George W. Bush's totals by an average of 3.5 percent. There was no question Bush had southern coattails, or that John Kerry had hurt Democrats both with his liberalism and his inattention. When Kerry conceded the region, fewer national Democratic resources—which might have indirectly benefited the party's candidates down the ticket—flowed there. Altogether, in only nine of thirty-four Senate races nationwide was Bush outpolled by his party's senatorial standard-bearer, and these nine included longtime and popular incumbents like John McCain (Ariz.), George Voinovich (Ohio), Charles Grassley (Iowa), and Michael Crapo (Idaho), who needed no help.

Many Democrats were quick to point out that they had held their own in House races outside of Texas and argued that Bush could not be credited with having coattails in the House elections. Mathematically, of course, they were right. However, Republicans also showed strength nationally, as demonstrated by their majority of the national House vote. And if Democrats failed to retake the House, it was not only because Republicans gained in Texas, but also because Democrats gained virtually nowhere. In

Connecticut, Democrats argued that they had failed to take away two vulnerable Republican seats partly because Bush did much better in the state than they had expected.[41] The effect of Bush on House races can to some extent be deduced by observing the degree to which each party's candidates were willing to attach themselves publicly to their presidential nominee. While some Republicans, especially in the Northeast, had to distance themselves from Bush, there seemed to be a larger number of Democrats who asserted their independence from Kerry, not least by avoiding the party's convention in Boston. Furthermore, gains due to redistricting, even if not indicative of presidential coattails, are indicative of something of perhaps greater long-term significance: more Republican influence in state government.

## State Elections

The state elections presented a mixed picture for the parties, though the slight edge the Republicans gained in 1994 was not seriously disturbed.

Each presidential election year, there are about a dozen governorships, thousands of state legislative seats, and a variable number of important initiatives and referenda on state ballots along with federal offices. The aggregate results of state elections are often affected by national partisan tides and by mobilization efforts aimed primarily at federal offices. However, they are also dominated by a different set of issues or represent a different perspective on national issues. Issues like terrorism, which might be debated in federal races in terms of war in Afghanistan and Iraq, were more likely to appear at the state level in the form of debate over funding for "first responders" (policemen, firemen, and paramedics). Overall, state budget issues dominated in 2004, as many states continued to struggle with reduced revenue and balanced budget requirements. According to Tim Storey, an analyst for the National Conference of State Legislators, "The three big issues are the budget, the budget, and the budget." States with budget problems—which is to say, most states from 2001 to 2004—"have frequently seen the Governor's races as referendums on the fiscal condition of the state."[42]

Republicans began the 2004 election year with a 28-22 edge in governorships, a majority they had maintained since 1994. Only eleven governorships were up for election—five controlled by Republicans, six by Democrats. Five of the eleven were open seats, as three eligible governors did not run again—one due to poor prospects generally and two due to lost primaries. The Democrats' one source of joy in 2002 came in the gubernatorial elections, where they gained four, and they hoped to repeat that feat in 2004. On the other hand, Republicans had been on a roll in 2003, gaining control of the governorships of Kentucky, Mississippi, and, in a dramatic recall election that put Arnold Schwarzenegger in the governor's mansion, California.

When all the votes were counted—and that was not until the end of December, if then—the overall party balance had not shifted at all. Indeed, the gubernatorial elections produced a paradox: stability in the partisan balance, masking significant turnover in governorships of individual states. Out of eleven governorships at issue, only four incumbents were returned. In 2002, there was a similar rate of change, as twenty-five of thirty-six governors elected that year were new.[43] Democrats replaced Republicans in Montana and New Hampshire, while Republicans took away Missouri and Indiana, where George W. Bush's former director of the Office of Management and Budget, Mitch Daniels, was elected. By far the most contentious race was in Washington state, in an episode eerily reminiscent of the 2000 Florida debacle. First, Republican Dino Rossi led Election Night returns. Then Democrat Christine Gregoire pulled ahead as absentee ballots were being counted. Then Rossi regained the lead. After a recount put him ahead by forty-two votes, he was certified the winner. When more than seven hundred ballots were discovered in Democratic-leaning King County, the state supreme court ruled they had to be counted, giving Gregoire a victory by 129 votes out of more than 2.8 million cast. Rossi vowed to challenge the results and called for a new election. A Rossi win would have meant a net GOP gain of one governorship.

In state legislatures, Democrats gained sixty seats across the country (though Republicans gained in the South), a small number out of the 5,809 at stake but enough to pull into a tiny lead over Republicans nationally. Democrats now controlled 3,660 state legislative seats to the Republicans' 3,657—a margin of three. Democrats also gained control of seven new legislative chambers and Republicans four. Control of state houses was divided twenty-five Republican to twenty-three Democrat, with 1 tied; state senates were split twenty-four for each party, with one tied. This left the GOP with complete control—possessing the governorship and the majority in both houses of the legislature—in twelve states. Democrats controlled eight, and twenty-nine were divided (Nebraska, with a nonpartisan unicameral legislature, is not included).

Altogether, though the results were inconclusive, Democrats saw reasons for encouragement, especially in Republican-leaning western states like Colorado, where they gained control of both houses of the legislature, and Montana, where they won a governorship, several other statewide offices, and control of the state senate. They attributed their successes to improved organization, skillful fund-raising, and pragmatic candidates who could appeal to rural voters, develop local issues, and escape the ill effects of the national Democratic label.[44] However, it was unclear whether or how Democrats would be able to turn this strategy for survival in hostile locales into a coherent strategy for a national majority. And Republicans, while not enjoying Bush coattails at the state level, could nevertheless take some satisfaction that they remained much more competitive than they had been twenty years before. Indeed, they still controlled a majority of governorships, a slim plurality of legislative chambers, and more full state governments than the Democrats.

Another notable feature of the state elections was the presence of more than 150 initiatives and referenda on the ballots of thirty states.[45] Numerous local jurisdictions also offered voters a variety of ballot issues. Subjects ranged from eight gambling issues on state ballots to twenty-one tax issues to term limits, which voters in Arkansas were asked to lengthen to twelve years from six in the house and eight in the senate (they said no). In a transparent slap at Frank and Lisa Murkowski, voters in Alaska handily passed a measure stripping the governor of the right to fill U.S. Senate vacancies by appointment. In California, voters approved a $3 billion state commitment to fund embryonic stem cell research after Governor Arnold Schwarzenegger endorsed it at the last minute. Of 161 conservation measures at the state and local level, 120 passed in blue and red states alike, including authorization of a total of $3.5 billion in land conservation spending.[46] Colorado considered, and then rejected, a proposal to split its electoral votes proportionally in accordance with the popular vote.

By far the most widely noted initiatives, however, were proposed amendments in thirteen states prohibiting same-sex marriage. About half of them also prohibited so-called "civil unions," a legally recognized relationship short of marriage. Two (Missouri and Louisiana) voted earlier in the year; eleven more voted on November 2. The impetus for these state amendments, as for the constitutional amendment proposed in the U.S. Congress, was the Massachusetts Supreme Judicial Court's decision of November 2003, as well as provocative conduct by some pro–gay marriage local officials. In a highly publicized instance, San Francisco Mayor Gavin Newsome, for example, ordered city clerks to violate California state law by issuing marriage licenses to gay couples, resulting in something of a national uproar.

The results of the initiatives were highly encouraging to social conservatives. All thirteen passed by wide margins. In only two states—Michigan and Oregon—were the amendments held to less than 60 percent of the vote, and even the prototypically liberal Beaver State gave the measure 57 percent. Yes votes totalled 71 percent in Missouri and 86 percent in Mississippi. All indications were that support for the amendments crossed party lines. Some analysts argued that the anti-same-sex marriage amendments were at least partially responsible for Bush's presidential victory. One observer noted that the measures "acted like magnets for thousands of socially conservative voters in rural and suburban communities who might not otherwise have voted."[47] In crucial Ohio, some thought that Republican turnout in the rural south and west of the state was driven partially by the amendment, and some credited Bush's improved showing in Appalachian Ohio to it as well. Likewise, Senator Jim Bunning's narrow escape in Kentucky was attributed not only to Bush's coattails but the effect of the amendment there.[48] Some Democrats, like Senator Dianne Feinstein (CA), expressed concern that gay marriage had been pushed "too much, too fast, too soon," bringing a backlash that hurt the party nationally.[49] However, some analysts questioned how much of an effect the amendments had on the presidential race. They pointed out that the amendments far outperformed Bush and that support for them was so broadly shared among Republicans, Democrats, and Independents that voters generally saw the amendments as an issue quite separate from the presidential race. Many inner-city precincts in Cleveland voted overwhelmingly for the marriage amendment at the same time they were delivering a microscopic fraction of their votes to Bush, and more than a few upper-scale suburban precincts voted for Bush but were less than enthused about the amendment.

Finally, in another sign of the increasingly partisan character of American elections in the system of 2004, 2004 saw, for the first time, expensive and partisan campaigns run on behalf of a large number of candidates in state judicial races. According to one published report, voters in eight states saw television ads for judicial races for the first time, and some judicial candidates were revealing their positions on issues that they might later have to decide from the bench. In one Illinois judicial race, two opposing candidates raised at least $5 million and waged an electoral battle around the issue of tort reform.[50]

## Consequences of the Vote

At the state level, the consequences of the 2004 vote were hard to predict, except that both parties would continue locked in combat in the majority of states that featured divided government. Looking ahead to 2006, Democrats can anticipate a particularly good opportunity to dislodge Republicans from their control of the majority of governorships. Thirty-six governorships will be up for election, and Republicans currently hold twenty-two of those, nine of which are in blue states. Democrats hold fourteen, seven of which are in red states. Thus Republicans will likely be on the defensive. The impact of state-level marriage amendments remains unclear. At a minimum, they will invite imitation by social conservatives in other states in 2006. California's stem cell initiative may also have its imitators.

The consequences of the congressional elections, at least in the short term, are somewhat easier to assess. As one journalist reported, the Republican Senate gains tangibly "altered the political landscape." The ranks of Democratic moderates were thinned, those of conservative Republicans expanded. With their bigger share of the chamber, Republicans can gain committee ratios that give them a margin of two, rather than one, on major committees.[51] Some analysts have argued that "Democratic moderates risk losing their nerve after watching Mr. Daschle's defeat."[52] Immediately after Election Day, no fewer than three key Democratic senators—Christopher Dodd of Connecticut, Charles Schumer of New York, and Jon Corzine of New Jersey—were said to be considering leaving the Senate to run for their states' governorships, ruminations that some interpreted as a "sign of growing Democratic powerlessness and despair in Washington." According to one Democratic strategist, "People are just giving up."[53]

Senate Republicans looked likely to flex their muscles, and they quickly voted to give majority leader Bill Frist the power to fill over half of all vacancies on the most important committees, a departure from seniority protocol that made the Senate more like the House. Trent Lott, senator from Mississippi and former majority leader, denied that Republicans were suffering from hubris: "I think it is excitement and enthusiasm about opportunities." NRSC head George Allen said simply, "We know what we want to do and now we have the ability to do it. And I think we will." For their part, Democrats sounded a cautionary note. Harry Reid (D-NV), who was quickly elevated to the post of minority leader in Daschle's stead, warned, "They'd better be very, very careful what they do."[54] Reid knew, as did Republicans, that fifty-five votes were still not enough to break a filibuster. Democrats might have been chastened, and would doubtless pick their fights more carefully, but they could not be expected to roll over once the shock of November 2 has sufficiently worn off.[55] (In response to the continued threat of Democratic obstruction, Republicans floated the idea of changing Senate rules to prohibit filibusters on presidential appointments.) In any event, prospects had at least improved for Bush policies such as the faith-based initiatives bill, an energy bill allowing oil exploration in the Arctic National Wildlife Refuge, and tort reform.

The urge to modify Senate procedures to make it more like the House derived largely from Republicans' frustration at their inability to enforce party discipline against wayward souls like Rhode Island's Lincoln Chafee, who openly admitted that he would not be voting for Bush, and at the ease with which Democrats could arrest the progress of Republican legislation. It may have been driven as well by the unprecedented degree to which the Senate consists of former House members. After the 2004 elections, the new Senate would contain fifty-two former members of the House, the largest number ever.[56]

The House itself saw less change than the Senate, but the results were still significant. In an era of uncompetitive districts and massive incumbent advantage, the Republicans padded their majority. Conservatives in the House were bolstered, not least because Tom DeLay's stature received a boost from the elections, despite his ethics reprimands. Unless he is indicted, most Republicans concur, he will be virtually assured of operating from a strengthened position. After November 2, conservatives indicated that they expected to be in charge of the House. Todd Tiahrt (R-KS), for example, remarked, "I think we [conservatives] are going to be driving the agenda." Others like John E. Sweeney (R-NY) emphasized that House Republicans could be expected to stake out their own direction, less constrained by the electoral imperatives of the White House: "Quite candidly, we've ceded some of our agenda to the White House in the last few years. In '06, the mid-term elections with a lame-duck presidency, we need to make a compelling case to the American people that we deserve to be re-elected."[57]

Indeed, both parties are already looking to 2006. Democrats are engaging in a reappraisal of message and strategy, with uncertain consequences. Their hopes derive in no small measure from the possibility that Bush will stumble and suffer from the usual six-year midterm blues. History will be on their side.

Republicans will seek legislative accomplishments and will place hope in their continuing structural advantages. In the Senate, eighteen of thirty-three seats up for election in 2006 are held by Democrats or Democratic-leaning independents (James Jeffords). Furthermore, five of the Democrats will be running in red states, only three of the Republicans in blue states. Because Republicans lost a net of four Senate seats in 2000, when they were defeated in seven of the nine closest races, there are no Bush Senate coattails to be withdrawn in 2006, which is the most frequently cited reason for poor presidential party performance in the six-year Senate midterms. In the House, to gain a majority of 218, Democrats will have to pick up 16 seats; yet neither party has gained more than nine House seats in any election since 1994. Days before the 2004 elections were held, a Supreme Court ruling gave hope to some Democrats that the Texas redistricting that harmed them so much might be undone. In *Vieth v. Jubelirer*, the court reaffirmed that partisan gerrymandering could conceivably be unconstitutional, though it declined to overturn the redistricting map at issue (in Pennsylvania). The court then asked the federal district court in Austin to reconsider its January ruling allowing the new Texas map to stand. In the wake of *Vieth*, other maps might be challenged as well, including Florida and Michigan (drawn by Republicans) and Maryland and Georgia (drawn by Democrats). But in the absence of a dramatic shake-up of House districts, the odds are fairly high that elections will continue being fought out at the margins. If House elections remain a game of inches, Democrats will find it hard to make up the yard or two that they lack. In any event, Democrats cannot count on history to work for them. Bush has already beaten history twice, once in 2002 and a second time in 2004.

## Notes

1. Isaiah J. Poole, "Party Unity Vote Study: Votes Echo Electoral Themes," *CQ Weekly Report*, December 11, 2004, p. 2906.

2. Poole, "Party Unity Vote Study."

3. Joseph J. Schatz, "Presidential Support Vote Study: With a Deft and Light Touch, Bush Finds Ways to Win," *CQ Weekly Report*, December 11, 2004, p. 2900.

4. "When the Presidency and an Open Senate Seat Share Ballots," *CQ Weekly Report*, October 23, 2004, p. 2496.

5. Richard E. Cohen, "In Hill Races, Hunting for Democratic Scalps," *National Journal Convention Special*, September 4, 2004, p. 2670.

6. "Narrow Battleground Limits Fight for Control of House," *CQ Weekly Report*, April 10, 2004, p. 871.

7. Peter E. Harrell, "House: Dearth of Close Races Makes Status Quo a Best Bet," *CQ Weekly Report*, October 23, 2004, p. 2506.

8. In January 2004, Gallup put congressional approval at 48 percent positive, 45 percent negative; NBC News/*Wall Street Journal* polls put the figure at 46-41 percent positive; CBS News/*New York Times* said 45-42. See www.pollingreport.com/job.htm.

9. See Gebe Martinez and Mary Agnes Carey, "Erasing the Gender Gap Tops Republican Playbook," *CQ Weekly Report*, March 6, 2004, p. 564.

10. See Helen Dewar, "Tight Race in S.D. Constrains Daschle," *Washington Post*, September 26, 2004, p. A5; Leigh Strope, "Democrats Unlikely to Fight Goss Nomination," *Washington Post*, August 16, 2004, p. A2.

11. Peter E. Harrell, "House Democrats Counting on a National Surge," *CQ Weekly Report*, June 19, 2004, p. 1462.

12. Harrell, "The House: Dearth of Close Races."

13. Different polls varied considerably regarding absolute levels of support, but showed the same trend. For example, CNN/*USA Today*/Gallup polls showed Republicans ahead of Democrats by 5 percentage points among likely voters in January, tied at the beginning of August, and back in the lead in mid-October; the George Washington University Battleground Poll showed Republicans tied with Democrats a year before the election, behind in the spring and summer of 2004, and pulling ahead in October. For these and other polls, see www.pollingreport.com/cong2004.htm (accessed December 2004). It should also be noted that for many years generic House polls have typically underestimated Republican vote shares.

14. Charles Babington, "Democrats Reassess Prospects to Win House," *Washington Post*, September 19, 2004, p. A9.

15. See Carl Hulse, "GOP Optimistic That It Can Keep Control of Congress," *New York Times*, October 3, 2004, p. A25; Carl Hulse, "The Battle in Pennsylvania Isn't Just for President," *New York Times*, October 25, 2004, p. A18.

16. See www.opensecrets.org/overview/stats.asp?cycle=2004; www.opensecrets.org/parties/index.asp (accessed December 2004).

17. See www.pollingreport.com/cong2004.htm (accessed December 2004).

18. See Harrell, "The House: Dearth of Close Races"; Eric Slater, "Safe Seats in House Keep True Races Rare," *Los Angeles Times*, October 11, 2004, p. A1; Kelly Beaucar Vlahos, "Competitive House Races Limited in Number," Fox News Channel, www.foxnews.com/0,3566,134014,00.html.

19. Carle Hulse, "DeLay's Troubles Give a New Focus to the House Races," *New York Times*, October 10, 2004, p. A1.

20. The Illinois Republican fiasco contributed to a new and short-lived political climate. Senate Democrats, like their House counterparts, saw an opening in the summer of 2004. DSCC chairman Sen. Jon Corzine (D-NJ) proclaimed in late June that, if the election were held then, "we'd be at 52-48" in the majority. Naturally, Republicans disputed that assessment. Outside observers were reluctant to back Corzine's claim, but agreed that Democratic prospects had improved, for two reasons: Kerry was gaining ground against Bush, and Democrats had done well in candidate recruitment in the key Senate races.

21. See Richard Simon, "Democrats Running to Right in Many Tight Senate Races," *Los Angeles Times*, October 12, 2004, p. A18.

22. Gregory L. Giroux, "Election Overview: An Uphill Fight for the Senate," *CQ Weekly Report*, February 21, 2004, p. 470.

23. Giroux, "Democrats Catch the Breaks in Senate," *CQ Weekly Report*, June 19, 2004, p. 1454.

24. Sarah Kershaw, "In Solidly Republican Alaska, a Charged Senate Race May Signal a Thaw," *New York Times*, October 21, 2004, p. A17.

25. Gregory L. Giroux, "The Senate: Democrats Trying to Tip The Close Tussles Their Way," *CQ Weekly Report*, October 23, 2004, p. 2500.

26. Sheryl Gay Stolberg, "Chasing a Coveted Democratic Scalp across the Plains," *New York Times*, October 24, 2004, p. A22.

27. John Fund, "How Daschle Got Blogged," *Wall Street Journal*, www.opinionjournal.com/diary/?id=110006018 (accessed December 2004).

28. See www.opensecrets.org/overview/stats.asp?cycle=2004; www.opensecrets.org/parties/index.asp; www.opensecrets.org/overview/hotraces.asp?cycle=2004 (accessed December 2004).

29. Giroux, "The Senate: Democrats Trying to Tip the Close Tussles Their Way."

30. Giroux, "The Senate: Democrats Trying to Tip the Close Tussles Their Way."

31. The House figure includes the results of the 433 races decided on November 2 plus two Louisiana run-off elections held December 4. By some calculations, Republicans gained five seats, but two of those merely filled vacancies of seats that had been held by Republicans (Porter Goss of Florida and Doug Bereuter of Nebraska). In either case, Democrats lost three seats from the 205 they had held before the election.

32. David Rogers, "Republicans Bolster Majorities in Congress," *Wall Street Journal*, November 4, 2004, p. A8.

33. Amy Schatz, "South Dakotans Decide Daschle Lost Touch with State's Values," *Wall Street Journal*, November 4, 2004, p. A8.

34. Gregory L. Giroux, "Red States, Blue States—Or Shades of Violet?" *CQ Weekly Report*, November 27, 2004, p. 2775.

35. See www.cnn.com/ELECTION/2004//pages/results/states (accessed December 2004).

36. Peter E. Harrell, "House Now a Slightly Redder Hue," *CQ Weekly Report*, November 6, 2004, p. 2621.

37. Harrell, "House Now a Slightly Redder Hue."

38. Available at www.opensecrets.org/overview/incumbs.asp?cycle=2004 (accessed December 2004).

39. This figuring excludes nonvoting delegates from the District of Columbia and U.S. territories.

40. Available at www.CNN.com/ELECTION/2004/pages/results/states/US/H/00/epolls.0.html (accessed December 2004).

41. Harrell, "House Now a Slightly Redder Hue."

42. Jennifer Mock, "At State Level, Budget Still the Make or Break Issue," *CQ Weekly Report*, October 23, 2004, p. 2515.

43. See Jennifer Mock, "For State Leadership, Change—and More of the Same," *CQ Weekly Report*, November 6, 2004, p. 2630.

44. Dennis Cauchon, "Dems Gain in 'Hidden Election,'" *USA Today*, December 14, 2004; John Nichols, "Democrats Score in the Rockies," *The Nation*, December 6, 2004, p. 20.

45. For a preelection overview, see David S. Broder, "Hot Issues Go Directly to State Voters," *Washington Post*, September 18, 2004, p. A1.

46. Will Rogers, "It's Easy Being Green," *New York Times*, November 20, 2004, p. A31.

47. James Dao, "Same-Sex Marriage Issue Key to Some GOP Races," *New York Times*, November 4, 2004, p. P4.

48. See Dao, "Same-Sex Marriage Issue."

49. Charles Forelle, David Bank, and Sara Schaefer Munoz, "Gay Agenda Is Seen as Rallying Point," *Wall Street Journal*, November 5, 2004, p. A5.

50. Adam Liptak, "Judicial Races in Several States Become Partisan Battlegrounds," *New York Times*, October 24, 2004, p. A1.

51. Carl Hulse, "Republicans Add 4 Seats in Senate," *New York Times*, November 4, 2004, p. A1.

52. Rogers, "Republicans Bolster Majorities."

53. Raymond Hernandez and Alison Leigh Cowan, "Three Senators Consider Bids for Governor," *New York Times*, November 6, 2004, p. A1. Not long after these rumors surfaced, Schumer decided to stay in the Senate to head the DSCC and Corzine announced he would pursue the New Jersey governorship in 2005.

54. Carl Hulse, "Larger Majorities and the Itch to Stretch G.O.P. Muscles," *New York Times*, November 19, 2004, p. A17.

55. For a discussion of the obstacles remaining for Bush and Republicans in the Senate, see Gary Andres, "Senate Dreams and Nightmares," *The Weekly Standard*, November 15, 2004, pp. 19–20.

56. See Alan K. Ota, "Senate GOP Gives Its Leader a Powerful New Tool," *CQ Weekly Report*, November 20, 2004, p. 2733.

57. Susan Crabtree and Jonathan Allen, "GOP Gains Strengthen Hand of DeLay, House Leadership," *CQ Weekly Report*, November 6, 2004, p. 2618.

*Chapter Six*

# Electoral Reform and the
# Future of the Parties

Presidential elections are most important, obviously, for deciding the great political question of who will serve as the most important official in the United States. These elections are studied, properly, for the insights they offer into the nature of the parties and party competition, the tendencies of voting behavior, and the direction of national policy and public philosophy. But there is another perspective that can be applied to these elections. They offer a chance to examine and assess the condition of America's electoral institutions and consider some of the key policy questions about their possible reform. As the Founders understood, the method and process of election have an effect both on what types of candidates win and on how the winners conceive and wield power. Those methods and processes are also a crucial link in the chain of consent of the governed that makes government legitimate. The nation has a great stake in the health and proper functioning of those institutions.

The elections of 2000 illustrated in a rather dramatic way a number of institutional issues in American elections. Many Americans concluded that the system of the Electoral College in particular, which permitted Bush to win the presidency but lose the popular vote, called out for constitutional or legal reform. Except for campaign finance reform, the events of September 11, 2001, drove reform efforts off of the national agenda; those that were dealt with went largely unnoticed. In 2004, institutional issues were not nearly as prominent in the public debate, but some questions emerged and are likely to continue to occupy the attention of politicians, activists, scholars, and journalists. If history is any guide, it is probable that policy makers will address some of these issues over the next four years. Intense waves of institutional reform are rare, and they generally require a powerful social movement or a triggering event or crisis to get them started.

Most of the time such change takes place in a piecemeal, often disjointed manner conditioned by the decentralized character of our federal system and the incremental character of our policymaking machinery.

## Electoral College

In 2000, when George W. Bush won the presidency even as Al Gore accumulated a narrow plurality of the nationally aggregated popular vote, a number of voices were raised calling for reform or abolition of the Electoral College. These reformers had little hope of success even before the terrorist attacks removed the issue from the public eye. Nevertheless, three items of interest in the 2004 election were sure to keep support for some modification of the system alive.

In Colorado, a ballot initiative (Amendment 36) was proposed that would have allocated the state's electoral votes in proportion to popular vote preferences. Although Colorado has voted Republican in every presidential election but one since 1964, it is a competitive state, meaning that its nine electoral votes could typically be expected to divide 5-4. Reformers who supported the measure asserted that it was "an affirmation of the basic principle of one person, one vote. It makes every vote count, and it gives greater weight to the individual."[1] Partisan Democrats also supported it, realizing that in most years, the practical effect of the measure would be to gain four electoral votes for the Democratic candidate. Partisan Republicans who realized the same thing opposed it. Also in opposition were some Democrats who perceived (on the basis of demographics) a future chance to win Colorado. Politicians of both parties feared that Colorado's national influence would diminish if it could offer to candidates the enticement of a net gain of only one electoral vote instead of nine. Ahead in the polls at the beginning of the campaign, Amendment 36 withered against a charge that it represented a form of unilateral disarmament in the electoral arena.[2] According to exit polls, Republican voters opposed the amendment by an 87-13-percent margin, while Democrats supported it by a 56-44-percent margin.

Had the Colorado initiative passed, it would surely have been imitated by other states, and it may yet be.[3] It was a powerful reminder that a constitutional amendment changing the Electoral College is not the only route available to reformers. It is also possible to instigate change from the bottom up. Indeed, two of the most important developments in the Electoral College historically were the decisions by states to embrace popular selection of the electors and to give their electoral votes winner-take-all.

The issue of the "faithless elector" arose again in 2004. Faithless electors are members of the Electoral College who do not vote for the candidate they were pledged to support. While only a handful have appeared in American history — and have never been decisive — they have been a focus of reformers. In 2000, some Democratic activists tried to pry loose the three Bush electors that Gore needed for a majority, but failed. Instead, a Democratic elector from the District of Columbia abstained as a protest for statehood for the District. In 2004, one Republican elector in West Virginia, South Charleston Mayor Richie Robb, threatened during the fall campaign to withhold his vote from Bush if Bush won the state.[4] In the end, Bush won West Virginia and Robb voted for him. However, when Democratic electors met in Minnesota to cast their votes for John Kerry, one of them (perhaps inadvertently confusing his Johns) voted for John Edwards.

These instances may cause states to reassess the enforcement of electors' pledges, and may renew interest in a moderate constitutional remedy that has long been suggested: an amendment providing for automatic casting of electoral votes without the intermediary of actual people serving as electors. Such a change would eliminate one objection to the Electoral College. However, it would also "lock in" the electoral votes, a potentially important disadvantage during the monthlong lapse between Election Day and the casting of the electoral votes. The current system allows for some flexibility in the event of the death, incapacitation, or disgrace of the winner.

Finally, the closeness of the presidential race again alerted citizens to the potential for the loser in the popular vote to win in the Electoral College. In 2000, that fellow was Bush. In 2004, Kerry came close to that outcome. Had he pulled 60,000 votes away from Bush in Ohio, he would have won the Electoral College while trailing by over 3 million popular votes nationwide. As Judith Best and other defenders of the Electoral College have pointed out, shifting votes around in that way is easier done on paper than in reality.[5] It is hard to envision an event or appeal that could have shifted 60,000 votes in Ohio without shifting tens or hundreds of thousands of votes elsewhere, too. Nevertheless, 2004 will go down as another example in a catalog of "close calls" for the winner of the popular majority. One could also envision a scenario in which the candidates tied with 269 electoral votes each, throwing the election into the House of Representatives for only the third time in American history.[6] This would have happened if Kerry had won Ohio and Iowa and Bush had pulled out a victory in Wisconsin. On balance, though, the pressure and momentum for Electoral College reform is much less evident today than after the 2000 election. As long as problems remain theoretical instead of real, pressure for reform will be weak. Perhaps the plurality-loser scenario will have to occur twice in a row, or at least become a much more regular occurrence, in order to produce action.

## Third Parties

In the nineteenth century, strong third-party showings in presidential elections were plentiful, not least because the legal barriers to them were minimal. Around the turn of the last century, state legislatures, at the behest of the two major parties, began to erect significant barriers to ballot access for third parties, mostly in the form of high petition signature requirements and very early filing deadlines. Not until 1968 did those barriers begin to come down. In that year, George Wallace's American Independent Party went to court to strike down some of the more onerous requirements; Eugene McCarthy in 1976 and John Anderson in 1980 completed the process of dismantling burdensome ballot access requirements. Consequently, Anderson and Ross Perot (in both 1992 and 1996) succeeded in placing their names on the ballots of all fifty states; Ralph Nader was on the ballot in forty-three states in 2000. Thus, it can be said that the tendency of American electoral politics in the last third of the twentieth century was to encourage third-party access. Many political scientists favored this trend as one that opened the political system to a wider variety of viewpoints.

In 2004, that movement came to a screeching halt. Democrats and liberal advocacy groups, fearful that Nader's candidacy would draw votes away from John Kerry, waged a vigorous legal campaign in more than a dozen states to keep Nader off the ballot. They succeeded in several key states, including Ohio and Pennsylvania, and forced Nader to expend precious resources in states like Florida and Wisconsin, where he ultimately won court challenges. When all was said and done, Nader appeared on the ballot in only thirty-four states in 2004. Nader contended, "The Democrats waged a bucketfull of dirty tricks and phony lawsuits and intimidation and harassment of our signature gatherers to get us off."[7] The consumer advocate was so incensed by his treatment that he vowed: "We'll make ballot access and electoral reform a prime civil liberties issue."[8]

This effort at what could impolitely be called the suppression of a third party was greeted with surprising silence by many of the celebrities and analysts who might have cried foul under other circumstances. Some of the Democrats' complaints had merit—in Pennsylvania, Nader petitions were filled with names like Daffy Duck, Bugs Bunny, and Roadrunner—but in many states the question of merit seemed to be incidental. In 2004, it seemed, all other considerations were to be subsumed under the overriding imperative of defeating George W. Bush. It remains to be seen whether the widespread success of a major party at blocking the ballot access of a third-party candidate augured the beginning of a new era—one more difficult for third parties—or simply a brief aberration.

## Primary Front-loading

We may be about to commence a new stage in the overlapping but distinct battles over primary front-loading and over when and how the official process of selecting delegates will begin. That battle will necessarily include a discussion of which is the bigger problem—front-loading as a whole or the privileged position of Iowa and New Hampshire.

In 1996 and 2000, Republicans seriously considered reforms to mitigate or reverse the process of primary front-loading that has become the signature feature of the modern presidential nomination system. In 2000, they awarded bonus delegates to states that held their primaries or caucuses later in the primary season. When that failed to have the desired effect, a Republican task force recommended a plan mandating that the small states go first and the largest states last. At the last minute, the Bush campaign convinced the Republican National Committee to kill the plan rather than risk a messy floor fight at the 2000 convention with California, New York, and other big states opposed to the plan. Democrats studied the problem but concluded that the front-loaded system had worked just fine for them.

With the parties' acquiescence to front-loading in 2004, some began to speculate that the front-loaded system is here to stay. For better or worse, in this view, all the issues have now been taken off the table, and there is no further place to go. Perhaps so. But before the celebrations (or lamentations) commence, it is well to recall two other possibilities. One would be a renewed attempt of some kind, undertaken with more rigor, to reinstitute a slower schedule. After the 2004 election, rumblings were heard that the front-loaded system had not served Democrats well this time. In the view of some, John Kerry rode the momentum of his Iowa win all the way to the nomination before Democratic voters could catch a second breath and assess more thoroughly some of his potential weaknesses as a candidate. The other issue is the privileged status claimed by Iowa and New Hampshire. This is a contentious point that has been kept off the agenda because of all the focus on front-loading. Some states in recent years have tried to challenge their status, although without much success, as candidates who openly participated in these contests have been threatened with penalties by politicians and leaders in Iowa and New Hampshire.[9] For people in these states, protecting their cartel is not just a question of pride and influence; it is big business for the travel industry and the media outlets. At the DNC meeting in 2002, the state party chair of Michigan, Mark Brewer, called for an end to the "unfair monopoly" of Iowa and New Hampshire, a view strongly supported by Senator Carl Levin, who insisted that "no states should have greater access to our candidates than any other state."[10]

Indeed, following the 2004 election, the outgoing Democratic Party chair, Terry McAuliffe, appointed yet another party rules commission to look into primary scheduling for 2008. The *National Journal* reported that some elder statesmen in the party were hoping to use the commission to end Iowa and New Hampshire's dominance of the earliest contests, and that the commission might consider spreading out Democratic primaries over a longer period or adopting a regional primary model.[11] If Democrats revisit the primary schedule issue, perhaps Republicans will as well, especially since they have no incumbent running for reelection with a vested interest in front-loading. If the parties want a fix, they will have to reach some sort of agreement on it. Such an agreement will not be easy to coordinate, since Democrats can change their nominating rules in the DNC anytime they want, while Republicans can take no action until their 2008 national convention. In any event, even if the goal is admirable, it is far from clear which alternative to front-loading could (or should) command assent.[12]

## Vote Casting and Counting

The Florida fiasco in 2000 prompted calls for reform in the area of vote casting and counting. At the federal level, Congress in 2002 enacted the Help America Vote Act (or HAVA), which authorized grants to states for the purpose of replacing punch-card and lever voting machines; created a federal Election Assistance Commission to help states with election reform issues; authorized grants for voting technology research and testing; established rules to ease military and overseas voting; and required the attorney general to report on the adequacy of fraud statutes. It also required states to adopt voting systems standards, state registration lists, and provisional voting, which allows voters who think they are registered but are not found on the roll of voters at the balloting location to vote anyway, subject to later verification of their eligibility. Of the fifty states, forty-one adopted noteworthy electoral reforms even before the passage of HAVA; the other nine followed more reluctantly, in response to the federal legislation.[13]

When put to the test in 2004, these reforms seemed to have worked fairly well. By and large, there were few complaints. Indeed, DeForest B. Soaries Jr., chairman of the Election Assistance Commission, declared, "The election went smoothly." A spokesman for an association of election and voter registration officials likewise contended that "for it to go off as well as it did was an absolute miracle," given the turnout.[14]

Nevertheless, like Florida in 2000, Ohio in 2004 provided critics at least three targets. First, some Democratic activists complained that there were still local disparities in voting equipment that favored Republicans, and they complained about long waits by voters in some jurisdictions, a problem that was undoubtedly owed to the unusually large turnout. Second, controversy raged over exactly whose provisional ballots would be counted as valid—specifically, in order to be counted, did provisional votes have to be cast in the correct precinct? Secretary of State Kenneth Blackwell said yes, but critics decried his ruling. A federal judge upheld him, but federal courts in Michigan ruled the other way, creating legal uncertainty. This confusion was an unfortunate consequence of HAVA, which required provisional voting but established no standards to guide it. The controversy opened up the possibility that the federalization of elections, begun by HAVA, cannot be stopped, as each ambiguity must be clarified with ever more precise federal dictation.

Third, consideration of the Ohio provisional ballots postponed resolution of the race until Wednesday morning. Had the initial results from Ohio been closer, the provisional ballots would have delayed the outcome by perhaps two weeks. Such a delay could be dangerous in a time of national crisis. The five-week delay of 2000 was the result of an unusual, if not bizarre, conjunction of events; provisional ballots now mean that we have deliberately chosen to increase the risk of such delay. This must be weighed against the desire not to exclude legitimate voters.

Despite the relative calm of 2004, journalists identified a continuing spate of difficulties related to vote casting and counting.[15] There may be a drive in the 109th Congress to modify HAVA. Voting reform advocates indicated they were preparing to continue their efforts. As one analyst argued, "The results should not slow down the crying need for comprehensive reform of the voting system. Just because it went well this time does not mean it will go well next time."[16] Citing supposed voting irregularities in Ohio, a handful of Democrats challenged the congressional counting of Ohio's electoral votes. This maneuver forced each chamber of Congress to retire from joint session for a two-hour debate. However, most journalists and the Kerry campaign itself had already declared that there was no evidence of voting irregularities sufficient to overturn the state's results. In the end, the challenge garnered one vote in the Senate and thirty-seven in the House; even most supporters claimed that they merely wanted to force a new nationwide examination of voting procedures.

## Voter Fraud

Issues of fraud are closely related to issues of vote casting and counting. In 2004, there were new allegations of fraud. Some centered on the registration of ineligible voters or other questionable means of promoting new registrations. There were a significant number of cases in which advocacy group canvassers submitted registrations that were invalid, sometimes registrations for nonexistent people and sometimes multiple registrations for the same real person. Aside from being illegal in itself, this tactic, when not discovered, clearly opened the door to voter fraud on Election Day. In one case, a canvasser paid people to register by giving them crack cocaine. There were allegations that both parties were shipping in volunteers from other states to establish phony residence and register to vote in Florida. There was enough credence to these charges that the Florida Secretary of State's website added a warning about the legal penalties for trying to register and vote in two states.

Controversy erupted in Ohio, Florida, and South Dakota when Republicans, fearful of fraud, vowed to conduct an aggressive poll-watching exercise. Democrats cried foul, claiming that such efforts amounted to an attempt to intimidate minority voters. Democrats sued unsuccessfully to stop Republicans in Ohio, and Senator Tom Daschle sued to try to stop Republicans in South Dakota. A Colorado law requiring provisional voters to show identification was also challenged.

After election day, the disappointment of liberals with the outcomes in Florida and Ohio led to a number of attempts to prove Republican voter fraud. The hopes of conspiracy theorists were nourished by the (highly flawed) exit polls leaked to the press on the morning of Election Day, which indicated a Kerry lead in those states. Vague concerns about fraud were also raised when some jurisdictions in Florida inexplicably lost large numbers of absentee ballots,[17] and in the Washington state governor's race when King County suddenly found more than seven hundred ballots that put Christine Gregoire over the top. (King County election workers also admitted that they had counted some provisional ballots without first verifying their eligibility. Overall, the Florida-like saga of the Washington governor's race illustrated once again the trade-off between finality versus accuracy.)

Whatever the validity of any of these allegations, it is clear that concerns over fraud have returned in recent years, due to relaxed safeguards and heightened partisan polarization. The bitterness of the partisan divide may have convinced some Americans that even illegal tactics are acceptable to prevent the victory of the "enemy." And, when there is a more innocent (and more probable) explanation available, increased partisanship may have made many Americans less willing to accept it and more willing to think the worst about their adversaries.

## Who Can Vote?

In 2000, many Americans learned that felons are disfranchised in many states, either temporarily or in some cases permanently. In Florida, some voters were incorrectly identified as felons and barred from voting, while hundreds of ineligible felons were inadvertently allowed to vote. In 2004, studies found that 14 percent of otherwise eligible black males in Atlanta, Georgia, were unable to vote due to felony convictions; in Providence, Rhode Island, the figure reached as high as 32 percent.[18] Critics called for the elimination of felon disfranchisement provisions.

Observers noted another challenge: how to treat voters suffering from dementia. Experts estimate that up to 4.5 million Americans suffer from Alzheimer's disease, and either are or will become incapable of exercising judgment. There may be more than 450,000 cases in Florida alone. Many of these citizens still vote by absentee ballot, but it is often their spouse or other close relation who actually casts the vote.[19] (This problem demonstrates one more general weakness of mass absentee voting today, which is that there is no guarantee of a secret or individual ballot.) There is no obvious solution short of some sort of competence test, but few are willing to voice support for this remedy, which would carry its own problems and may not pass constitutional muster.

In the debate over immigration, some urged that noncitizens be allowed to vote. If this policy were applied nationally, it would be the most radical expansion of the electorate in American history. Several communities in Massachusetts began considering whether to allow noncitizen residents to vote, on the theory that they pay taxes and are affected by the laws and public services. Chicago and New York now allow noncitizens to vote in school board elections; San Francisco considered such a law on November 2 but turned it down.[20] Such proposals are likely to become more widespread in coming years and must be considered extremely carefully, as they hold the potential of eviscerating the very meaning of citizenship.

## Who Can Run?

The U.S. Constitution prevents a foreign-born citizen from running for president. Some have recently suggested that the Constitution be amended to allow naturalized citizens to run for president. The idea is not new; such an amendment has been proposed twenty-six times and was discussed as recently as the 1970s, when it was referred to as the "Kissinger Amendment," on behalf of the foreign-born secretary of state who might have benefited. This drive did not arise in a vacuum, but rather as the result of a mini-boom for California governor Arnold Schwarzenegger, who was born in Austria and is ineligible for the presidency. (Perhaps the "Kissinger Amendment" has now been "terminated" and should be renamed the "Schwarzenegger Amendment.") Once the topic was introduced, it was obvious that a handful of Democrats might someday take advantage of such a change, too, including Michigan governor Jennifer Granholm, born a Canadian citizen.

Advocates included Senator Orrin Hatch (R-UT), who, as chairman of the Senate Judiciary Committee, held hearings on the idea in October 2004. Hatch argued, "It is time for us, the elected representatives of a nation of immigrants, to begin the process that can result in removing this artificial, outdated, unnecessary and unfair barrier."[21] Skeptics argued that it was a bad idea to change the Constitution merely for the benefit of one office seeker, and proposed that any amendment require a twenty- to thirty-five-year residence in the United States before becoming eligible or a ten-year delay before the amendment becomes operational, so that the merits of the issue do not become entangled with partisan calculations about potential candidates like Schwarzenegger or Granholm. Senator Diane Feinstein (D-CA) defended the current limitation, saying, "I don't think it is unfair to say that the president of the United States should be a native-born citizen. . . . Your allegiance is driven by your birth."[22] There was also widespread agreement, quite sensibly, that naturalized candidates should be required to renounce any dual citizenship they might hold—Schwarzenegger, for example, continues to hold Austrian citizenship. In early 2005, prospects for such an amendment were uncertain. A Gallup poll in November 2004 showed Americans were opposed to an amendment by about a 2-1 ratio.[23]

## Congressional Districts

The uncompetitive nature of the vast majority of U.S. House districts led to calls in 2004 for new redistricting processes. In the critics' view, uncompetitive districts have led to both meaningless elections and greater partisanship in the House, as members work to satisfy their core supporters. In California, activist Ted Costa, who spearheaded the recall of former Governor Gray Davis, adopted redistricting as his next reform project. He tried to place an initiative on the ballot to strip the legislature of its power to draw district lines, placing authority instead in the hands of a neutral panel of retired judges, but failed to procure sufficient signatures in 2004. He has declared he will try again. Others have proposed different remedies. Some looked to the Iowa model, which legally mandates competitive districts, and explicitly prohibits unnecessary splitting of counties and drawing lines to protect incumbents. The Center for Voting and Democracy favored the use of larger multimember districts. In Costa's view, "There's a hundred ways to do it. But the one way not to do it is the way we do it, to let [politicians] have any say in mapping their own districts."[24]

Congressional districting is the sort of arcane, though important, issue that the general public typically finds uninteresting, and there is not much reason to believe politicians will willingly divest themselves of the power of drawing district lines. Nevertheless, this could be an important reform for American democracy. Although there is little evidence that a large margin of electoral victory makes incumbents unresponsive, there is something incongruous and troublesome about a House of Representatives in which fewer than one in ten races might realistically shift in any election. The critics' arguments—that the current system foments extreme partisanship and institutional rigidity—are worth a closer look than most Americans are likely to give them.

## Campaign Finance

It is virtually assured that some members of Congress will revisit the 2002 Bipartisan Campaign Reform Act (BCRA). The authors of the legislation were not pleased with the use of the 527 loophole. Many observers judged it a failure when independent advocacy groups totally evaded the intent of BCRA. If one considered only the 527s and issue ads, it was difficult to see that BCRA had made any difference at all. All of the advantages of advocacy group spending (stimulation of voter interest and a counterweight to incumbents) increased, as did the disadvantages (loss of control and accountability by candidates and parties). Even at the height of soft money excess, no individual contributed $27 million to the defeat of a presidential candidate, as billionaire George Soros did in 2004. The law was thrown into turmoil when a federal judge struck down fifteen of the nineteen rules written by the Federal Election Commission to implement BCRA as insufficiently strict.[25] Before the 2004 campaign was even over, the original sponsors of BCRA—Senators John McCain and Russ Feingold and Representatives Christopher Shays (R-CT) and Martin Meehan (D-MA)—had drafted legislation to close the 527 loophole, and committees in both houses held hearings to consider whether the Federal Election Commission needed to be made into a tougher watchdog.

On the other hand, some observers contend that BCRA performed much as was intended. Despite the ban on soft money, neither party lacked resources. Both parties were forced to rely more heavily on relatively small contributions rather than the six or seven figure gifts they had been receiving up to 2002. Democrats, in particular, adjusted better than many analysts had predicted, actually outraising Republicans in hard money in Senate races and remaining competitive in the presidential sweepstakes.[26] Of the top-ten corporate givers in 2000, none gave money to 527s in 2004. Many corporations that four years before would have written large checks to the national party committees instead encouraged greater grassroots participation by their employees.[27] All in all, Shays, one of the original BCRA sponsors, argued that "we're seeing thousands and thousands and thousands of people contributing. The parties are turning to far more people than just a few, and that's what we intended. . . . The campaign finance law has been a home run. . . . It hasn't been a grand slam."[28]

Democratic-leaning groups got into the 527 game first and most vigorously, but it was the Swift Boat Veterans for Truth that had the most impact. George W. Bush sued to stop 527s but also benefited from them, so it is hard to predict how the parties will end up calculating their interests on this question. The 527 issue will reignite the debate over the relationship between campaign money and political speech. If Congress does take up the issue of campaign finance again, it would be a good opportunity to establish a much larger increase in the individual contribution limit, at least for presidential nominations. Such a change might be necessary if the parties are serious about reversing primary front-loading, as it would extend the viability of candidates who lose early contests.

The 2004 elections also accelerated another campaign finance trend: the demise of the partial public financing of presidential nomination races. In 2004, three major candidates, including the two eventual nominees—Bush, Kerry, and Howard Dean—shucked the spending limits and the matching funds and raised record amounts. The trend is now unmistakable and probably irreversible.

## Election 2004 and American Politics

Politically, 2004 illustrated the outlines of a new electoral system, long in the making but now fully revealed. That system consists of a (slight) Republican majority, built on a reshuffling and rationalizing of party coalitions over several decades that has, on balance, favored Republicans; the ascendancy of a conservative public philosophy, which occurred hand-in-hand with the development of an infrastructure of conservative intellectual institutions; and the gradual rise of the new media, which fundamentally transformed the delivery of news and commentary in America, aiding Republicans in the process.

Any account of the rise of the Republicans must admit the importance of contingency. The GOP might still be the minority party, it could be argued, if not for vexing events in 1968 (Vietnam, race riots, and the rise of the counterculture), 1980 (stagflation, Iran, and Afghanistan), and 2002 and 2004 (September 11). But almost every majority party has owed much to events, many of them traumatic and unforeseen, which the public perceived that it handled better than its opponents. Where would the New Deal coalition have been without the Great Depression and Pearl Harbor, or McKinley without the Depression of 1893, or the first Republicans without Fort Sumter and Appomattox? In any event, if Republicans owed their political success after 2001 to September 11, it was largely because they had spent more than a generation establishing their bona fides as the national security party.

The 2004 election has a number of implications for the future. Republicans in Congress seem to possess a number of structural advantages that present a steep hill for Democrats to climb in their quest for a takeover. In presidential politics, the tide in 2004 ran in the Republicans' favor, making red states redder and blue states purpler. Bush's win was broad, as he gained ground in almost every demographic group. And, to a greater degree than at any time in recent American history, a president and Congress of the same party successfully pursued a comprehensive and unified strategy that wove together the political, the electoral, and the legislative.

A variety of analysts, each with their own partisan agendas, have different answers to the question of what it will take to dislodge the Republicans. Democrats like John Judis and Ruy Teixeira argue that recent Republican successes are short-term deviations from a long-term Democratic trend that will produce a Democratic majority by 2010. They base their view on a demographic claim that Democrats are increasingly the party of professionals, working women, and minorities, groups whose share of the electorate is growing.[29] However, even Judis and Teixeira admit that their coalition does not add up to a majority without white working-class voters, and it is here that Republicans have made great inroads. Furthermore, they simply extrapolate from the past without accounting for the possibility that events or Republicans might disrupt the trends. If 45 percent of the Hispanic vote begins regularly to vote Republican, or if Republicans increase their share of the black vote to 15 or 20 percent, or if the percentage of women who work outside the home peaks (as it may have already), Judis and Teixeira's hypothetical majority will have evaporated. Their scenario also depends on the national security issue quickly receding, but it is impossible to say when that will happen.

On the Republican side, Karl Rove, whose aim has always been to forge a durable Republican majority using William McKinley's elections of 1896 and 1900 as a model, perceives signs that his durable majority is in the process of being cemented. Like Judis and Teixeira, he assumes existing trends are likely to continue. He simply emphasizes the trends favoring Republicans. Regarding Republican dominance of the South, for example, Rove asks, "If you accept my underlying assumption that this is the result of a trend that has gained momentum over the years and has been reinforced under President Bush, what is the act that is going to stop it and reverse it? Once these things get set in motion, they require something on the landscape done by one or both parties, or events to intrude, to stop it and reverse it."[30] Other analysts have pointed out that the fastest-growing parts of the country are also the most reliably Republican parts, and that, in the long term, conservatives are simply having more children than liberals, though it will take some time for that phenomenon to affect the voter rolls. To hold their own, Democrats—like the Shakers of the eighteenth and nineteenth centuries—will have to depend on conversion rather than fertility.[31]

It is clear that much of Bush's second-term legislative agenda will consist of attempts to use policy innovations to build a stronger Republican coalition, not least by turning Social Security taxpayers into small investors. However, Democrats in the Senate may block Bush's agenda. Other factors may work in favor of the Democrats. Continued immigration on a large scale may help Democrats make up for their low fertility rates; Republicans have not come close to winning the mother lode of electoral votes, California, since 1988, which means that they begin each election ceding one-fifth of the electoral votes needed for victory; and, above all, unexpected incidents are always in play. A majority—especially a slender one—that was made by events is one that can be undone by events. In the end, neither Rove nor Judis and Teixeira can be as confident as they claim.

In any scenario, certain features of the system of '04 would survive a declining Republican vote share. A Democratic presidential victory will not necessarily mean the end of the ascendancy of conservative ideas, as Bill Clinton's tenure demonstrated. Even John Kerry pledged not to raise marginal tax rates above Clinton's top rate, which, at 39.6 percent, was a far cry from the 70 percent that Ronald Reagan inherited in 1981. In addition, in the same way that the massive expansion of the welfare state in the New Deal and the Great Society probably created a floor under which the national Democratic Party could not fall, the conservative idea infrastructure and the rise of the new media may establish a floor supporting Republicans. As long as these features of the system of 2004 are in place, Republicans will remain competitive for a national majority, at least in the absence of a total national catastrophe on their watch.

The election of 2004 not only confirmed the importance of the new media (and some of its benefits, like the enforcement of accountability in the old media); it also hinted at the challenges the new media will present the American polity in the future. Perhaps the most troubling aspect of the growth of the new media is that it seems to facilitate and perhaps even encourage a process of ideological "cocooning." After the 1972 election, the film critic Pauline Kael famously remarked that she could not understand how Nixon had won, considering that she did not know anyone who had voted for him. At the time, Kael's statement was taken to demonstrate how out of touch she (and her intellectual circle) was with America. As the new media allows for more niche-oriented news and opinion delivery, such provincial views may become more common. Book-buying patterns at Amazon.com reveal little crossover in the readers of books by right-wing flamethrowers such as Ann Coulter and left-wing propagandists like Michael Moore. The recommended links to other sites on conservative-oriented blogs are markedly different from those offered at liberal sites. The result of this bifurcation could be an ideological echo chamber in which the most radical views can reverberate and in time gain a veneer of respectability while opposing arguments and views are marginalized. Although the growth of a media that serves niche interests may allow for greater individual choice, it may also hamper the ability of the country to unify around cultural norms of civic respect that are necessary to sustain a liberal democracy.

Another issue bearing on the long-term well-being of the republic is the relationship of war and politics. A potentially problematic pattern has emerged since the 1970s and was laid bare in 2004: The growing unwillingness of partisans to give a president of the other party the benefit of the doubt in wartime. During the Kosovo war in 1999, House Republicans voted down a resolution approving the air strikes, after they had already begun. During the 2004 campaign, many Democrats and liberals accused

Bush not of poor judgment but of deliberate bad faith in Iraq, despite the fact that intelligence assessments from around the world had been almost unanimous that Saddam had WMD. Indeed, throughout the year they made a series of statements that helped their campaign but could only hurt the war effort. To the degree that these positions were the result of genuine conviction, they should be stifled only with great care. But who believes that House Republicans would have opposed the Kosovo operation if George Bush had been the one undertaking it, and who cannot notice that Democrats raised no protests when Bill Clinton launched Operation Desert Fox against Iraq in December 1998 in order to stop its WMD program? The whole 2004 campaign must leave open the question of whether extreme partisanship will ultimately render America incapable of pursuing a difficult course for an extended period of time.

Thus, the partisanship that serves as one characteristic of the system of 2004 is a mixed bag. It has focused debate, advanced the cause of collective responsibility, and served to politically mobilize a greater portion of the American public, driving up voter turnout and other forms of participation. But it has also made communication across the partisan divide more difficult, has eroded trust, and has made it harder for presidents to function in wartime.

Where does each party go from here?

For Democrats, the debate will undoubtedly be long and agonizing. They will begin by trying to build on their two successes of 2004: gains in some state elections and among the youngest cohorts of voters, the only age group to give Kerry a majority. Minority parties typically adopt one of three responses to their predicament. Sometimes, they go into deep denial, changing nothing in the hope that they will wake up someday to find themselves back in their natural place in the majority. This reaction can be accompanied by a kind of fatalism. Republicans often suffered from this psychology in the decades after 1936. Sometimes, defeat serves as the prod for innovation, much as the U.S. Army transformed itself after the Vietnam War. Republicans also went through such a period after 1964, which helped lay the foundation for a turnaround in their fortunes. Finally, defeat can produce civil war within a party, as it turns on itself to cast blame, find scapegoats, and determine who will chart its course.

Among other things, Democrats will have to confront one of the most difficult judgments in losing campaigns: how much blame should be assigned to the messenger, and how much to the message. If the campaign was decided based on personality more than policy, the Democrats need only to find a more appealing vessel for their policies. If, however, the election represented a rejection of Democratic policies, a retooling of the party would seem to be in order.

Since 1964 only one Democratic candidate for president has received more than fifty percent of the popular vote—Jimmy Carter won 50.1 percent in 1976 in the wake of Watergate, Ford's pardon of Nixon, and the fall of Saigon. In that period, five Republicans have done so, including two by landslides. Even the charismatic Bill Clinton could not get over the 50 percent threshold. This failure to win a majority for its presidential candidates coupled with the GOP's takeover of Congress and state houses in the 1990s suggests that the Democratic Party is facing a problem bigger than the alleged quirks of its nominees. Even if Democrats come to accept this notion, however, there is no way to know how they will address it.

For Democrats, two central policy questions will be how to establish credibility in national security and how to manage the tough social issues. As long as Iraq is an issue—and more broadly, as long as the war on terror continues—Democrats will be torn between hawks and doves. They will also be torn between those who want to mitigate the hostility the party now engenders among traditionalist red voters and those who want to press the party's advantage among the secular blues. Even before the election results were known, books like *Retro vs. Metro* and *What's the Matter with Kansas?* displayed contempt for traditionalists. These analysts assert that traditionalists should either be ignored or converted by pointing out to them the foolishness of making $30,000 a year and voting Republican on the basis of gay marriage. (Somehow, it is never foolish to be in the $100,000 a year tax bracket and vote Democratic because of abortion.) If many Democrats want to move the party to the center—not just in appearance but in substance—they will face a fight from dovish, highly secular intellectuals who, in a certain respect, serve as the "brain" of the party. Democrats will have to decide whether to de-Clintonize or re-Clintonize themselves. Bill Clinton headed an administration that was, paradoxically, both more moderate and highly partisan. One possible choice would reduce conflict in Washington—greater moderation and less partisanship—but will leave the party's activists flat. Another choice would be to copy Clinton's entire formula—political moderation combined with partisan combativeness. This option will appeal to many who want a return to the glory days of the 1990s, but the liberals had already grown tired of Clintonism by the end of his presidency and do not want to return. A third option would be to combine intense partisanship with a rejection of moderation and a sharp lunge to the left. This course was nearly adopted in 2004—in the form of a Howard Dean nomination—and centrist Democrats argue that a milder form actually was adopted, especially when one reviews the whole Democratic campaign (including the 527s). The fourth option—more left-wing and less partisan—is theoretically possible but highly unlikely. There is no easy choice here for Democrats.

Democrats will not be the only ones facing a challenge, however. It may be a difficult process to construct a majority, even a narrow one, but it is also no easy thing to maintain one. Republicans will discover, especially in Congress, that the bigger their majority, the harder to satisfy it. They will also face a potentially frustrating and even politically dangerous situation: As the majority in unified partisan government, they will be held responsible for the course of the country. Yet, remaining short of the sixty votes in the Senate that is required to stop filibusters, they will not have as much power as their responsibility implies. Their majority status also makes them particularly vulnerable to the political backlash that might come with any serious national setback.

Republicans will have to contend with the potential for significant splits within their own ranks. This possibility has increased now that Bush's successful reelection releases congressional Republicans from the sometimes onerous duty of staying in line with the White House. In foreign affairs, the president's policy will face challenges from some Republicans who consider it overly ambitious; Bush may provoke a virtual rebellion over immigration in the GOP ranks; Social Security reform, with its high transition cost, will not be swallowed whole by some fiscal conservatives; and, of course, social issues will continue to divide Republicans. As Bush's term runs out, his power will decrease, leaving a vacuum that will need to be filled. Without an heir apparent, Republicans will be highly distracted after 2006 by their presidential nomination contest. At that point, depending on the shape of the Republican presidential field, the GOP may too be forced to make a decision. They might seek to continue the mixed ideological direction set by Bush, but the odds on that happening will largely depend on Bush's standing at that time. A considerable contingent will prefer to return to a purer limited-government Reaganism. Yet a third faction will seek to jettison the social issues, either out of conviction or in order to secure a charismatic candidate, but such a course will put at serious risk the pivotal Republican gains among evangelicals and Catholics.

The greatest intangible of all will be the course of events. This applies to Iraq in particular. Will there be a continued economic recovery, renewed stagnation, or, in the worst case, some sort of economic catastrophe? A large terrorist attack within the United States, the capture of Osama bin Laden, or both? A deficit reduced to smaller proportions, or fiscal profligacy? What about Iran, North Korea, the Palestinians? And how will Bush's ambitious second-term agenda play out in the court of public opinion?

A new system—the system of 2004—is in place, culminating a long process of partisan change. Yet even if Republicans gained ascendancy through a "rolling realignment" that resulted in an undisputed national majority in 2004, there can be no telling how long it will last. When Democrats looked out from the summit of their landslide of 1964—a victory much more impressive than the Republican win forty years later—they perceived an endless horizon of electoral success stretching before them. In retrospect, though, 1964 was the apogee of their power. They were undone not by the mechanistic workings of an inevitable cycle, but by events, their own mistakes, and a Republican Party agile enough to take advantage of those errors.

Someday, the reds and the blues of America in the twenty-first century will seem as quaint and curious as the blues and the greens of Byzantium or the whites and blacks of Florence. For the moment, red stands atop blue in the "51 percent nation," like Hercules standing astride the world itself. Only Hercules has a narrow toehold indeed. Like a mythic Greek, Republicans may find that hubris and fate are their most threatening enemies.

## Notes

1. Jo Becker, "Colorado Initiative Could Be Key to Presidential Race," *Washington Post*, September 18, 2004, p. A12.

2. Governor Bill Owens, "Plan Would Hurt Small States," *USA Today*, September 19, 2004.

3. Had it passed, it would also have been challenged in court on two grounds. It was written to be applied to the 2004 vote, and some argued that this retroactive feature was improper because voters on Election Day could not cast their vote for president with knowledge of the effect of that vote. Others pointed out that the Constitution reserves to "the legislature" the role of determining how electors will be chosen.

4. Chris Stirewalt, "Robb's Vote May Not Go To Bush," *Charleston Daily Mail*, September 8, 2004, p. 1A.

5. Judith Best, *The Case against Direct Election of the President* (Ithaca, N.Y.: Cornell University Press, 1971).

6. Susan Page, "Remember the Mess in 2000? How About a Tie?" *USA Today*, September 3, 2004, p. A1.

7. Peter Goodspeed, "After Strong 2000, Nader Not a Factor this Time," *Ottawa Citizen*, November 3, 2004, p. A8.

8. Rodney Dalton, "Nader Defiant despite Savaging," *The Australian*, November 3, 2004, p. 10.

9. In fact, the District of Columbia held a nonbinding primary in 2004 before Iowa, on January 13, but no one paid it much attention.

10. "Democrats Finalize Ground Rules for 2004," Eric M. Appleman/Democracy in Action at www.gwu.edu/~action/2004/dnc0102meet.html.

11. See Dan Balz, "DNC Chief Advises Learning from GOP," *Washington Post*, December 11, 2004; Emily Goodin, "Enough Blame to Share," *National Journal*, December 4, 2004, p. 3630.

12. For a comprehensive examination of the front-loading problem and possible solutions, see William G. Mayer and Andrew E. Busch, *The Front-Loading Problem in Presidential Nominations* (Washington, D.C.: Brookings Institution, 2003).

13. See Daniel J. Palazzolo and James W. Ceaser, ed., *Election Reform: Politics and Policy* (Lanham, Md.: Lexington Books, 2005).

14. Seth Stern, "No Election Day Meltdown, But Problems Remain," *CQ Weekly Report*, November 6, 2004, p. 2590.

15. Jo Becker and Dan Keating, "Problems Abound in Election Systems," *Washington Post*, September 5, 2004, p. A1; "Voting Technology: Old, New and Recount Redux?" *CQ Weekly Report*, p. 2362.

16. Stern, "No Election Day Meltdown."

17. See Manuel Roig-Franzia and Dale Russakoff, "In a Changed Florida, The Acrimony Remains," *Washington Post*, November 1, 2004, p. A1; Peter Wallsten, "Casting Votes, Claims of Fraud, Come Early in Florida," *Los Angeles Times*, October 31, 2004, p. A29.

18. Daryl Kean, "In Atlanta, 14% of Black Men Can't Vote," *Washington Post*, September 23, 2004, p. A10.

19. Shankar Vedartam, "Dementia and the Voter," *Washington Post*, September 14, 2004, p. A1.

20. Matt Viser, "Proposal Would Let Non-Citizens Vote," *Boston Globe*, November 25, 2004, Globe West, p. 1.

21. Michael Janofsky, "Senate Examining (Again) Constitutional Ban on Foreign-Born Presidents," *New York Times*, October 6, 2004, p. A16.

22. Martin Kasindorf, "Should the Constitution be Amended for Arnold?" *USA Today*, December 3, 2004, p. 1A.

23. See Kasindorf, "Should the Constitution be Amended for Arnold?"

24. Eric Slater, "Safe Seats in House Keep True Races Rare," *Los Angeles Times*, October 11, 2004, p. A14.

25. See Helen DeWar, "Bill Would Curb '527' Spending," *Washington Post*, September 23, 2004, p. A27.

26. See David Miller, "Democrats' McAuliffe on the Campaign: 'Unprecedented Money,'" *CQ Weekly Report*, June 19, 2004, p. 1448.

27. Jeanne Cummings, "In New Law's Wake, Companies Slash Their Political Donations," *Wall Street Journal*, September 4, 2004, p. A1.

28. David Nather, "The $4 Billion Campaign: Better, or Just Louder?" *CQ Weekly Report*, October 30, 2004, p. 2546.

29. John Judis and Ruy Teixeira, *The Emerging Democratic Majority* (New York: Scribner, 2002).

30. Ronald Brownstein, "GOP Has Lock on South, and Democrats Can't Find Key," *Los Angeles Times*, December 15, 2004, p. A41.

31. Much like modern liberals, the Shakers believed in common property, equality of men and women, and pacifism. Because they also believed in celibacy, the continuation of the sect depended on winning over new converts to replace the old. Modern liberals clearly do not believe in celibacy, but they do believe in abortion, small and late-starting families to accommodate the needs of career women, and below-replacement-level childbearing to save the Earth.

# Index

# About the Authors

**James W. Ceaser** is professor of politics at the University of Virginia, where he has taught since 1976. He received his Ph.D. from Harvard in 1976. He has also held visiting appointments at Marquette University, the University of Basel, Claremont McKenna College, Harvard University, and Oxford University. In 1996 he was awarded "The Joint Meritorius Unit Award for Total Engagement in the Creation of the the George C. Marshall Center for European Security Studies" by the U.S. Army. Professor Ceaser is the author of several books on American politics and American political thought, including *Presidential Selection*, *Reforming the Reforms*, *Liberal Democracy and Political Science*, and *Reconstructing America*. He is coauthor with Andrew E. Busch of *Upside Down and Inside Out*, *Losing to Win*, and *The Perfect Tie*.

**Andrew E. Busch** is associate professor of government at Claremont McKenna College. He received his Ph.D. from the University of Virginia in 1992. Professor Busch is the author of *Outsiders and Openness in the Presidential Nominating System* and *Horses in Midstream: U.S. Midterm Elections and Their Consequences, 1894–1998*, as well as as numerous articles on elections, American politics, and Ronald Reagan. He is coauthor with James W. Ceaser of *Upside Down and Inside Out*, *Losing to Win*, and *The Perfect Tie*.